Dear D...

Merry Christmas!

Love

Victoria

25.12.96

The Operators

Inside 14 Intelligence Company –
The Army's Top Secret Elite

The Operators

Inside 14 Intelligence Company – The Army's Top Secret Elite

by

James Rennie

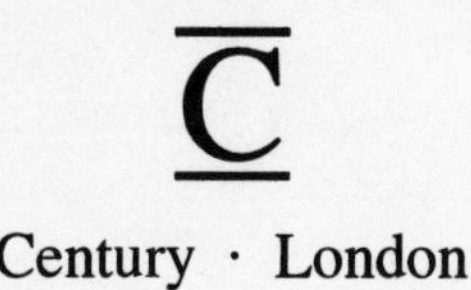

Century · London

First published by Century in 1996

First published in the United Kingdom in 1996 by
Century, 20 Vauxhall Bridge Road, London SW1V 2SA

Random House Australia (Pty) Limited
16 Dalmore Drive, Scoresby
Victoria 3179, Australia

Random House New Zealand Limited
18 Poland Road, Glenfield
Auckland 10, New Zealand

Random House South Africa (Pty) Limited
PO Box 2263, Rosebank 2121, South Africa

Random House UK Limited Reg. No. 954009
A CIP catalogue record for this book
is available from the British Library

Papers used by Random House UK Limited are natural, recyclable
products made from wood grown in sustainable forests. The
manufacturing processes conform to the environmental
regulations of the country of origin.

ISBN 0 7126 7730 5

Typeset by SX Composing DTP, Rayleigh, Essex
Printed by Mackays of Chatham PLC, Chatham, Kent

Glossary of Surveillance Terminology

Zero	The radio net callsign of the control station, usually the detachment operations officer. He or she would normally be based in the Det ops room, but if circumstances demand may be mobile or airborne.
Alpha, Bravo and Charlie	These are often reserved as radio designations for surveillance locations, targets and vehicles respectively. For example, Bravo 1 could be the primary human target of an operation, and would live at Alpha 1 and drive Charlie 1. The use of Alphas, Bravos and Charlies assists the very rapid radio voice procedure that surveillance operations demand, and reduces the potential for confusion if communications are poor or operating conditions stressful.
Click and double-click	If conditions do not permit an operator to speak over the net, one click of the radio transmit button means 'no' and a double-click means 'yes'. The clicks are not available to passers-by.
Complete	Inside. For example, 'Bravo 1 is complete Alpha 1'; or an operator returning to his car would say 'I am going complete', meaning getting into his vehicle.
Contact	Visual contact with armed terrorists.

CTR	Close Target Reconnaissance operation.
Delta through to Zulu	These are reserved as radio callsigns for individual members of each 14 Company detachment, who are known as operators. The only exception is foxtrot, which is never a personal callsign. An operator retains the same callsign on an operation whether he is on foot, mobile or airborne.
Dickers	Local youths or aspiring terrorists employed by the major terrorist organisations to keep watch for and give advance warning of security force activity, particularly during weapon and bomb moves.
Foxtrot	Travelling on foot. For example, 'Bravo 1 is foxtrot towards Charlie 1.'
Green army	Regular, uniformed army, as distinct from special forces.
HMSU	Headquarters Mobile Support Unit. A highly trained and heavily armed, uniformed RUC squad, used in support of covert operations.
To have	To have visual contact with the target. For example, 'Golf has Charlie 1 mobile.' He who 'has' the target has priority use of the radio net.
Intending	Likely or intending to turn towards. For example, 'Golf has Charlie 1 intending left.'
Mobile	Travelling by vehicle. Thus, 'Bravo 1 is foxtrot from Alpha 1 to Charlie 1 and mobile.'
Off	No longer having the target. For example, 'Charlie 1 is towards Alpha 1 and I'm off.'

Two up, three up, etc.	Refers to the number of people in a vehicle.
Possible	Used to qualify an operator's certainty about the identity of a target. It is always vital to make clear any element of doubt that exists, in order not to mislead and distract the rest of the surveillance team. For example, 'Echo has a possible Charlie 1 mobile. Checking.' The next transmission from Echo would be either 'Standby, standby, Echo has Charlie 1 mobile,' or 'Cancel, that's a negative.'
Spot and colour codes	Each road junction or other prominent topographical point in the area of operation is designated a colour and a two-digit number. This allows the rapid description of road or foot movement of targets and team members over the radio net. In small towns and villages, individual streets are allocated colours. For example, 'Charlie 1 is mobile from Red Two Three towards Red Two Four,' or 'That's Charlie 2 mobile on Purple towards Brown.'
Shorts and longs	Generic terms for hand guns and rifles.
To stake out	To box the target into an area by controlling all the routes.
Standby, standby	The expression used to warn a surveillance team of significant movement by a target. It is used with great care because it usually triggers movement by the entire team, breaking up the stake out, which may take some time and difficulty to re-establish if it is a false call.

Surveillance voice procedure	In order to keep radio transmissions during surveillance operations to a minimum, standard military radio voice procedure is severely abbreviated. For example, 'Hello Zero, this is Echo, the target has come out of his front door and is walking towards his car, he's got his keys out, over,' becomes 'Zero, Echo. Bravo 1 foxtrot from Alpha 1 intending complete Charlie 1.' Rather than answering with the usual 'Zero, roger out,' the acknowledgement is simply 'Zero'. In areas of poor radio reception Zero often repeats other callsigns' transmissions.
To have a trigger	To have visual or electronic control of a target, usually when waiting for movement or action.
VCP	Vehicle Check Point, usually manned by the security forces but occasionally set up by armed terrorists in hard republican areas.

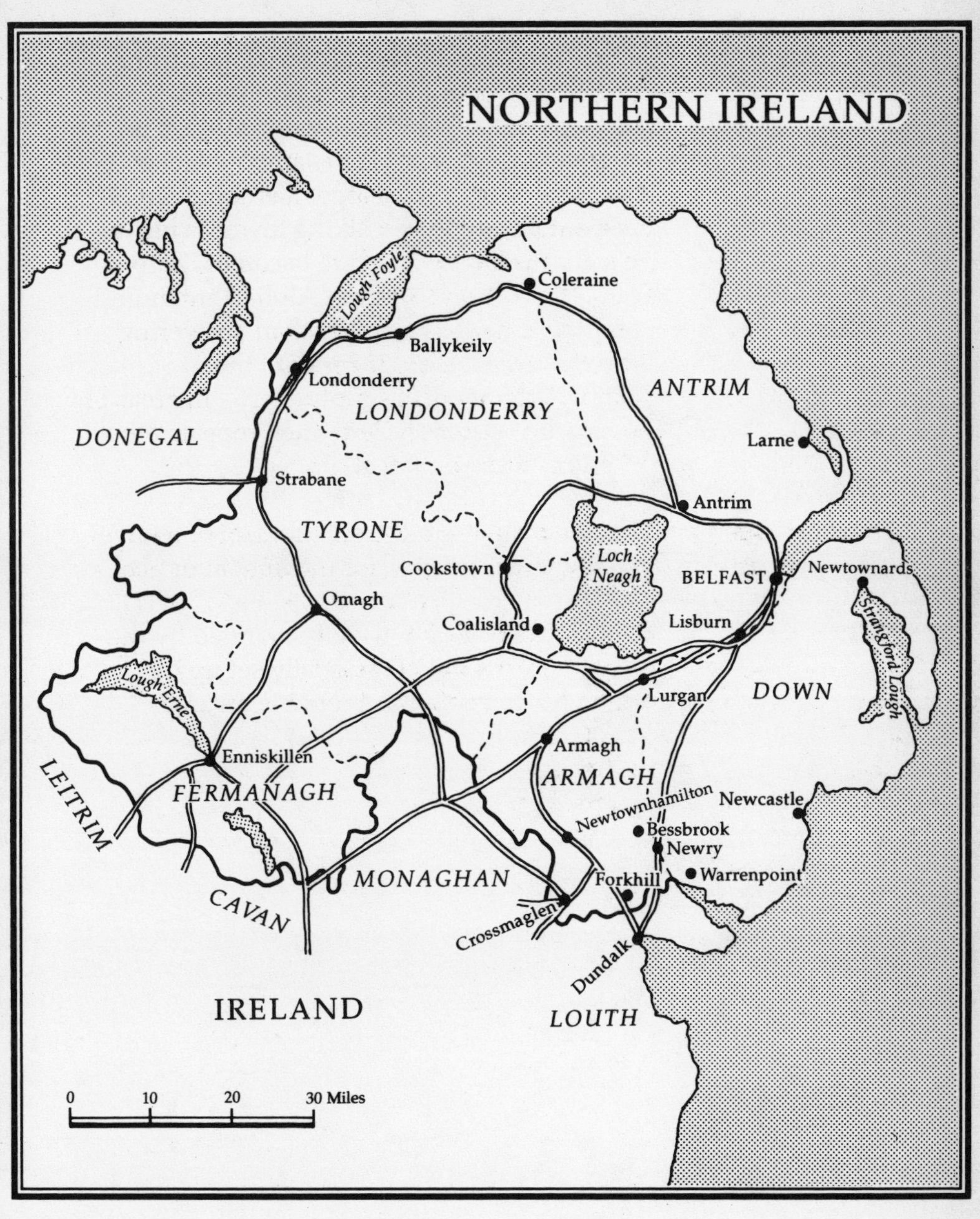
NORTHERN IRELAND
Lough Foyle
Coleraine
Ballykeily
Londonderry
LONDONDERRY
ANTRIM
DONEGAL
Larne
Strabane
Antrim
TYRONE
Loch Neagh
Cookstown
BELFAST
Newtownards
Omagh
Coalisland
Lisburn
Strangford Lough
Lough Erne
Lurgan
DOWN
Armagh
Enniskillen
LEITRIM
ARMAGH
FERMANAGH
Newtownhamilton
Newcastle
Bessbrook
Newry
Forkhill
Warrenpoint
MONAGHAN
CAVAN
Crossmaglen
Dundalk
IRELAND
LOUTH
0
10
20
30 Miles

Authors Note

Given the sensitivity of the contents of this book I submitted the manuscript to the Ministry of Defence prior to publication. At the request of the MoD a number of changes were made to the text in order to protect the work of a unit which continues to play a key role in the fight against terrorism.

Chapter One

'Standby, standby. Zero, Oscar. I have Bravo 1 foxtrot from Alpha 2 towards Charlie 2.' The tension in callsign Oscar's normally calm voice set my pulse racing. I could see Keith further up the busy street, sauntering along carelessly in a shiny suit, carrying a battered briefcase.

'Zero. Standby, standby from Oscar.'

'Zero, Delta. I have a trigger on Charlie 2.'

'Zero.'

The surveillance team was quietly casting itself about the surrounding streets and alleyways, melting into the routine of the area.

'Delta. Yeah, but not for long. And now I have Bravo 2 with Bravo 1 at the back of Charlie 2.'

A double-click from Oscar's hidden radio sounded the acknowledgement. He continued up the street, passing a group of four youths sitting on a low wall. Dressed in parkas and heavy boots, they were ten years behind the times, as usual.

Suzy and I were leaning up against each other in a bus shelter, watching Oscar's walkpast through the slight drizzle that was beginning to fall. Suzy was pretending to coo into my ear and nibble my neck, for the benefit of two middle-aged women who stood at the other end of the green lean-to, ignoring us. As I craned over her shoulder, my windcheater pulled tight and I felt her move her hand over the protruding buckle of my shoulder holster, screening it from the women. The barrel of the MP5K submachine gun that was suspended in a quick-release holster from my right shoulder was jutting into my hip bone, and the twin thirty-round magazine was pressing awkwardly into my ribs.

Past Suzy's left ear I was watching the hooligans, who were now showing a distinct interest in Oscar as he sauntered away. The squattest one levered himself off the wall and stood in the middle of the pavement. Probably just yobs, I thought, but they could be dicking as lookouts for the weapon move. A second one slid from the wall and they conferred briefly, still looking towards Oscar. Maybe they were muggers. They set off purposefully. It was time for me to warn him. 'Oscar, November. Yobs are following you, ten metres. Suggest a pick-up pronto.'

Double-click.

'Zero. Who can?'

'X-Ray's mobile to Green One Four.' Steve would now be casually pulling out into the late-afternoon traffic, heading north.

'Roger, X-Ray. Oscar, Green One Four?'

Double-click.

'Delta. Bravo 1 and 2 foxtrot back to Alpha 2 with a holdall. Looks like the longs to me.'

So far so good. This was what we were expecting. Once the two terrorists were alone with the rifles in the narrow terraced house, the options would crystallise. A few nights previously we had covertly located the weapons as they lay in their hide, and carefully deactivated the firing mechanisms. If we hadn't been able to do this in advance of the weapon move, we'd have had to stake the terrorists out until an SAS assault team was in place to take them on. Although the Regiment – as 22 SAS are known within special forces circles – had a troop permanently stationed in Ulster, today we were using uniformed HMSU police to perform the interception, hoping thereby to conceal the fact that we had been tipped off well in advance about this weapon move. Unfortunately there hadn't been time to place one of our operators in an HMSU vehicle, so we were relying on the police HQ to relay the targets' positions to them. That was fine, as long as we maintained radio contact.

A note of alarm from Delta sounded over the radio net. 'They've gone left left left through the alley. Delta's unsighted, going foxtrot.'

'Zero. Anyone have?'

Silence, just the low *hish* of the net.

Then, 'Lima. I have both Bravos foxtrot with holdall towards Green Two Nine. They're speeding up. Came straight out of the alley, don't think they did a drop.

'Lima. That's through Green Two Nine, now right towards Two Seven, speed steady.'

Time for Suzy and me to move into the follow. We set off up the street, hand in hand. As we approached Alpha 1, Suzy decided to get some footage of the alley and Charlie 2 for the record. She reached into the cheap handbag slung over her shoulder and switched on the miniature video camera that I had spent hours the previous month helping her bury into the bag's fabric. She felt under a loose flap of plastic for the remote button, casually swung the bag over her hip as we crossed the mouth of the alley, then carried on past the car. The tiny noise from the bag, really nothing more than a gentle vibration, reassured us that it was recording.

'Tango's got Alpha and Charlie taped.'

'Zero.'

'Delta. Good possible dicker at Green Two Seven – on the left, blue trainers.'

'Zero.'

'Lima.'

The team's invisible web was holding the targets in its centre as they moved through the streets. Suzy and I knew the plan of the area like the backs of our hands. We walked as fast as we could without making it obvious, overtaking several shoppers and an old man out for a stroll with his dog. If the targets drifted over towards us, we would take over.

'Lima. Bravos've gone right to Red One Two. I'm off. Whisky, do you have?'

Double-click from Whisky. A pause, then Sally added, 'Looks like they're heading for the park.'

'Zero. Roger. We're checking the cops' progress now.'

This was becoming serious. If they reached the estate at the far side of the park we'd lose the weapons for sure. I could tell from his voice that the ops officer was concerned, and would now be trying to steer a uniformed police patrol on to them, to make it look like a chance arrest.

'Whisky. That's a left towards Red One Three. The park it is.'

'Zero. Roger. Fucking comms with the cops are out, we're trying landline.'

Christ, I thought. If Phil's swearing on the net this really is a cock-up.

'Lima's mobile towards Green One Seven. Tango November want a pick-up?'

'Yeah, pronto. Drop off Green One Nine,' I muttered. A lift from

Lima in his car would put Suzy and me neatly ahead of the field without having to break into a run. Green One Nine was at the south end of the park, so we could cover that route if necessary.

'Whisky. That's crossing right to left, fifty short of Red One Three.'

'Zero.'

'Whisky, X-Ray. I'll take if they go right.'

Double-click.

We went through the game of flagging down Lima as he approached, smiling – just friends cadging a lift. We bundled in, me in the front and Suzy behind. We travelled in silence, each concentrating furiously as the car meandered through the busy streets, trying to keep a mental note of where the individual members of the team were.

Andy dropped us off in a garage forecourt. As we waved cheerio to him he pretended to check his tyres. We were satisfied that we had not aroused any unwelcome curiosity from the locals. Suzy and I both knew that by the time our targets cleared the rise at the park's western side we should be innocently seated in front of them. We crossed the road that bordered the park.

'Zero, Lima. November and Tango are foxtrot into the park from the Green One Nine side.' As Andy pulled out into the traffic I heard him again. 'Lima's mobile to Red Two Two.' He was driving round into the estate, so that he could come in from the far side of the park if needed, although this would be difficult.

'Whisk, that's the Bravos into the park and I'm off.'

'Zero.'

'Oscar has, foxtrot slowly on the main path.' Keith had now altered his appearance by dumping most of his kit in X-Ray's vehicle. Now he looked like a reluctant middle-aged jogger in crushed trainers, baggy nylon shorts and a loose grubby sweatshirt. It had to be loose to conceal the radio set and Browning pistol with two spare 13-round magazines. His ruffled hair blew around his ears as he shambled into the park 100 metres behind the terrorists.

I used the side of my hand to wipe rain droplets from a bench just off the main path and Suzy and I settled down to wait. From here we could take over the follow without having to move or loiter unnaturally. The drizzle had stopped now, and I scanned the other occupants of the park, looking for any sign of a handover. We'd passed two teenage mums on a bench, watching their toddlers play with a bottomless litter bin and absently rocking empty pushchairs as they chatted. They had shown no interest in us and I felt sure they were not involved. A couple of yobs were hanging around at the edge of some back gardens about 150 metres away. Maybe they were sniffing glue; they certainly looked too young to be dicking. I noticed Suzy lightly (and probably subconsciously) touch the holstered bulk of her concealed pistol, drawing comfort from its hard outline. I casually opened the three poppers on the front of my windcheater, so that I could draw the MP5K more quickly if necessary. Suzy was murmuring into her shoulder mike, but I was hearing her voice over the radio net.

'Zero, Tango November. We have Bravos foxtrot towards us, Bravo 2 has the bag.'

'Oscar's off, going complete.'

'Zero.'

It seemed to take an age for them to walk down the gently sloping path towards us, but it was probably only a minute and a half. Suzy maintained a running commentary for my benefit. They were both in their early twenties, a bit scruffy, wearing grubby slacks, bagged and sagging at the knees, one in a parka and the other in a dark donkey jacket. They seemed pretty jumpy, twice looking behind as they walked. It was possible that these characters would be carrying pistols for personal defence.

'Zero. We're considering the options, wait out.'

I could imagine the scene in the ops room. Phil would have the radio net speakers on, booming into the stuffy room so he could hear everything while he was talking on the secure phones to Special Branch and our own headquarters ops room. He was good in a crisis – which was just as well, I thought.

The rest of the team was already repositioning to cover the few exits from the park. We all knew that we'd lose them if they reached the line of broken fencing that divided the park from the rabbit warren of the crumbling housing estate, even with Lima mooching about as best he could. In order to keep control of the weapons and lift the terrorists, somebody would need to act quickly.

'Zero. Bad news. We've lost comms altogether with the HMSU and the local plods are still at least five minutes away. We're trying the local green army. Wait out.' Shit. We had only two minutes at most, or we'd lose them all!

Suzy was continuing to mutter her reports as they progressed along the path. I was gently stroking the inside of her thigh with the finger of one hand. She had a rather strange grin fixed to her face, and I hissed quietly at her, 'For Christ's sake look as if you're enjoying this!'

She put on a lopsided smile. I felt the butterflies starting to swarm in my stomach and reached up to stroke her hair. I noticed my fingers were shaking a little, but not too much. That's OK, I said to myself, it's only natural.

I could almost feel the terrorists' eyes on us as they approached, and I worried that parts of my equipment might be protruding. I could feel my Browning pistol held firmly in its holster inside the waistband of my jeans, its butt against my right kidney. I was confident it was covered by the loose folds of my windcheater.

I was turned sideways on the bench, facing away down the slope, watching the kids on the path behind us. Suzy was sitting next to me, also turned and watching the terrorists' approach over my shoulder. Our feet seemed hopelessly mixed up together. The two men were now fifteen paces away. I could feel Suzy's pulse – or was it mine? – beating away where my knee touched hers. I swallowed hard, trying to control my breathing.

'Tango November, Zero. Could you intercept?'

Suzy swung her eyes round to meet mine, and for a split second we stared at each other from a distance of three inches. Although I was an officer, she'd been in the Province longer, so I'd defer to her on this. She screwed up her nose and widened her eyes so that she looked for all the world like a naughty child, and raised a quizzical eyebrow. I gulped and gave her the smallest nod. She double-clicked our assent.

'Zero. Roger. Wait.'

I mouthed into her ear, 'If we do, you take the MP5.' This was sensible, since she was already facing them. She lightly pressed the tip of her finger twice into my thigh. OK. I watched a shaggy black crow wheel overhead, flap twice and drop like a discarded overcoat on to the grass fifty metres away. It slowly stalked about, throwing back its head from time to time.

'Tango November, Zero. Intercept now!'

They were only five paces away. I felt as though Suzy and I were communicating brain to brain, thinking as one. Time slowed. I began the double-click. As the first click sounded I felt Suzy's hand reach up into my armpit and fold round the pistol grip of the suspended submachine gun. Her other hand grabbed the short handle at the front of the weapon, and in one firm and easy swinging motion she ripped it from under my arm and clear of my jacket. The second click sounded as her legs unfolded from under us. She launched herself in an enormous bound to the far side of the path and faced them, the gun barrel extended towards them at eye level.

I had instinctively braced my back against Suzy's pull on the shoulder holster, and as the gun barrel cleared the hem of my jacket my right hand slipped inside, on to the butt of my pistol, drawing it in one seamless motion, thumb releasing the safety catch, second pad of the index finger firm on the trigger. Turning on my heel in a semi-crouch, I brought the pistol up into the textbook position, right arm rigid, other elbow and wrist cocked inwards, and looked past the sight and into the eyes of the terrorist on the left.

We had been astonishingly fast on the draw. One moment they were looking at a young couple petting on a park bench, and three-quarters of a second later they were looking the wrong way up the barrels of our weapons. In the excitement Suzy's voice cracked, and the 'FREEZE' she tried to shout came out as a shrill 'PHEEEEEE' – piercing enough to shatter any glass within range. I was yelling hoarsely at them, 'LIE DOWN, LIE DOWN, LIE DOWN!'

The effect on the terrorists of our lightning transformation was stunning. Two jaws dropped open, four eyes widened, and the one on the left put his hands to his chest and fell to his knees. Oh God, I thought, we've killed him, he's having a heart attack. He toppled forwards face-down, arms dropping sideways on to the ground. Meanwhile, the other had dropped the holdall, which bounced once on the tarmac path with a loud clattering rattle. He gaped wide-eyed at Suzy, trying to back away from the dancing barrel of the submachine gun waving inches from his chin, but tripped over his own feet. He fell heavily to the ground and lay on his back with his hands covering his face, knees drawn up to his chest. They clearly thought we were about to execute them.

Suzy struggled to recover her voice, and now it came out harsh and loud. 'FACE DOWN, FACE DOWN! ARMS OUT!' I scurried about, encouraging them into position with my foot. I shot a glance back at the women further down the slope and puzzled briefly at the sight. They were in a tangled heap on the tarmac, the toddlers roaring as they ran towards their mums. As I swung back to the terrorists it dawned on me that, when we leapt up shouting, they must both have tried to run across each other's path to reach their kids, and collided. Now they were scrambling to their feet and letting out low wails. I registered that they were still no threat.

'Search them! Quick!' Suzy said breathlessly. I knelt hard on the back of the first, rapidly frisking his body with my free hand, covered by the submachine gun. I felt the bulk of a pistol in his anorak pocket and dragged it out. It was a Czech model, quite old. I rolled him bodily on to his side and quickly ran my hands around his front, but there was nothing else, not even a knife.

I could hear Suzy on the net as I moved to the other one to complete the search. 'Zero, Tango. Got 'em, got 'em, both Bravos and the holdall – three longs, at least one short. We need some police or something here pronto.'

'Roger that. Feds and green army are blue lighting to you. Any trouble with the locals?'

Suzy looked round and into the distance. Other than the mothers and children, who were now scuttling away towards the park gates, the area seemed deserted. Then she noticed that the two louts had reappeared with two older men. While she watched, one ran back into the estate, the other continuing to observe us. A faint siren note rose in the distance, faded out, then reappeared more strongly than before, approaching from the south. Now two middle-aged women had joined the man. Word would be spreading outwards through the estate like the shockwave of an explosion. A hostile, even murderous crowd could form within minutes round here.

'No, not yet, but vultures are definitely gathering. I can hear the Feds now.'

'Tango, X-Ray. Watch out for the cops, they don't know you're here. Stand on your weapons.' Good point. Even if the local police were expecting to find us here with the terrorists we wouldn't want them to get confused. The standard emergency procedure was to surrender to them first and establish who was who later.

As I finished searching the second one I stood up and looked about. I could hear the team arranging for a lift for Suzy and me, back to our car. At the edge of the park I could make out the shapes of two grey police Hotspur armoured Land Rovers and two drab green, decrepit-looking army ones. The lead vehicle bounced over the kerb and tried to barge open one of the wrought-iron gates, but the massive bolt protruding into the tarmac wouldn't give. The vehicle reversed briefly, jerking to a halt inches from the bumper of the one behind it, and an officer raced round the front of the bonnet to open the gate. The vehicles began to spill through the gap and lumber up the incline towards us, their back wheels slewing left and right in the soft ground.

Still keeping the terrorists flat on the deck, we found ourselves surrounded by the four armoured vehicles and the troops and policemen who were pouring from them. We had put our weapons down on the ground and stood with our hands in the air, holding our identity cards aloft. An enormous RUC sergeant approached us, taking in the scene.

'Hi.' I smiled nervously at him. 'We've caught these two with a bag of rifles and a pistol. They're all made safe.'

The Sergeant looked puzzled and wary. He was joined by the army patrol commander, a sick-looking corporal in a flak jacket. His rifle was pointing directly at my stomach; I could see a small patch of rust on it, just behind the foresight.

'And just who the fuck are yous?'

'I'm Captain Williams and this is Corporal Anderson,' I replied, using our cover names. 'Don't worry – we're on your side. These two aren't, though – or weren't,' I added. 'You can claim the credit for this if you like, but I'd search them again, I wasn't very thorough.'

As his mind digested these bits of information as fast as it was able, we allowed our hands slowly to drop. I gently pushed the barrel of his rifle to one side with my ID card.

The corporal's face registered something resembling glee as the consequences of being able to report a double arrest like this – with weapons – slowly dawned. He turned to organise another search, but was countermanded by the sergeant, who said, 'OK, John. We'll deal with this now. Just secure the area if you would.'

As the corporal moved away I said quietly to the sergeant, 'We're 14 Company – your control room should be able to confirm it. We had a bit of bother with our own police support.'

'I know who you are,' he replied quietly. 'Thin out if you want. I'll clear this up.'

Suddenly I felt an enormous sense of anti-climax, and a little sick as the tension ebbed out of me. Without a word, Suzy and I reholstered our weapons and set off at a gentle jog, up the slope to the point where X-Ray was waiting to give us a lift. As we crossed the park in the growing dusk we chatted quietly about the consequences of the intercept. There was no doubt that a dozen locals had taken a hard look at us from outside the scattered cordon of troops. They could even have taken photos. As covert surveillance operators our usefulness here had just been blown. It hadn't been practical to put on the balaclavas we usually carried for just such a compromise: while we could trust the uniformed HMSU and the SAS not to shoot us by mistake, it would have been suicidal to wear them in front of green army and local police. The consequence of this public exposure was that we'd be unable to work this patch for a bit – at least until we'd allowed time for memories to fade. Never mind, I thought, there are plenty of other areas to work.

We slowed to a brisk walk as we turned out of the park gate. As I stepped off the kerb towards X-Ray's car, parked on the other side of the road, I glanced down and noticed that the kerbstones were neatly painted in the tribal colours of the area. It reminded me of the only other place I had seen painted kerbstones. They were outside the guard room of the infantry regiment that I joined in Germany after leaving Sandhurst. There, they were always kept freshly painted by that week's party of defaulters.

Now, light-headed with adrenalin, it seemed like a thousand years before.

Chapter Two

In the 1980s, the British Army of the Rhine was a significant contribution to the security of Western Europe. My regiment's role within it, as an Airmobile Battalion, was to locate and then ambush any Soviet armoured thrusts heading for the Channel ports. This we practised endlessly across the German countryside, in the baking heat of summer and the thigh-deep snow of a continental winter.

As the seasons passed, the annual training routine began to lose its appeal for me, and I started to cast about for something different to do. I volunteered myself for a six-week jungle warfare training course in Brunei, a small state, still ruled by a Sultan, occupying a corner of the island of Borneo. Here, after ten days' acclimatisation in Hong Kong, we learnt how to survive and fight in the sweltering primary jungle that swathes its steep ridges and narrow valleys. We spent days patrolling tactically through the bush in the company of hunters from the indigenous Iban tribe, who instructed us in tracking and trapping techniques.

On our return to base from one patrol we saw a bunch of SAS recruits setting out for their own training camp deep in the jungle. Their instructors looked grizzled, fit and vaguely menacing. As the two groups assembled on the helipad at the barracks, we ignored each other. This encounter made me think of my own situation. Although I was enjoying the rigours of the jungle, I'd soon be back in Germany again, suffering the same old exercise routines. I idly wondered whether I should try the selection course for the SAS. But I'd heard it said that the SAS spent most of their time training for situations that very rarely arose – which would surely be pretty tedious.

No sooner was I back in Germany than the battalion was ordered to prepare for a four-month emergency tour in West

Belfast. We flung ourselves into the specialised training necessary for this, pleased to be deploying to an operational theatre at long last.

Our role in Belfast was to escort the two-man RUC beat patrols around the fiercely nationalist areas, protecting them against sniper attack by throwing a fast-moving and unpredictable cordon of soldiers around them. We achieved this by splitting each rifle platoon into teams of four men, known as 'bricks'. A brick commander was a corporal or lance corporal, and a patrol of four bricks was commanded by the platoon commander or platoon sergeant.

Two out of the three platoons from D Company were based in Macrory Park Security Force Base, a small outpost of a dozen Portakabins on a piece of wasteground in the middle of the exclusively republican Whiterock housing estate. An eight-foot-high breeze block wall ran around the camp, which was about sixty metres square, with armoured observation posts at each corner. These were permanently manned. The walls were topped with a ten-foot screen of corrugated, grey-painted steel sheeting, above which was a further ten feet of wire netting, designed to prevent the locals from lobbing nail bombs or grenades over the fence into our compound. From the outside it looked like a modern version of Fort Apache, right down to the massive double gates that swung open to let us in or out. The main difference was that the American Indians hadn't had ready access to heavy machine guns or explosives, either of which would make short work of our defences.

The three platoons rotated around a six-day cycle. This was composed of forty-eight hours patrolling the southern half of the patch from Macrory Park, covering the Whiterock, St James and Beechmounts estates, then forty-eight hours patrolling the northern half based at New Barnsley, concentrating on the Ballymurphy and Springhill estates. The final forty-eight hours were spent acting as guards, mobile reaction force and ops room watchkeepers at Macrory Park. This routine meant that every member of the company worked twelve hours on and twelve hours off, every day of the week, for four months solid – broken only by one four-day leave period roughly in the middle.

This level of patrol activity was extremely demanding – all the more so because we fully appreciated that every second we were outside the camp perimeter we effectively became walking targets. Fortunately D Company suffered no serious casualties during the tour, only the odd broken bone from the bricks and bottles that were frequently hurled at us. However, B Company, based to our east at North Howard Street Mill in the Lower Falls area, sadly lost a young NCO, killed by a bomb which had been concealed in a derelict building near the infamous Divis flats. Half a mile to our west, a patrol from A Company was ambushed by an IRA gun team, who opened up on them with an M60 machine gun before escaping in a stolen car. By chance there were no casualties.

In reality, this situation was a significant improvement on what had gone before. It was only relatively recently that the residents of the hard republican areas had begun to tolerate the appearance of RUC constables. For years the army had been acting in place of the police, and although the IRA was actively waging war against us, the local populace had become relatively inured to the presence of soldiers. At first, the sight of RUC constables had roused the locals into a fury bordering on a riot, but as the months passed they seemed to have become more and more used to the idea. By the time we arrived in West Belfast, two constables were able to walk their beat protected by only sixteen soldiers, whereas a year or two before a whole company of troops would have been required.

Being patrol commander, I would walk beside the policemen as they moved at random around their patch. My job was to direct the four satellite bricks – using a simple code over our small and extremely unreliable radio sets – into positions from which their very presence would deter or prevent a terrorist shooting at the policemen. Since the police were always in the centre of a defensive circle with a radius of about 150 metres, the greatest threat was in fact to the soldiers on the outside of the protective ring. The concept of the four-man brick had been developed specifically so that it could provide itself with all-round defence in an urban area, the individual members covering each other across road junctions and open areas which might provide a terrorist sniper with an opportune target.

It was routine when out on patrol to stop and question suspicious-looking individuals or known former terrorists. We always took the trouble to chat to them in as civil and friendly way as possible, because we understood that the Catholic population had good historical reasons to resent and mistrust the Protestants in Ulster. Since 1969 the streets that we were now patrolling had effectively been a no-go area for the police.

On two occasions during my tour the individuals we stopped for questioning were undercover soldiers, one male and one female. They had been operating individually in the hardest republican ghettos, dressing and behaving exactly like the locals. On each occasion their reaction had been the same: 'Don't make a scene, just treat me like any other civilian and I'll be on my way. Don't worry about what I'm up to; you don't need to know.' We had no idea who they were or what they were doing, but we certainly admired their courage.

At the end of the tour we returned to barracks in Germany and, as the last snowplough rumbled back into its shed at the end of spring, the battalion set off again on another season of exercises, range practices and training events. Having been through this mill twice before, I now realised that there was little new or novel in the battalion's programme. We had another two years to serve in Germany.

It was with mixed feelings then that, having been summoned to the CO's office one morning, I learnt that I was to become the next regimental intelligence officer, combining the role with the job of assistant adjutant. This meant promotion to the rank of captain – which was welcome – but it also meant that I was going to be deskbound for a couple of years, which wasn't quite what I had had in mind. Nonetheless, I was prepared to give anything new a go.

The adjutant's office handled all the administration for the battalion, and the adjutant himself – a rather serious, dark-haired senior captain called Charlie – was the official guardian of military discipline in the unit, with the ferocious assistance of the regimental sergeant major. One of my duties was to co-ordinate the publication of Battalion Routine Orders, which appeared daily on company noticeboards. One morning, the chief clerk handed me a single sheet of paper for inclusion the next day, on which was a short typed paragraph:

> FROM TIME TO TIME THERE IS A REQUIREMENT FOR MEN AND WOMEN TO VOLUNTEER TO UNDERTAKE SPECIAL DUTIES OF A HAZARDOUS NATURE IN NORTHERN IRELAND. THE SELECTION AND TRAINING FOR SPECIAL DUTIES ARE BOTH RIGOROUS AND ARDUOUS.

FOR FURTHER DETAILS SEE DEFENCE COUNCIL INSTRUCTION 11/80/21A.

'What on earth is this, Chiefie?' I asked.

'Secret Squirrels in Ulster, sir. If I told you about it I'd have to shoot you! Anyway, it's of no interest to the likes of you, sir – you should be concentrating on passing your staff exams.'

He went out to answer his ringing phone. I waited for him to finish his call, then stuck my head through the small hatch that connected our offices. 'Yeah, no doubt . . . but what is it, Chiefie?'

'Er, well, to be honest, I don't know much about it myself. It's all very sensitive. I've never read the DCI.'

'Oh, well, I'll take a look myself, then. There's a full set of DCIs in the orderly room isn't there?'

'That particular DCI is classified secret; it's in the safe. I've got to do the weekly check of the secure docs this afternoon. You can look at it then if you want.'

After lunch I joined him outside the secure room. It was a large, windowless cell at the heart of the Battalion HQ complex. I'd been inside several times before with the company commanders, because hanging on one wall was a large map showing our wartime deployments. (If the Soviets came pouring over the border, these were the positions that the battalion would crash out to occupy, and so the map was classified Top Secret.)

Dominating the room was a vast steel safe, which Chiefie quickly opened. He rummaged through two shelves. 'Here you are, 11/80/21A. There's not much to it, I'm afraid.' He handed me a flimsy sheet of paper, and I took in the scanty details. Volunteers from all three services, men and women, were required for selection and training for hazardous independent intelligence operations in Northern Ireland . . . The unit was known as Intelligence and Security Group . . . Applicants should preferably be unmarried . . . Six months' training after selection. The contact office was a room in the M.o.D. Main Building in Whitehall.

As I read I could feel the hairs on the back of my neck begin to prickle. Here was something different! Everyone knew about the SAS, but this couldn't be them because the SAS didn't recruit females. Intelligence and Security Group? I'd never even heard of this lot. Maybe this is what those two undercover soldiers we'd come across in Belfast had been up to.

'Thanks, Chiefie,' I said, handing back the sheet, deep in thought.

He looked at me hard. 'Don't you go spoiling your career over some special forces malarkey, sir! They're not very nice people in my experience.'

'No, no. I expect you're right.' But as I walked back down the long corridor I was thinking to myself, he said those words – *special forces*. Images of Bodie and Doyle, *Harry's Game*, James Bond and the Man from U.N.C.L.E. flickered in front of my mind's eye. Could the good old-fashioned, traditional British Army really offer this? It seemed unlikely. I had to find out more.

The next morning, the adjutant and I strolled up to the officers' mess for coffee. As we started across the playing fields I said casually, 'I had a look at that special duties DCI yesterday. It seemed quite interesting. Do you know anything about Intelligence and Security Group?'

Charlie glanced sideways at me. 'Yeah, we had a presentation from them at Junior Staff College, they're also known as 14 Company.' He paused. 'Don't even think about it!'

'That's exactly what Chiefie said! What the hell does everyone think is wrong with me? If they're looking for volunteers, why shouldn't I consider it?'

'James, you're nuts. You don't know what they do to you. OK – for instance, on day one you all line up and they introduce you to your buddy for the next two weeks. Only it's not a person, it's a six foot log – and where you go, it goes, 'cause you're tied to it! Drop it and you get a kicking!'

'For Christ's sake, Charlie, that's got to be crap! Who told you that? What'd be the point?'

'A chap on my course said he'd tried the selection but got kicked off on day three. Said it was absolute hell, totally pointless shit. And after twenty-four hours he'd changed his mind anyway.'

'Well, he would say that, wouldn't he, if he couldn't hack it, for goodness sake!' Despite my bravado, this information did shake me a bit. I changed the subject as we approached the mess. The last thing I wanted was to make a fool of myself by biting off more than I could chew.

The summer routine continued, but still I was fretting. Although life in the battalion was still great fun, it simply wasn't challenging enough.

The turning point came when D Company was tasked to relieve a neighbouring regiment as guard for a nearby nuclear weapon storage site. The instruction was to man the watch towers and perimeter fence surrounding the bunkers, which were hidden beneath a clearing deep in the German forest. For this job the soldiers were required to carry live ammunition in their magazines at all times, because in the event of war these secret nuclear sites could be an early target for eastern bloc special forces, known as Spetznaz.

Out of curiosity I accompanied Tony, whose platoon was detailed for the first week's stint at the site, on his initial visit to the area to discuss the handover. As Tony was shown round by his opposite number, I sat outside the low guardhouse in the sunshine with the resident platoon's company commander, a major called Nick. Nick commented that this was an enormous change from his last job in Northern Ireland, where he had been in plain clothes.

'That wasn't special duties, was it?' I enquired casually.

'Yes, it was – and to be honest I was hoping to stay a while longer, but I've got to do a spell as a company commander here or I won't get to Staff College.'

I studied him closely as we sat side by side. He looked ordinary enough, and seemed a nice chap. He'd said he was an English graduate, and I couldn't imagine him putting up with being tied to a log. 'Would you recommend it? Special duties, I mean? I once thought of volunteering myself.'

He sat up and looked at me directly. Then he looked away, taking in the clearing and the watch towers. He answered quietly. 'For most soldiers this is about as exciting as it gets – guarding nukes with twenty rounds in your magazine. It's OK, but by God it isn't very exciting, is it? If you want a bit of adventure, just go for it. Every one'll try to put you off, or fill your head with horror stories. They're either ignorant, jealous or gutless. You make up your own mind. But, yes, I'd recommend it. Just make sure you're fit before you go. *Really* fit.'

'But what's it like? What's involved?' I pleaded.

He thought for a while. 'I can't say. I'd like to, but it wouldn't be fair. The selection is bloody hard. It needs to be, because the consequences of the wrong type getting through are serious. But you could pass it, no problem, if you really wanted to. We always need more officers.'

He'd used the word 'we' so casually. Now I knew that I desperately wanted to be able to talk about 'we'. I wanted to be where it's at, to be on the inside, to be part of a select band, the happy few. At that moment my mind was made up.

A week later I put in a written request to my Commanding Officer, volunteering myself for special duties.

Clutching my Joining Instructions in one hand and the steering wheel in the other, I peered out into the gathering dusk. With the light failing, it was becoming increasingly difficult to read the typed directions to the disused army camp.

Ignoring the urge to stop and pee again, I caught myself mentally checking off once again the list of kit and equipment that I was supposed to have brought with me. It seemed surprisingly short, little more than two changes of lightweight army working dress, PT kit, and a set of scruffy civilian clothes, to be packed in no more than two bags.

At least I felt fit. I should do, I thought, having spent the last two months slogging round the hills that circled our barracks in Germany. I was probably almost as fit as I had ever been.

Five weeks earlier, I had been summoned to our Divisional HQ to participate in a one-day programme of PT, an interview and IQ tests. It was run by three mysterious people in plain clothes who, to my frustration, having quizzed me about what I thought might be involved, imparted no information whatsoever about the job. They did say, however, that any distinguishing physical marks – such as scars, birthmarks or tattoos – would instantly rule a candidate out of the running.

The following week, I received a letter from the M.o.D. saying I had been graded as suitable to undergo further selection, and enclosing Joining Instructions for a two-week selection course in England.

I yawned again. It was mostly nerves, but I was a bit tired too. I was still irritated with myself for not having allowed enough time for the drive over from Germany – via home – to this God-forsaken corner of the Midlands. Here was I, about to start a two-week selection course, and already I felt weary.

The crossroads I'd been waiting for grew in the headlights. I swung the car left and, after a mile and a half, slowed as the camp entrance appeared on the right. A large sign, which had been peppered with buckshot from someone's shotgun, read: MOD PROPERTY – KEEP OUT – TRESPASSERS WILL BE PROSECUTED. No buildings or lights were visible from the road, but I could just make out a section of perimeter fence, sagging and rusty. I drove carefully up the rough track which led towards a patch of tall scrub in the distance.

A hundred yards into the scrub, the track twisted and I faced a lowered barrier. Either side of it, a new seven-foot chainlink fence snaked away into the dark, topped by a loose roll of razor wire. A uniformed policeman, wearing the insignia of the M.o.D., flagged me to a halt and checked my registration against a sheet on his clip-board. A moment later he signalled to a colleague, who raised the barrier. He said crisply, 'Stay on this road. Follow the signs to the reception car park and park up.' I nodded to him and drove on into the darkness, swallowing hard. What the hell am I doing here? I asked myself out loud.

As I pulled into the car park behind a series of low, old-fashioned barrack buildings, I looked around. The solid brick two-storey blocks probably dated from the 1930s; now they had that vacant and depressing air found in so many disused army camps. I could see a deserted parade ground in the distance, and beyond it, at the edge of some playing fields, a large and gaunt gymnasium. A row of unlit upper windows above its sloping roof resembled the clerestory of a cathedral.

There must have been about twenty civilian cars already in the car park when I arrived. I slipped into a vacant slot and turned off my headlights. There were few lights on in the eight or so barrack blocks I could see from here. Half a dozen four-ton trucks and the same number of minibuses stood beside a low block that looked like a kitchen and canteen. A hundred metres behind that building, lit by pools of orange light from floodlights set on tall poles at regular intervals, the thin birchwood scrub of the training area crowded up to the shiny perimeter fence. The training areas surrounding every infantry base are pretty similar, and at first sight this one looked no different. Acres of low, scratching gorse scrub alternated with swathes of heather or bracken dotted with spinneys of pine and birch trees. Doubtless it would be criss-crossed by miles of stony track. From the map I guessed that it was at least a thousand acres. Odd, though, that there was so little life in this camp, I thought. Sitting quietly in the car, I couldn't see a single soul anywhere, even at the lighted windows.

Suddenly, I was startled by a loud tap on my window. I quickly wound it down. A stocky chap in his late twenties stood beside the car. He had sandy hair and was fit-looking, but was otherwise nondescript. He wore army boots, olive green lightweight trousers and a sweatshirt, with no indication of his rank showing. Through the open window he said, 'Turn off the engine, lock the car, bring your kit and keep up with me. Do exactly as you're told, and address all instructors as "staff".'

'Right-oh . . . staff.' Christ this takes me straight back to Sandhurst, I thought. I picked my two holdalls out of the boot, locked it, and turned to follow him – but he was already twenty metres away, jogging briskly towards the corner of a building. Shit! I broke into an awkward run and cantered after him, loose change and keys jangling wildly in my pockets, bags crashing about my knees.

'Stand here, at ease, face against this wall. Don't talk and don't move until you're spoken to.'

We were now outside a two-storey building. I stood with my nose inches from the damp brick. Two other people were standing in a similar position next to me, and behind me I could hear a couple of instructors pacing up and down.

After about five minutes, something touched me lightly on the shoulder and a voice said, 'Leave your bags where they are and go into the first room on the left.' As I entered the room a pale-faced, skinny clerk in barrack dress hung a board round my neck with the number thirty-seven written on it in large figures. I was surprised by the pop of a flash as someone took a Polaroid of me. Then the clerk thrust a small card mounted on a safety pin into my hand, also with the number thirty-seven on.

'From now on you are number thirty-seven, nothing else,' said the fair-haired instructor. 'Wear that tag on your right chest at all times. Don't reveal your real identity, rank or unit to anyone else during your stay here. Got that?'

'Yes, staff.'

'Leave your ID card and car keys on the table here, then collect your bags and follow me.'

We doubled away towards another tall brick block, where he led me up two flights of stairs and into a large, high-ceilinged dormitory on the first floor. It was like any other old-fashioned barrack room, with a dark-grey polished floor and a neat row of ten beds down each side. Between each bed stood a tall grey metal wardrobe and a low grey bedside cabinet. Bare bulbs hung from the roof and there were no curtains at the window. It was very clean and smelt faintly of disinfectant. Neatly stacked on each striped, plastic-covered mattress of each grey-painted, metal-framed bed were two sheets and a pillowcase, two grey army blankets, a striped pillow and a dull orange counterpane. The washroom for our floor, I was told, was across the other side of the stairwell. About a dozen of the beds had already been bagged, judging by the sundry suitcases and holdalls that were disgorging their contents over them.

'Get changed into boots, lightweights and jersey, and be seated in the lecture theatre opposite in five minutes. Any questions?'

I nearly said, 'Yes – where's the mess?' but realised just in time that flippancy might not be appreciated right now. 'No, staff,' I replied meekly.

I slung my bags on to a bed half-way down on the left, and frantically began changing out of my civvies. Just then a different instructor arrived with another puffing red-faced volunteer, and gave him the same brief. We glanced at each other warily as we struggled into our kit.

Four and a half minutes later, perspiring gently, I took my seat in the large room. It was brightly lit and crammed with rows of school desks on each of which was a pad of paper, a pencil, a rubber and a sharpener. I looked nervously around. The room was already half full of volunteers, who were seated and seemed to be scribbling frantically. I counted five women among our number, one of whom was quite tall with light brown hair and who looked, from her slightly patrician bearing, like she might be an officer.

An instructor appeared behind me and said quietly, 'Start writing a detailed account of your journey here today. Write at least five sides of foolscap.'

Damn, it was hard to concentrate. This was a strange and disconcerting set-up. A steady stream of new faces was entering and sitting down. The room was far too hot. I sharpened my pencil, then realised there was nowhere to put the shavings. I fumbled them into my pocket, picked up my pencil and began to write.

After about forty minutes had passed, an impressive-looking figure, six foot tall, lean and with greying cropped hair, strode into the room from one side and joined a group of instructors, which included two women. I studied the group surreptitiously, counting about a dozen of them in all. Both of the women were pretty, one blonde and one brunette, probably in their mid to late twenties. I guessed from the slight deference paid to the new arrival by the other instructors, and from the fact that he looked about forty, that he was a senior officer, perhaps a lieutenant colonel, although you couldn't tell from his dress, which was the same as the others. He stood on the small stage at the front and looked impassively at us. Then he cleared his throat, which was sufficient for him to secure the full attention of everyone in the room. After a short silence he spoke in a quiet but firm voice.

'It's nothing personal, but I suspect that very few if any of you will meet the high standards we are seeking. Just do as you're told at all times and try your hardest. Remember that you're free to leave here at any time. Just ask one of the staff. I promise you that failure is no disgrace. We have a very particular requirement that we need to fill and we cannot afford to compromise. Good luck to you all! Chief instructor, carry on.'

One of the instructors took over. He was quite short but powerfully built, with brown hair. He looked about thirty-five. 'Right, everybody, you've got five minutes to change into PT kit and parade in three ranks outside. Drop what you've just written into this burnbag on your way out,' he barked. 'GO!' The room erupted in a scraping clatter as over a hundred desks were pushed forward at once and we surged towards the exit, hearts thumping.

The next day – beginning at 6 a.m. – flashed past in a disorienting whirlwind of punishing PT sessions and strange tasks. We were the only occupants of this otherwise deserted barracks.

After the first two sessions of PT, one conducted around the training area and the other in the gym, we were told to walk through a room one at a time, entering by one door and leaving by another, and not to touch anything or loiter for more than two minutes. Obviously we were supposed to make a mental note of the contents. The room was furnished like a bedsit, with a TV playing quietly in the corner. It was as if whoever lived here had just walked out of the door ahead of me. Looking round, I tried to memorise the scene: a tin of milk powder on the window sill; a stocking draped over the back of a chair; a cigarette butt ground out under a table; a suitcase ajar on the end of the bed, a newspaper protruding from it.

Back in the lecture theatre again, we had one hour to answer a detailed questionnaire about the room. The first task was to describe the person who spoke to you last before you entered the room. Damn! Which was it? The tall gangling one who looked like John Cleese or the one with fair hair . . . I couldn't be sure. Next question: what had he said? Was he left- or right-handed, and how could you tell? Then there were questions about the position of the individual items in the room, and about other details – what channel the TV had been tuned to, what make it was, what was in the waste paper bin, and so on. The last task was to sketch a plan of the room from above, showing the location of the windows, doors and furniture.

Next we were split into groups and shown how to strip and assemble the SLR, SMG and Browning pistol, which were the army's standard rifle, submachine gun and side arm. As an infantry officer I already knew how to do all this, but it brought home to me that some of the volunteers were probably from the Navy or the RAF, and therefore wouldn't be particularly familiar with these weapons. Nor would the five women on the selection course. As we practised on the weapons the blonde female instructor moved around the room taking notes, presumably logging our individual dexterity and facility with weapons.

Although I would never have described myself as a particularly competitive person, I found that I was subconsciously measuring myself against the other volunteers on the course. Knowing no details of anyone else's rank or background, all I had to judge them against was my own performance at the various tasks. In spare moments I observed my colleagues. Like some amateur Professor Higgins, I tried to guess what rank they had or service they might be by listening to their accents and use of language. One slightly effete and languid type seemed almost certain to be a cavalry officer. There was a real Biggles lookalike, with the regulation RAF aviator's moustache. There were lots of junior NCO-types from the infantry and the paras (paras stick out anywhere with their air of aggressive independence). There were also some Royal Marines, identifiable from their barrack-room slang – words like 'yomp' and 'heads' – and one or two sailors, who seemed completely out of their element and didn't stand to attention or at ease in the army fashion, and referred to the 'galley' instead of the cookhouse. It was striking that there was no common thread of character or personality running through us; we were a very mixed bag indeed. The only thing we had in common was that we had all volunteered for an unspecified and dangerous duty.

The disconcerting thing was never knowing what was coming next. Life in the forces had always been very structured, fully briefed in advance and working to a strict programme. And now here we were, being confronted with a series of unexpected and unwelcome tasks to perform in an environment where suddenly one's rank seemed to have no bearing on anything. I'd noticed that some of the instructors who cajoled us, several of whom were undoubtedly officers, kept swapping rank insignia with each other, alternating between corporal and major.

Sometimes the senior officer appeared and observed us, but he never spoke to us.

'Take a map, a Silva compass and a torch from the table, and depart individually when I call your number! You are now . . . here . . . ' The instructor indicated with the tip of a billiard cue a series of grid references chalked on to a blackboard at the front of the room. ' . . . And you have one hour to get to . . . here . . . Odd numbers must visit this point *en route*, even numbers must visit this point . . .'

Without looking at a map, I could tell from the relationship of the first and last grids that they must be at least six kilometres apart, even as the crow flies. Shit! I'd have to run to cover that distance in an hour, allowing for map reading errors, and we'd only just had a hasty supper of fish fingers, chips, beans and tea. It was 9 p.m. already. I sighed and bent to tighten the laces on my boots again. I could hear the rain spattering out of a broken gutter on to the tarmac outside. Why am I doing this to myself? I wondered.

'Thirty-seven. Go!'

I stepped out into the darkened camp, turning the collar of my combat jacket up against the cold drizzle. My legs were stiff and painful from my exertions earlier in the day. As soon as I got my bearings I hobbled away, and once the blood began to warm my tired muscles I broke into an easy jog.

I lost track of my position a couple of times as I alternately walked and ran across the bleak training area. There was no moon to help, and a steady drizzle ensured that we would all be soaked through. At last I arrived at the destination, a derelict shed below the crest of a low rise that was bisected by a track. A couple of instructors stood in the lee of a four-ton truck parked alongside the shed. One came forwards to me.

'OK, Thirty-seven. This morning you practised stripping and assembling weapons. Under that tarpaulin over there you'll find three weapons, already stripped, laid out on three mats. Crawl under the tarp and reassemble them as quickly as you can. You can use your torch, but don't let any light escape. Any questions? Good. Start now!'

Squirming under the thick canvas sheet, which smelt faintly of diesel oil and old rubber, I quickly found the first weapon. It was an SMG, and I methodically assembled it in the stuffy dampness. As I tried to compress the thick return spring beneath the round end cap, it somehow slipped out and whacked me across the chin, drawing a tiny line of blood. Bastard, I muttered. I was lucky it missed my eyes. Clipping the spring home, I worked the action and squeezed the trigger to let the breech block slip forward, restrained by my hand on the cocking lever. It settled firmly into its recess with a satisfactory hollow clunk. I then moved on to the next weapon, a pistol. No problems with that. Then came the SLR. Because it had been my personal weapon for the last three years, I could strip and assemble it blindfold. With the task completed I crawled out into the fresh night air, conscious now of the discomfort of my wet and muddy clothing. Another volunteer had arrived and was waiting for his turn to strip the same weapons down again. I got to my feet and patiently stood at ease in the light rain, waiting for the next chore.

'Right, Thirty-seven, make your way back to camp now. That's all for today. The quickest way from here is to follow that track. There's a container of tea and some sandwiches in the lecture room. Get your head down and parade dressed for PT at 0730 tomorrow.'

It was 1 a.m. by the time I'd doubled back to camp, showered and sorted out my kit. At least there was no bullshit here and we didn't have to worry about ironing kit or polishing boots. Others were still arriving back at camp and I chatted to some of them. We were all firmly determined to stick it out, but no one knew what lay ahead and there seemed no point wasting breath or precious time in pure speculation. I reckoned the best plan was simply to take everything as it came, without trying to anticipate anything.

The regime had proved too much for some, who had arrived too unfit to cope with the punishing PT. Already about a dozen volunteers had asked to be returned to their parent units. As I dropped into an exhausted sleep I thought, well, I'm still here for the moment.

The damp tarpaulin was weighing me down, pressing my head into the wet, spiky heather. Someone was shouting at me from the outside, but I didn't want to leave the cocoon I was in. The shouting was becoming more insistent and I could ignore it no longer. Reluctantly I was being dragged, exhausted, from a deep sleep.

'Rise and shine you lazy lot! Get your PT kit on and parade outside in ten minutes. Wakey, wakey!'

God, it can't be 7.30 already, I thought. I squinted at my watch. It said 5.50. The bastards, they've tricked us . . . I quickly joined the disgruntled migration to the washrooms, the sting of the icy tiles beneath my bare feet compounding my depression. We jostled along a row of washbasins, wiping the condensation from the mirrors as we shaved, yawning uncontrollably, hardly speaking, each locked in his own thoughts. The one thing that everyone in the forces can do on auto-pilot is wash, shave and dress in ten minutes flat.

We stamped about outside in three ranks wearing our thin PT shirts and shorts, chilled by the pre-dawn February air. The party of girls joined us from another barrack block where they were quartered together, chased along by the pretty blonde instructor, whom I'd heard one of the other instructors refer to as Sally. We were all very apprehensive, our muscles still sore from yesterday's exertions. Now half a dozen instructors appeared and we began some warming-up exercises. We were split into three groups and led off on a long run around the training area. Soon my group was strung out over about five hundred metres as we struggled to keep up, lungs aching with the frost. The instructors ran ahead of us with that seemingly effortless loping stride that signals extreme fitness.

By the time we stumbled back into camp the sun was up. I was almost on my knees as we jogged on the spot, warming down and waiting for the last stragglers to catch up. The moment everyone was in we were fallen out for thirty minutes for breakfast, before mustering again, still in our sweat-soaked PT kit. We were then led off to the gym and spent an agonising hour and a half in a whirl of circuit training and sprint relays – running backwards, sideways, on all fours, crabwise, piggy-back, wheelbarrow; interspersed with rope climbing, push-ups, pull-ups, star jumps and bunny hops. This was absolutely shattering. At times a few of us had to stumble grimly out of the double doors at the back of the gym, on to the playing field, where our breakfast reappeared involuntarily. Three volunteers threw in the towel in the face of this severe beasting, and were led away.

The blessed relief of hearing the words, 'Get back to your block, shower, change and parade in fifteen minutes in working dress!' was tempered only by the fear of what might come next. I felt seriously exhausted now – and it was only 10.15 – but in fact the next two hours involved sitting in the lecture theatre taking a variety of isometric tests. These were of the disquieting type that demand an immediate response to a sequence of questions. The combination of the enormous variety of themes running through them and the lack of time to consider the reply makes it impossible to try to fool the examiner or analyst. There were hundreds of questions, many quite odd. For instance, would you rather do two jobs quite well or only one job very well? Do you love anyone more than yourself? Would you rather be a tractor driver or a plumber? Do you ever lie? Do you prefer to travel or to arrive? Do you read a book every week? Do you always wash your hands when you go to the lavatory? Are you the life and soul of the party? Do you take trouble over things that don't matter? Which do you prefer – dogs or cats? Would you deceive a friend to spare his feelings? Which is more appealing to you – satisfaction or happiness? Are you a modest person? Do you always want to be told the truth? God only knows what significance could be attached to the results! They must certainly have been boring to mark and evaluate.

After a brief lunch we paraded once more outside our accommodation block, dressed in boots and lightweights. Four four-ton Bedford trucks appeared, we climbed aboard, and were driven for forty-five minutes into the surrounding countryside. We were then dropped off in pairs, with the object of progressing around a fifteen-kilometre circuit, visiting checkpoints every so often. Typically, the weather worsened considerably as my partner – a young Scottish NCO – and I leapt down from the tailboard of our vehicle and jogged slowly along the rolling country lanes and tracks in high wind and rain. Every so often we would pass pairs of volunteers going the other way round the circuit, and we'd swap encouragement and information about the location of the next checkpoint.

At last, as dusk fell, we were met by the welcome sight of a four-tonner with a container of tea. We dozed, huddled together in the back of the draughty unheated lorry, all the way back to camp, finally clambering down footsore and stiff. Fortunately, each washroom in our block had an excellent drying room at the far end, so we changed into our now dry spare working dress and quickly hung up our wet kit.

After supper, our faces glowing with windburn, we gathered for a very dull lecture on signals theory given by Jill, the brunette instructor. It seemed odd to me that the subject matter was extremely technical – irrelevant to anyone but a signals boffin – but then I twigged that this material would surely form the basis for a test. I could see a number of volunteers around the room dozing off, but the instructor ignored them. I forced myself to stay awake in the warm room and make notes as Jill, reading monotonously from a thick manual, droned on about frequency modulation, antennae wattage, resonance and so on. After about forty minutes she stopped abruptly and started to pass round a questionnaire covering the topics she'd just spoken about. There were looks of panic in some faces as they glanced through the fifty detailed questions.

It was with a feeling of luxury that I climbed into bed at 10 p.m., determined to catch up on some of the sleep I'd missed over the last couple of days. I slipped into a deep slumber. The next thing I knew, two enormous and very close explosions ripped me awake, shocked and bewildered. There were voices shouting nearby. I came to with little idea of where I was. Because my legs were tangled in the bedsheets I tumbled straight over the side and on to the floor. The man from the next bed trod on me as he leapt out. Now the lights snapped on and we were blinking stupidly at each other, mouths open. The room was hazy with smoke and I recognised that distinctive, fireworky, cordite smell. Thunderflashes! Two instructors were standing grinning in the doorway.

'You've got five minutes to parade outside in working dress! Move yourselves!'

Our hearts racing, and still in slight shock, we lined up outside in the darkness. Someone started calling the roll. As we stood in the frosty night beneath a wonderful array of stars, shivering with cold apprehension, the gaps in the numerical roll call showed that more than twenty volunteers had already cracked.

I looked at my watch. It was a quarter past midnight. We were led back into the lecture theatre, which was bathed in an eerie glow by a single table lamp with a blue bulb. On a screen in front of us, an ancient documentary film flickered into life. We goggled at the black and white images, as a year in the life of a tribe in a remote rainforest unfolded before us. It lasted about forty minutes, during which the urge to sleep in the dark, warm room was almost overwhelming.

Once it was over, the lights went up and again we were required to answer a long series of questions about what we had viewed. How many different animals lived in the long house? What were the women mashing in the wooden pot? How many sons did the chief have? Describe the youngest white man in the film, and so on.

We handed our answers in, then trooped back to our barrack block. It was well past two o'clock, but to my intense frustration I found I couldn't get back to sleep. Every noise or cough now woke me, heart thumping, fully expecting to be hauled out of bed once more.

All too soon – I still felt that I hadn't slept at all – an instructor appeared quietly at 6 a.m. and told us to turn out in PT kit. Again, we set out for a long, hard run around the training area, breaking only for punishing relays up and down a short, steep slope or squat-thrusts or sit-ups or star jumps. Then it was back to camp for a shower and breakfast before a map-reading lecture followed by a theoretical test, using map and protractor, at our desks.

My heart sank when we left the classroom to change for yet another session of PT.

Lying outside our block was a row of stretchers, each with a six-foot railway sleeper lashed to it. We formed up and were divided into ten teams of eight, the four remaining females being dispersed around the male teams. So far, the girls had done everything alongside us, to the best of their ability, and we were full of admiration for them.

A stretcher race forms part of the climax of all recruit training in the British Army, and we were therefore under no illusions about the unpleasantness of what lay in store. We set off at an alarmingly fast pace, four to each stretcher, the other four tailing along behind, ready to swap with the carriers the instant they flagged. The next forty-five minutes were a blur of burning muscles, straining lungs and aching arms as each team lumbered with its dread burden around the five-kilometre course. It was made much worse by the fact that most of the teams were within sight of each other throughout the race, so the instructors were able to goad us on relentlessly to beat the others. The route itself was wickedly planned to include hills, obstacles and streams. All but the very fittest of us were on our knees by the time we approached the accommodation block at the end of the last leg. I couldn't recall ever being subjected to a more gruelling test of endurance. At Sandhurst, we'd usually been well rested before each major test of stamina. Now I felt my reserves of strength and determination were being eroded.

A handful of individuals had performed badly in the stretcher race, becoming a burden to their teams. They must have realised that they were unlikely to pass the selection course now, even if they hung on till the end, and so they dropped out and were doubled away out of our sight. Our numbers were shrinking rapidly as individuals chose not to continue, some because of injury, but most because they couldn't stand the pace.

We were given twenty minutes to stagger indoors, change into civilian clothes and be seated in the lecture theatre, where the next task was explained to us. We heard that after a quick lunch we would be paired off, then each pair would be dropped by minibus on the outskirts of a local small village or hamlet. Our task was to sidle around the village as inconspicuously as possible, logging in our notebooks every detail we could, such as the position of individual houses, post-boxes, telephone poles, culverts under the road, hedgerows, ditches, etc. We were not to let it become obvious to the villagers what we were doing, but if questioned we could say that we were on a territorial army initiative exercise. On our return to camp we would have three hours to prepare a 36-inch-square plan of the village showing all the details that we had collated.

I was partnered with one of the women, who I guessed was an NCO in the WRAC. It felt good to be away from the claustrophobic camp environment, engaged on an unusual non-military task. Our morale was high as we padded around our hamlet for a couple of hours and we nipped into the Post Office to stock up on chocolate. Twice I spotted an instructor driving through the village in a blue Volvo, presumably checking up on us.

When our time was up, we returned to the rendezvous to meet our minibus, and dozed in the back as we meandered slowly back by a circuitous route, picking up more pairs of volunteers.

The novel task of creating a large-scale sketch plan absorbed us completely. We selected a scale of 1:1,000, and transposed the main topographical features from the 1:50,000 Ordnance Survey map on to our grid. We soon realised that this wouldn't help with the location of the roads and buildings, because they appeared disproportionately large on the OS map. Next we constructed a detailed key of features like hedgerows, ditches, footpaths, etc., using coloured crayons. The allotted three-hour period sped past, the large lecture room buzzing with voices as pairs of volunteers pored over their sketches.

By the finish at 7 p.m. my partner and I were satisfied with our efforts. As we packed up our drawing instruments and handed in our maps, now feeling very tired and looking forward to supper, again came the order, 'You've got five minutes to change into PT kit and parade outside! Go!' An involuntary groan went up and we jostled each other through the door.

We changed, then doubled over to the gym to find it had been set up as an indoor obstacle course, with benches to run along, boxes to vault, ropes to climb, beams to crawl under and so on. We split into teams, and for the next forty minutes raced around the circuit – first one way, then the other. The emphasis here was on agility rather than brute strength, and I actually found myself rather enjoying this session, tired though I was.

After a late supper of steak and chips and sponge pudding, sluiced down with a pint of sweet tea, we were told we had earned an early night to make up for the fact that we had been dragged out of bed the night before, and that the next activity would be after breakfast the following morning. In our dormitory we discussed this, cautious about such unlikely magnanimity, but on balance we decided that the instructors probably needed a night off themselves after the intensive activity of the last few days. Even so, as I lay in bed at 11.30, I found it difficult to relax, still haunted by the memory of the explosions in the darkness the night before. I could hardly believe that that episode occurred less than twenty-four hours ago; it seemed like last week, so busy had we been since dawn. I fell into a deep and dreamless sleep.

A slight click sounded and instantly I was awake and alert. I peered around in the darkness and fixed on the door. I guessed it was about one o'clock. Was it my imagination, or was the door swinging slowly open? Now a hand reached round and gripped the frame, followed by an arm and shoulder. A head appeared – and I recognised the silhouette of one of the instructors. He tiptoed silently into the room, looking around. In the half-light he caught my gaze, and at once put his finger to his lips, motioning me to stay silent. I lay and watched him. He stopped in the centre of the dormitory. He checked his watch, then slowly raised his hand to his mouth. A shrill, ear-splitting whistle pierced the night, taking me completely by surprise. Now he was shouting at the top of his voice, 'Everybody out, PT kit, three ranks outside in five minutes!' I could hear a similar commotion from the dormitory above mine, as once again we tumbled out of bed. At least this time I hadn't been sound asleep. As I dressed I glanced at my watch: 1.20 a.m.

For the second night running we shivered in the starlight. After a rapid rollcall we doubled over to the gym, which was ablaze with lights. As we jogged in through the wide doorway we were met by the sight of a proper boxing ring, set up in the middle of the floor. Oh Christ, I thought, here we go. We were told to line up in one row by height, tallest on the right, shortest on the left – which we achieved after a bit of confused wandering about. The four girls formed a separate line. Then we numbered off from the left into pairs.

The chief instructor stood in front and addressed us. 'Each pair of you in turn will put on boxing gloves and enter the ring. You will then have three minutes to batter the shit out of your opponent! Girls will box girls. We are not looking for fancy footwork, just guts and determination. Just do your best, and I will decide who's won. First pair, step forward!'

The rest of us sat on benches around the ring. I exchanged glances nervously with my partner. Although he was about the same height as me he looked much broader and heavier. Shit!

'Have you ever boxed before?' I asked him quietly.

'Yeah, I had a trial for the Navy team once,' he said with a slight smirk, looking completely unconcerned.

Goddamn! Just my luck to have to fight a Jolly Jack Tar with previous for Actual Bodily Harm.

Being fairly short, we were about the fifth pair to enter the ring. I had watched the preceding fights with mounting horror. I'd never boxed before and it looked pretty painful. Next to me, King Kong seemed amused rather than intimidated. He said to me, 'Don't worry, it'll be a piece of cake!' I smiled weakly at him in reply. That's what I'm afraid of, I thought to myself.

Now someone was tying the laces of some boxing gloves around my wrists . . . Now I was in the ring facing my opponent, breathing hard, hands up in what I hoped was a guard position. A bell sounded behind me and we moved towards each other. I made a half-hearted jab at the back of his raised gloves. Like a bolt of lightning his gloved fist burst through my defence and landed square and very hard on my forehead. Ouch! I was taken aback by the pain. I'd supposed that it wouldn't actually hurt much, being so keyed up, but it damn well did. Thump! This time he landed one on the left side of my head. Now I was beginning to get cross. I was vaguely aware of the shouts of the onlookers, yelling at me to get stuck in. Another thump, this time on the side of my chest, and I lost my temper. Fuck you, you bastard, I cursed inwardly as I launched myself at him, trying to get inside his clubbing fists. I jabbed successfully at his nose, which spurred me on, and then we were trading blows wildly, hitting hard, my shots mostly glancing off his gloves. Furious now, I gritted my teeth and battered on, taking far more punishment than I dispensed. I flailed recklessly, sometimes scoring, mostly not – but at least if I could sustain this tempo, I could perhaps keep him off balance.

The very effort of repeatedly punching as hard and as fast as I could was wearing me down; my legs were slowing, my arms becoming numb with weariness. Still we hammered away at one another, blood from my nose and lip slicking his gloves. A blow to my stomach winded me and I felt as if I was underwater, desperately wanting to take a deep breath but unable to. My body was working without conscious control and my mind was trying to count off the seconds. Already it felt like at least four minutes had passed. Why hadn't the bell rung? Surely it couldn't be another trick! Then I heard it . . . *clang* . . . and we stumbled apart. I tripped with fatigue. The judge declared that the Navy lad had won convincingly, but I was well beyond caring.

As she helped undo my gloves Jill said to me, 'Don't worry about it . . . you did fine.' She gripped my cheeks firmly in her hands and peered deep into my eyes, presumably to check if I was concussed. She was very attractive and I enjoyed the touch of her fingers – but all too soon she released me and I had to resume my place on the bench.

Grateful that this trial was now out of the way, I could sit back and watch the others battle it out in turn. I gingerly took stock of my condition. I was pretty badly bruised across my head and chest, one eye was closing, but the cuts were superficial. More seriously, my left thumb felt as if it had been temporarily dislocated. The joint began to swell ominously and was too sore to touch. Humiliatingly, my opponent appeared to be completely unscathed and had obviously thoroughly enjoyed himself, so much so that when someone further up the line bottled out and left his partner matchless, the stupid gorilla volunteered to have another go. To my great satisfaction his new partner was heavier and taller than him and had clearly boxed before, so it was a much more evenly balanced contest. Finally there were the four girls, who fought in pairs like alleycats, cheered on by everyone.

We jogged back to our accommodation. I washed the dried blood from my face, ran my thumb under a cold tap for a bit, and settled into bed once more. It was now about half past three, and this time I had no difficulty in dropping off to sleep at once.

We were left undisturbed until 7.15, and mercifully today there was no early morning PT. Instead, after breakfast, and feeling like death warmed up, we were driven out to a nearby range and spent most of the morning shooting the SLR, SMG and pistols in a variety of practices which were clearly designed to test our facility with weapons. My performance was marred somewhat by having to juggle everything away from my damaged thumb, but at least the swelling was subsiding.

On arrival back in camp, we had a brief lunch and were told to parade in boots and lightweights again. We doubled off in three ranks to the training area and then spent an hour and a half on the assault course, running round and round the sandy tracks between the individual obstacles, before returning, bruised again and exhausted.

The next task we faced seemed bizarre at the time. We were instructed to go through a door one by one, that led into a small windowless lobby. We were to shut the door behind us, enter an inner room, and to make our way slowly across it and leave by the far door, taking care not to leave any tracks or disturb the contents in any way. Simple enough, I thought.

When my turn was called, I entered the lobby and shut the door behind me. It was pitch dark, but I had seen where the inner door was. I edged over to it and gently swung it open towards me. I couldn't see a thing in the absolute darkness. I took a step carefully into the room and closed the door behind me. I waited for a moment to let my eyes adjust, but it soon became obvious that there were no leaks of light into the room, so there was little point in waiting any longer.

Feeling like a blind man I set off slowly across the room, carefully lifting one foot at a time. As the tip of my boot came down I felt a slight grittiness under it. I stopped, and bent down carefully to examine it. I traced a smooth layer of fine sand spread on the floor in front of me, so I gently followed the forward edge of it round to the left with the tip of my finger. I shuffled around it on my hands and knees.

Then I became aware of a light pressure against my left shoulder. Hardly breathing I froze, then eased back fractionally and put my hand up to examine the object. I felt a cold, rounded shape, like a large tin. It wobbled a little when my fingers touched it. I let my hand move slowly down its side, tracing its outline. Ah! It was a loose tower of tin cans, stacked one on top of the other. I skirted around it, still on all fours, keeping between it and the sand patch that would show my footprints if I strayed on to it.

Now I felt another gentle pressure, this time across the top of my hair. Reaching up, I touched a thin thread stretching tight about two feet off the ground. I ran my fingers left and right along its length as far as I could reach. Should I go under or over it? I started to stand up slowly, and almost at once my rising head knocked against something perched in the darkness above me. A second later there was a resounding crash as a heavy object tumbled to the floor. Shit! It must have been balanced on a beam or something above me. Keeping my head bent low, I cautiously stepped over the thread, then waved my hands delicately in front of me as I continued to advance in a crouch.

After the shock of the unexpected noise I wasn't sure which way I was now facing, and in the utter blackness I was beginning to have difficulty keeping my balance. To make matters worse my eyes seemed to be playing tricks on me; little flashes of light were popping inside my head. Here was another obstacle . . . only a table. I stroked its surface to check if anything was on it. A row of small metallic objects stood side by side in the centre of it. As my fingertips pattered lightly around them an image formed in my head. It was a circle of a dozen or so 9mm pistol rounds, standing on their ends towards the left hand end of the table. I tried to count the individual rounds, but found it impossible in the pitch dark. I moved on.

Then I encountered something like a mop propped at forty-five degrees against a wooden chair. I moved around to the right and kicked the edge of something on the floor. Reaching down, I made out a large tray, which seemed to be full of water. I gave it a wide berth and eventually reached the wall. Painstakingly I began to edge round to the right, searching for the door. Here it was, the thin handle protruding. I checked the space between the jambs and found another thread, vertical this time, which seemed to be attached to an object above the lintel. I eased the door open and slipped sideways past the thread and into the lobby beyond, which was also windowless. As I was doing so I almost jumped out of my skin when a voice from about two feet behind me in the darkness said, 'Shut the door behind you, wait thirty seconds, then go out the other door, round the front and send the next man in.' Whoever was speaking had obviously been observing me all along, presumably using night-vision goggles and an infra-red torch. Back in the classroom we drew a sketch of what we thought was in the room and where the objects were located.

Once more it was into PT kit for another beasting in the gym, followed by a quick change before supper. Then we gathered again in the lecture room in civilian clothes, and learnt that tonight we were to conduct another village reconnaissance, this time in the dark.

Again we were paired off and driven out far into the countryside. It was cold, very dark and drizzling, and within half an hour my partner – a young Geordie this time – and I were chilled to the bone and wet through. We sloped about the village for a couple of hours, feeling miserable as hell, before being picked up again. Back in camp we set to to produce another detailed plan, finally finishing at about 2.30 a.m.

Falling into bed, utterly exhausted and depressed, I discovered that I could only sleep fitfully, waiting for the inevitable rousing in the night. Typically, it didn't come, and we were up as usual at 6.30 for a punishing run around the training area before breakfast.

Then we were instructed to write a biographical life story, starting from the age of ten. It was very difficult to concentrate on this boring task, because by now we were beginning to suffer from lack of sleep.

After an hour we were told to stop, hand in our essays and muster again in boots and lightweights for more PT. Outside, the sight of a line of telegraph poles sent a shiver through me. Oh God, I pleaded silently, not a log race . . .

I must have died and gone to hell.

The man directly in front of me stumbles, tripping on the rough ground, then sinks to his knees. I can hear the pounding as the blood pumps through my inner ear. My brain, stalling from lack of oxygen, registers his fall in slow-motion, and I feel myself being dragged down behind him, unable to bear the additional weight of the rough log that's suspended in a cat's cradle of thick hemp ropes between the team of eight volunteers. The front pair are both now on their knees, but the dead weight of the log is still pressing onwards, carried forward by its own momentum, and we are becoming tangled together as we struggle wildly to regain control.

'Get up, you idle bastards, get up now! Sort yourselves out and run!'

The skin on my left wrist is chafing and burning from the torsion of the rough hemp twisting round it like a tourniquet, but I know that right now that's the least of my problems. We are barely 400 metres into the five-kilometre team race, a twelve-foot section of telegraph pole slung between the eight of us, and already my lungs are on fire as I fight desperately for breath in the cold air. My shoulder joint feels as if it could dislocate at any second, and my gorge is rising. As I run I turn my head to the right and spew a thin gruel of whitish fluid down my side, then wipe my mouth on the sleeve of my sweatshirt.

'Well done, Thirty-seven. Keep it up, better out than in!' shouts an instructor from behind me.

We run on across the undulating turf, I with renewed vigour. The heaving, jerking, log swings between us like a roped alligator. I think to myself, this is a nightmare . . . this is a nightmare . . .

My lungs are bursting as we approach a muddy stream. We are following an instructor who is running in front. Suddenly he plunges waist-deep into the stream and we stumble obediently down the slippery bank behind him. My feet momentarily disappear from under me, and I feel the skin scrape off the back of my thigh beneath the thin cotton fabric of my trousers as I'm dragged over a rocky outcrop by the weight of the log. The shock of the cold water galvanises us into action again and we push hard through the current, slipping on the uneven stream bed and cursing each other hoarsely. The log is bucking and heaving in the flow, but at least it feels lighter when it's in the water.

After 200 metres the instructor turns a sharp right and hauls himself up a muddy bank between two gnarled and twisted oaks. We're beyond coherent speech now; instead, a crescendo of groans and shouts rises from the eight of us as we encourage the log over the lip of the bank. For a frantic few seconds we are swept back down the slope by its weight. The two men at the rear are pushed neck-deep into the stream, overwhelmed by the burden. Instructors wade around us, yelping encouragement, and I tug with all my strength, my boots skating off the shaly incline. We finally regain enough forward momentum to clear the rise, and use a hummock on the bank as a fulcrum to swing the back end clear of the water. My throat is rattling unnaturally with every lungful of air. I see that my hand, still bound tight round the wrist, is a greyish blue. I become aware of someone yelling in my ear, and thumping my shoulder hard.

'CHANGE HANDS! CHANGE HANDS! SWAP SIDES!'

Still running, I slip my fist out of the prickly hemp loop and skip around the back of the log to the other side, swapping with the man next to me. I can't believe how light I feel when I'm free of the dead weight, but as I take up the strain again on the other shoulder I feel despair brimming at my throat.

The enormity of the task remaining starts to overwhelm me. Now I'm shouting rhythmically to myself inside my head, 'Ten more steps . . . ten more steps . . .', desperately trying to close down my world to something I may be able to manage. Suddenly, something inside my brain gives, and a surge of power propels me forwards. I break into my second wind and let the searing, blazing, brilliant pain wash me onwards, and now I too am hectoring and spurring the others on.

I feel drunk and dizzy with fatigue, past caring about anything except reaching the end of this torture. But I'm not going to let the team down. If they can hack it so will I, and I slog on. Every step is an effort, but every step takes me closer to the finish. Now we are entering the camp again – here is the road leading to the accommodation block. Now we are struggling to a final juddering, jerking, swinging sprint over the last 100 metres, everyone cursing incoherently, lungs shrieking. And at last we drop the ghastly burden and stagger around, leaning on each other, gulping breath, falling flat on the damp ground, limbs steaming, eyes closed, ribs heaving, hearts leaping – and it's over.

Instructors mill around us. Sally says, 'OK, let's do this one more time!' Nobody laughs, in case she isn't joking, and if she is, it's not funny. I've never felt so weak in my life. Slowly we gather our wits and hobble back to the block, where we shower and dress like old men. I feel truly drained of energy and for the first time I seriously consider chucking my hand in. Then I think to myself, it can't get much worse, what a waste to give in now. I'll give it another twenty-four hours.

As I came down the stairs to head out to the lecture room, I heard a low sobbing sound from a washroom on the floor below mine. I stopped and listened. It sounded female, so I quietly put my head around the door. There she was, leaning against a washbasin, her face covered by her hands, her wavy brown hair flopping forward and her shoulders heaving rhythmically as she cried gently to herself. I hadn't spoken to her before and I guessed she was a private soldier or perhaps a lance corporal. She looked about twenty. She had obviously found the log race traumatic (the girls had had a smaller log to carry between the four of them).

I cleared my throat and said, 'You're not thinking of packing it in now, are you?' She glanced up at me, nodded slowly once and then broke down again, the tears running down her pale and drawn face. At that moment I realised how much harder this all was for the girls. At least we blokes were generally used to this sort of harsh treatment, but it must have been pretty shocking to the girls. My heart went out to her.

I moved beside her and put my arm round her shoulders, saying softly, 'You can't leave now – you're the only reason I'm still here. I say to myself, if she can hack it, I bloody well can too! You're doing so well and trying so hard, you're bound to pass. Don't surrender to them now!' I smiled at her, trying to look imploring.

She glanced at me again and sniffed hard but it got caught up in her next sob. She smiled back self-consciously and I handed her a crumpled and not very clean tissue. She blew her nose.

'I'm sorry, it's the best I've got. Come on, we'll be late for the lion taming or whatever's next,' I said.

She smiled again then turned and looked into the mirror behind us. Between sniffs she said, 'But I look like I've been crying!'

'Yeah, well, who cares? The lads won't, I assure you. Quick, let's go or we'll be in trouble!' She followed me out and together we trotted stiffly over to the hall.

Fortunately, the next session was a series of simple Kim's Games, which involved trying to memorise a variety of pictures of objects, faces and places. These were set out on montage boards around the room. The subjects on the boards became progressively less obvious and less noteworthy. After studying them each for three minutes, we had to write down all that we could remember and sketch the location of each in relation to the others.

After a quick lunch, we climbed aboard four-ton trucks and were driven about twenty miles to the west, the road rising gradually until we reached an area of rough heather-clad hills laced by dry-stone walls. We were dropped off, individually this time, to navigate ourselves around a fifteen kilometre course – only today the routes between checkpoints avoided metalled roads and forced us on to higher ground. A weak February sun in a cloudless sky lit up the views around me as I walked and trotted around the course. It was still chilly, but as long as I was moving it was tolerable. At least we weren't carrying any kit other than a map, compass, water bottle and a spare jersey. The map reading itself was pretty simple and my morale soared.

As I travelled along the rough paths I took stock of my situation. Physically, I felt run down and my feet were quite badly blistered, but as an infantryman I was used to this sort of routine discomfort and it didn't bother me particularly. It is amazing how quickly the body can recover from physical stress, especially if it's basically very fit. My thoughts turned to the instructors. They were a strange bunch, quite unlike any I'd come across in the army before. Nor were they like the few SAS troopers I'd known. They seemed far more sophisticated and much less aggressive than SAS types.

They displayed a quiet, reassuring confidence, and although they'd been giving us a real beasting lately they were very matter-of-fact about it all and not a bit vicious or vindictive. They were obviously extremely fit and very robust. The selection course itself was being run with awesome efficiency. I knew from my own experience just how difficult it is to keep a body of troops fully occupied from day to day. Here the activity was constant and unremitting. When we paraded for PT, they were there five minutes beforehand, goading us on. They were around too when we fell out for the night, and they were there to wake us. Yet we weren't aware of any special effort on their part. It was difficult to judge them, however, because to date, other than issuing instructions for the different tasks, they'd hardly spoken at all to us. I liked the way that there was nothing formal or stuffy about them and the way that they treated the two female instructors as absolute equals. I was certain that I very much wanted to be a part of this unusual unit. I just wished I knew precisely what it was that we were being selected to undertake!

Having reached the final rendezvous at dusk, I again dozed in the back of the lorry as we wound back to camp. By the time we turned into the approach road I was cold, stiff and hungry, but we were ushered straight into the lecture room.

We sat and watched a video of a street scene, somewhere in Britain, which looked as if it had been filmed from a vantage point at a second- or third-storey window. For the first ten minutes or so the activity seemed perfectly ordinary to me, but then I began to perceive a vague pattern within it. After about twenty minutes I was sure. That white Transit van had passed several times already. We weren't close enough to read the registration, but I was convinced it was the same one. Now it parked in the street. Two men got out and walked further up the street. Why didn't they simply park further up? I wondered. I kept an eye on them among the other pedestrians and traffic. They passed in front of a Lloyds Bank branch and both stopped to light cigarettes, but they were definitely having a good look round as they did so. Then they carried on up the road and disappeared out of shot. I checked the Transit again – shit! It had gone, and I didn't see who was driving or which way it went. I concentrated on the vicinity of the bank, watching cars and people pass it. Ten minutes later a bus pulled up in front of it and for a second I thought I spotted one of the two men walking back along the pavement towards the bank. But he was obscured by the bus, and when it pulled away there were only a couple of women visible. He'd either got on the bus or entered the bank. After another couple of minutes, the Transit appeared again from the left and pulled up outside the bank, the driver remaining at the wheel. Then the man ran out of the entrance, leapt into it, and it sped away. Hah, bank robbers! Ten minutes later, the video sequence ended and I hoped that I'd witnessed the main action.

We then had to answer a series of questions – such as how many floors did the row of shops have, what was the last shop visible on the left, describe the man with the ladder and so on – and from the nature of them it was clear that there had in fact been two separate noteworthy incidents unfolding concurrently. Bugger it, I'd only seen the one!

My belly was rumbling with hunger now, but instead of being dismissed to our supper we were told to parade in twenty minutes with waterproofs on over our combat jackets and lightweight trousers, making sure that we had a jersey and a spare pair of socks with us. We did so, suddenly subdued at this unexpected twist. Again we were paired off, then issued with an exercise book, pencil, torch and a lightweight groundsheet for each pair. We doubled out into the frosty night, heading for the desolate training area. Once there, each pair was directed to a patch of scrub by an instructor and told to set up a simple observation post. The task was to observe the area of track fifty metres to our front, and we were to keep a detailed log of any activity. My partner this time was number forty-two, an officer from a technical regiment, and together we set about securing the groundsheet's corners to twigs so that it was stretched about a foot above the ground. We then camouflaged our position with branches and debris, so that we were concealed and also protected against rain or snow. Next we gathered some dead bracken and stuffed it under the cover, spreading it around on the ground as insulation and hoping it would help to keep the cold wind out. Even while we were moving about we were beginning to shiver and so we quickly burrowed into our uncomfortable new home.

Lying flat, side by side, we arranged the bracken as best we could and settled down to watch the track. In normal circumstances we might have been able to alternate the task of keeping watch between us, doing four hours on and four hours off, but we were so tired and cold that it wasn't practicable – whoever was on watch would certainly fall asleep before the four hours were up. Therefore we decided to try one hour on and one hour off. Even this was difficult for us because it was too cold for the non-watcher actually to sleep properly, lying on the rough heather which became wet as soon as our body heat melted the light frost. We wore the spare socks as gloves. God, I was hungry – and it was only 11 p.m.

We kept watch as best we could, but saw little in the faint starlight. At about midnight, a light crunch of footsteps behind us heralded the arrival of an instructor. He crouched beside us and lifted a corner of our roof.

'Just checking up on you lads. Nippy, isn't it?' he said.

'Er, yes, it is a bit, staff,' said forty-two.

'Well, the good news is that, as a special concession because of the atrocious weather, I'll fetch you two items from your bunk. What's your order?'

This was more like it! We conferred rapidly. 'A sleeping bag and some chocolate would hit the spot, staff! Thanks very much!' I replied, trying to keep the eagerness from my voice. Although it would have been more comfortable to have a sleeping bag each, we both knew that a sentry or observer should never be in a bag while on duty. The temptation to sleep invariably becomes overwhelming.

The instructor held a small torch between his teeth as he wrote our request into a notebook, the pages flapping in the wind. In the beam of his torch I could see tiny flakes of snow driving past.

'OK, no problem. See you in a bit – I've got to visit the other OPs round here first. Cheerio.' With that he was gone.

'Thank God for that. Whoever's not on watch can use the sleeping bag,' I said. 'Maybe we'll get a bit of sleep now.'

'And maybe these bastards have a heart after all!' whispered forty-two. 'Hey, look there!'

On the track in front of us a car's headlights appeared in the distance, waving up and down because of the potholes. A little Fiat appeared and drove slowly past us, but we couldn't see the registration number from this angle. There was only one occupant. As soon as the car departed we scribbled down the time and details of this sighting.

The minutes passed and I lay shivering, pressed against forty-two's side in an effort to share our body heat. The wind cut straight through our pile of bracken, chilling us to the bone, but there wasn't much we could do to screen it because we were directly downwind of the target area and we needed to be able to see clearly. It was definitely too cold to sleep now, and we concentrated all our energy on keeping warm.

'This is no good, we're going to freeze to death here if we're not careful,' I whispered to forty-two. 'Let's try stuffing bracken inside our clothes, at least until the sleeping bag arrives.' We crept out and furtively stalked around in the dark, grabbing handfuls of the stiff, dry ferns and stuffing it up between our waterproof outer layers and our combat jackets and trousers. This seemed to make a difference and, for a short while as we huddled together once more, we stopped shivering, but the sensation of warmth didn't last long with the wind howling and flapping around us.

For the hundredth time I glanced at my watch. 2.15 a.m. Suddenly, we heard the wonderful sound of footsteps approaching quietly through the frosty scrub. Here was the instructor back, kneeling down beside us, clutching a kitbag.

'Do you know, I wouldn't be surprised if we had a foot of snow before morning, it feels cold enough for it,' he said amiably. 'Oh, I almost forgot, I couldn't get what you wanted, so I've brought you something else.' He reached into the kitbag and drew out a small, white paper bag and a glass bottle. He put them on the ground and rose to leave, saying, 'See you about this time tomorrow night. Cheerio.'

As soon as he departed we pounced on the items. As forty-two examined the contents of the bottle, I stuck my hand into the bag and pulled out a slightly soggy sandwich and an orange.

'What's in the bottle?'

'Water! What's in the bag?'

'A marmite sandwich and an orange!'

'Fucking twisted bastards!'

We split the sandwich and the orange in two and ate our respective shares in a miserable silence. Although we felt frozen to our very cores, we still needed the extra water and sipped at the bottle from time to time. For the rest of the night we lay together, unable to sleep and desperately hoping for dawn and the heat of the sun. Twice we got up and jumped about on the spot, trying to reintroduce some warmth into our limbs and taking the opportunity to have a pee. At about half past four the little Fiat drove back the other way along the track. My fingers were now so cold that I could hardly write in the logbook. Later, as a faint, grey, watery light began to steal over the clearing in front of us, I noticed two figures moving swiftly along the track.

I shook forty-two and we stared at them, trying to make out some detail in the dim light. Then I realised that the front man was dragging a groundsheet. As they drew level with us I recognised him. It was the naval gorilla! Hah – so he wasn't as tough as all that, I thought to myself. He and his buddy had obviously decided that enough was enough and were on their way home. This gave me some small satisfaction and our spirits rose with the sun. Gradually, our shivering died down and, when the wind dropped at about nine o'clock, we were able at last to doze fitfully between watches.

Throughout the day the little Fiat came and went, sometimes stopping while the driver deposited something in the ditch at the other side of the track or picked up a bulky object. We logged as much detail as we could, filling several pages of the now grubby notebook. Eventually the shadows lengthened as the sun dipped, and forty-two took the opportunity to crawl around behind our position, collecting an enormous mound of dead bracken to bolster our defences against the inevitable cold.

Our second night was considerably more comfortable than our first, and we briefly amused ourselves by listening to the incredibly loud groanings and rumblings that emanated from our empty bellies. Time passed slowly, but we were now into a steady routine and, so long as nothing changed unduly, I was content enough. The ubiquitous Fiat appeared intermittently through the gloom and at 1 a.m. the instructor appeared and left us exactly the same provisions as the previous night.

'See you the same time tomorrow night,' he whispered as he departed. Christ, my stomach felt as if it was shrinking from lack of food. Another day of this and I'd have to consider eating forty-two!

Back came the damned Fiat for another pass, only this time the driver stopped the car, lifted the bonnet and examined the engine for about five minutes by torchlight. Then he got in again and drove off.

The hours passed slowly as we alternated between watching and resting. My thoughts kept drifting back to the subject of hot food, plates and plates of it, piled high and smelling delicious. I began to visualise every detail of the last meal I'd had, which was a snatched lunch of pizza, chips and a mug of tea in the canteen before yesterday's hill walk. Or was it the day before? I couldn't remember for sure. Thinking about food made me feel worse, so I decided to recite to myself all the poetry I had ever learned. I struggled as best I could through *The Old Vicarage, Granchester, Death in Leamington,* a fair bit of *Horatius,* then *Vitae Lampada, Cargoes* and *Seafever, Abersoch* and the one that starts 'A garden is a lovesome thing, God wot'. When I got to *Invictus* it seemed so particularly appropriate that I shook forty-two awake, so he could appreciate it too.

'Hey, listen to this,' I said quietly, and began:

'Out of the night that covers me,
Black as the pit from pole to pole,
I thank whatever Gods may be,
For my unconquerable soul.

'In the fell clutch of circumstance,
I have not winced or cried aloud,
Under the bludgeoning of chance,
My head is bloody but unbowed.

'It matters not how straight the gate,
How charged with punishments the scroll,
I am the captain of my fate,
I am the master of my soul.

'What do you reckon, just about sums us up, eh?' I said.

'Fuck off, will you? I'm depressed enough already!'

'Well, you tell me one then.'

He thought for a moment. 'OK, how about *Gunga Din*?' He cleared his throat and began: 'You may talk of gin and beer, when you're quartered safe out . . .' He stopped. A twig behind us had snapped. We both froze, silent, and looked at each other in the inky darkness. Another twig behind us cracked. Someone was definitely creeping up on us.

A loud voice said sharply, 'You've got two minutes to pack up your kit and muster on the track in front of you! Stow your waterproofs in your pockets!'

Our hearts racing, we leapt to our feet and began to rip the insulating bracken out of our clothes, then stuff the waterproofs away down the fronts of our combat jackets. We rolled the groundsheet up and I carried it under my arm as we bounded out on to the track. From all around the clearing other pairs of volunteers were appearing from the scrub. I glanced at my watch – 6.15 a.m. – and now that we were clear of the scrub I noticed the first glimmer in the east as the night receded. I could see that we were all in a pretty bad way, our dirty and unshaven faces deeply etched with exhaustion. My limbs felt oddly stiff and swollen, which I put down to lying around in the cold and damp for the best part of thirty-six hours.

'Form three ranks, turn to your right! Double MARCH!' We doubled away behind two instructors, the pace fierce as always. Once more I was struggling for breath and trying to ignore my aching legs as we clattered along, the weaker runners gradually falling behind.

After about a kilometre and a half we rounded a bend and there before us stood three Bedford trucks, their tailgates hanging open welcomingly. We halted, and were told that we were going back to camp for breakfast. Gratefully we clambered aboard, settling ourselves around the inside, and I began to fantasise about breakfast.

However, as the last stragglers were just climbing aboard, the instructors reappeared and blew their whistles. 'Everybody out! Everybody out! There's one last job to be done! Leave groundsheets and waterproofs in the vehicles.'

Jesus Christ, I thought as I awkwardly eased my tired frame back down to the ground. I'm not sure I can take much more of this.

'Form three ranks! Move yourselves, you idle lot.'

As we shuffled into a semblance of order in the grey light, I noticed that each truck had a long tow-rope attached to its front towing hook. Oh shit, I thought, I can guess what's coming next.

'Each rank will pull one of the vehicles back to camp! Last team back misses breakfast! Take your marks!'

We formed up along the ropes, and at the signal we pulled frantically to get each truck moving. Once my team picked up a bit of momentum, it wasn't too difficult to keep it going. The worst problem was that we were still wearing all our warm clothing, so after a few minutes of exertion we began to drip with sweat. The instructors danced around, encouraging us with shouts. Fortunately the road was fairly flat and smooth, but even so after several hundred metres we were really struggling. As we laboured on I felt weaker at every step.

Suddenly we were called to a halt. I sank down on to one knee, trying to catch my breath. 'Leave the ropes and follow me!' shouted one of the instructors. We doubled off after him, and soon we came to the sandy bank of a small lake, about 100 metres square. It was in a slight hollow, surrounded by scrub and bracken, except for the point where we were now gathered. The surface of the water had iced over, and to our horror and disbelief we saw two instructors in a small inflatable boat, poling themselves around near the bank, smashing at the ice with oars. On the bank was a jumbled heap of empty oil drums, planks, bits of rope and so on, alongside a pile of yellow life vests.

Jill was waiting for us. 'OK, each team has five minutes to construct a raft using these bits, then ferry a casualty to the other bank. Strip down to your underwear and put on a lifejacket before getting into the water! Go!' she shouted. We stared stupidly at each other for a second, shocked at this new prospect, but self-discipline took over and we began to sort ourselves out into our respective teams. Two lads who refused to participate any further were immediately doubled away.

Muttering oaths and imprecations under our breath, the rest of us grimly set about building the three rafts. It was a pretty shaky construction which my team carried down to the water's edge. The girl in our group volunteered to be the casualty.

We all began to strip off in the biting cold. Our precious cargo, wearing only bra, pants and life vest, balanced precariously on top as the rest of us shuffled forward barefoot on the mud and down into the icy water. Broken shards of ice half an inch thick piled up against our thighs as we pressed on. It was wickedly cold, and there were loud squeaks and groans as the water rose up over our midriffs. By the time we were chest-deep and gasping for air we were past caring, so we kicked out wildly, trying to propel the raft towards the far bank. However, the moment we were underway our vessel began to come apart. Soon our casualty was dunked shrieking into the water as the plank she was lying on dipped below the surface. This little bit of comedy cheered us up considerably.

Having now lost both the raft and the casualty, we were told to return to the bank, where the instructors had sensibly lit a bonfire in an old oildrum. We quickly dried ourselves on our shirts and dressed, rotating ourselves in front of the huge brazier and sipping hot sweet tea from polystyrene cups.

The truth was, as is usually the case, that the anticipation of stripping off and swimming in icy water when we were so cold, tired and hungry had been much worse than the reality of it. Once you're in, you go so numb that you don't feel particularly cold. Indeed, I felt much better for that dip – and as soon as all three groups were dressed, we jogged the remaining kilometre back to camp, our bellies still grumbling loudly.

We were left alone to savour an enormous and leisurely breakfast, after which we showered, shaved and then slept on our beds for two hours. Once you are into the routine of catnapping, a two hour kip is as much as you need. We mustered for a light lunch of soup and rolls at 12.30, now feeling thoroughly invigorated.

That afternoon, we doubled out on to the training area to undertake a series of initiative and command tests which had been set up around a five-kilometre course. We jogged round in teams of six and at each location the team had to solve a practical problem – for example, transporting a sand-filled ammunition box across a gap without touching the ground between two points, and using a minimum of equipment. We each took it in turns to command the group for an activity. My task was to give vocal directions to the rest of the team, who were all blindfolded, so they could collect together a set of different coloured ammunition boxes which had been scattered over an area of about fifty metres square, then line the boxes up in a specific sequence at a central point. The end result was not very impressive, but we did at least have a good laugh as the volunteers, unable to see, bumped into each other and generally fell about.

Back in camp, the small number of officers among the volunteers were taken to one side and briefed individually to carry out an appreciation of a particular military problem, work out a solution and prepare a formal set of orders for the operation. This was to be delivered at 9 p.m. to an audience consisting entirely of instructors. We read through our briefs over supper. Mine required an attack on the jungle base of a group of rebels – the information supplied about the logistic support available to my troops was very detailed, and forced me to consider a variety of options. For instance, there was just one passable road that led to within four kilometres of the target. However, I had only two trucks available and the road might be mined. To clear the road in advance would take twenty soldiers six hours, but after that the speed of the trucks could be thirty miles per hour. (Whoever wrote this has obviously never tried to drive along a jungle road themselves, I thought to myself.) I also had at my disposal three boats which could carry ten men each and cruise at six knots. The river led right up to the target, but there was a rebel lookout post (consisting probably of three men and a machine gun) on the bend immediately downstream of the base. One kilometre upstream of the base was a native footbridge, which might or might not be guarded.

The enemy numbered about fifteen men in all, and I had forty-five men at my disposal, with the usual small arms, plus an option on three 81mm mortars. These can be man-packed but are very unwieldy to carry, each mortar requiring three men with the ammunition being split among the remaining party. My brief informed me that if I took them along the rate of advance on foot through the jungle would be reduced from 2.5 km per hour to 1.5 km per hour.

The most direct route was to cut straight through the jungle on foot, a distance of fifteen kilometres. The routes by road and river were thirty and forty kilometres respectively. A sheaf of appendices showed ammunition scales, weather and moon states, rations and water available, radio callsigns and equipment and so on, and there was a detailed map with rough sketches of the rebel base and the lookout post. Now I had to absorb the information and formulate my plan, and I had an hour and a half to do it in.

By 9 p.m. I had considered all the options and come up with a workable solution. I decided that I would send a small diversionary party by river, with the mortars, to attack the lookout. They would then defend the post against a possible counter-attack and prepare to mortar the rebel base. Meanwhile, the main party would advance through the jungle on foot, cross the river by the bridge if it was unguarded (or swim it further upstream if it was guarded) and be ready to attack when the mortars opened up. I was pretty confident that this was a good solution and I looked forward to delivering the set of orders I'd prepared. In good infantry fashion I'd also constructed a rough model to help my explanation of the plan.

The instructors gathered in the small classroom were in an exuberant mood, and even before I began I could overhear some of them making rude comments about the accuracy of my model. When I got started, the criticisms began to flow thick and fast. Every assertion I made was abruptly challenged, and when I came to detailing the plan itself it was greeted with incredulous laughter. This was most unnerving, but I ploughed on. When I reached the end, red-faced and irritated by the barrage of interruptions, I asked with trepidation if there were any questions. They all had points to make about facts I had incorrectly interpreted or factors I had ignored. Under their brutal scrutiny, I began to doubt that my plan was any good after all. I had the distinct impression that they didn't rate my analytical skills very highly. Frankly, this was a bit of a shock to me; I was an infantry captain, and if I couldn't come up with a decent plan under pressure of time, what use would I be to them?

Afterwards, I made my way back to the accommodation. Two of the other officers had arrived before me, and they too looked a bit stunned. We compared notes about the experience and I was mightily relieved to discover that all of us had apparently merited the same hostile reaction to our orders. We realised that this was just another ploy to see how we dealt with criticism under pressure. It had certainly been an uncomfortably effective test.

After another bout of early-morning PT and breakfast, we mustered in civvies to be briefed about the next exercise. We were to be dropped off individually, and each of us had to make our way overnight to one of a number of small market towns spread across the Midlands. Our instructions for each stage of the journey would be left in dead letterboxes or passed verbally by agents *en route*. We could take no more than £2.50 in change, and were each issued with a sealed envelope containing emergency instructions in case of accident or a missed rendezvous. Everyone we came across, other than the agents, was to be considered as passively hostile; we were to avoid speaking to anyone except when hitching a lift, and if challenged we should again claim to be in the TA.

The only other items we were permitted to carry were a photocopy of an AA road map and a notebook and pencil.

We were split into groups of ten, and then we awaited our turn to be ferried out to our respective drop-off points.

As the minibus drove out into the countryside, I felt a mounting excitement. This was quite unlike anything I'd done before in the army, and I was enjoying the prospect of a new challenge. As I climbed out of the side door at a bleak crossroads, the driver handed me an envelope through the window before leaving.

Although it was a lovely day, with a bright sun and clear skies, the wind was chilly, so I sheltered in the lee of a stone wall to read my instructions. I was to make my way to a telephone box in a village about twelve miles away, but I was not to arrive in the village before 6 p.m. Stuck to the underside of the coinbox would be a piece of card with new instructions on. I should read them and then replace the card securely. Checking the map, I quickly decided to hitch and started to walk down the road in the right direction. It was noon. I decided to try to get as close to the place as I could before dusk, lie up somewhere and then walk in at six o'clock.

There was hardly any traffic at all, and the few cars that did pass were understandably wary of this wild-looking young man – but at last a coal lorry offered me a lift to the next village. I was sorely tempted to buy myself a pasty from the village shop, but decided to keep my change intact in case there was a more pressing use for it ahead. I sat in a bus shelter and consulted my map. My target was the next major habitation along the road, now only five miles away. If I hitched another lift it was likely to take me all the way there, and it would look odd to ask to be dropped short of the village. It was only 1.30 p.m. and the weather was fine, so I decided to walk from here. The map showed a minor road on the other side of the stream, running along the broad valley bottom parallel to the main route, which if anything would be a slightly shorter if more hilly route. I set off at a brisk pace, my Blakeys ringing out on the tarmac.

By 3.30 p.m. I was on a rise overlooking the village, and I looked about to find somewhere to lie up. My feet were rather blistered, since I was now wearing my ordinary brown brogues. I hopped over a wall and settled down in the corner of a sheep pen, out of the wind, where I watched a spectacular sunset across the valley before setting off in the dark to find the phone box.

Typically, the light inside the booth didn't work, so I couldn't read what was on the card. I took it outside and held it up to the light spilling out of the village shop. The instructions were clear enough: 'Make yourself known to two agents in the left-hand bar of the Red Lion in XXXXXXXXX at [7.45 p.m. plus your own personal two- or three-digit number] precisely.'

My number was thirty-seven, so I had to be there at exactly 8.22 p.m. It was a good ten miles away, so I'd never make it on foot. I'd need to hitch or take a bus if there was one. I replaced the card and had a quick scout round for a bus shelter with a timetable, but I couldn't find one so I decided to hitch. I scribbled the name of the town in big letters on a piece of discarded cardboard and set off for the outskirts of the village.

Two lifts later I had arrived, and found I had forty minutes to kill. As I wandered around, I couldn't escape the smell of frying that wafted from the busy chippy. Sod it, I thought, I may be on the go all night – so I spent 70p on a large portion of chips and a pot of beans which I ate in a bus shelter.

Feeling much better, I pushed open the door to the public bar of the Red Lion at 8.21 p.m. and sidled over to the bar. It was a typical old coaching inn, the blackened beams festooned with the usual assortment of horse brasses, bedwarmers and similar highly polished knicknacks. A spectacular log fire spat and hissed in the inglenook. This was more like it. There were about a dozen customers dotted around the bar and I ordered a half of bitter and a packet of nuts.

I casually scanned the room. There, at a corner table, was Sally and the fair-haired instructor, quite smartly dressed, chatting over their drinks. I approached them, smiling, and sat with them for five minutes while they quizzed me about what I'd done since I was dropped off and traced out my route on the map. It was wonderful to sit in the warm, smoky atmosphere, taking the weight off my aching feet – but all too soon I was receiving my new instructions from Sally.

'Meet me at noon tomorrow in the BR ticket office at XXXXXXXXX. Bring a sketch plan of the building which is at the junction of these two roads.' She pointed to a spot on my road map. 'Also, find out who is the area secretary of the National

Farmers' Union and the name of the president of the local Chamber of Commerce. Any questions? Good. Cheerio then,' she finished, and they smiled broadly as I took my leave. Outside, I bumped into another volunteer about to make his way in. We grinned self-consciously at each other as we passed.

I set off once more and quickly walked the three miles to the road junction. A petrol station, clearly shut now, was the only building there – and so I moved around it in the shadows, sketching its outline dimensions, the positions of its windows and doors, stopping whenever a car passed by on the road. After about half an hour I had sufficient detail. I'd draw it up properly in my notebook in the morning.

As it wasn't yet ten o'clock, I felt it was reasonable to hitch to the target town, so I filled out the other side of my cardboard sign and stood at the junction. My luck was in, and within half an hour a group of drunken students in a battered Transit van offered to take me all the way.

In the morning I would need to find a public library, but in the meantime I wanted to stay away from the town centre. I waved goodbye to the van on the outskirts and headed back the way we'd come until I was in open fields again, searching for a barn to spend the night in.

I spent a cold night catnapping in a draughty lean-to shelter which was propped in the corner of a muddy field. I was pretty thirsty, but I didn't think it was wise to drink from the slimy cattle-trough next to the shed. Instead, I promised myself a full fried breakfast and a pot of tea in a greasy spoon – if I could find one. At 7.00 a.m. I hobbled out of my shelter feeling awful and certainly looking the worse for wear. I was stiff, cold, tired and hungry. To make matters worse, I had mud all over my jeans, I was unshaven and generally looked thoroughly disreputable.

I walked into the town and discovered what every tramp or homeless person must know: it's very difficult to find anywhere comfortable to sit for any length of time. If you don't have enough money to buy a constant stream of food and drink you can't sit in a café, and the only alternatives are public libraries or train and bus stations. The former didn't open till 10.00 a.m. and the latter were both draughty and uncomfortable, so I wandered round the town centre, examining the shop displays and feeling sorry for myself. Eventually, I could stand it no more and bought myself a breakfast of beans on toast and a mug of tea, which I spun out into an hour's stay in the warm fug of the café.

At last the public library opened, and I quickly found the two names I needed by searching the reference section. I then sat and neatly drew out my sketch again, before settling down with a copy of *National Geographic*. I kept dozing off, and I could tell the staff were disapproving, but I simply ignored their foul looks.

Soon I was joined by two other volunteers and we exchanged gossip. They too were meeting Sally in the ticket office, though slightly later. The library staff now seemed to be alarmed by our presence – and when a fourth volunteer appeared, also unshaven and bedraggled, we decided to leave before we were ejected.

In the booking hall, on the dot of noon, Sally greeted me and said, 'Give me your sketch and the two names and get into the minibus parked out the back.' With enormous relief, I climbed in and promptly fell asleep, but was woken every ten minutes or so as another volunteer arrived. Sally accompanied the sixth.

'OK, it's back to camp for lunch!' she said, slipping into the driving seat. I relaxed, letting out the breath that I'd subconsciously held. Thank God for that, I thought. It was an interesting exercise, but I felt completely shattered.

After a late lunch, over which we swapped stories about how we'd fared, we had another session of weapon handling, followed by an hour of PT. Again I was dragged to the edge of despair as we pounded across the gym floor in a series of relay races and circuit training, my chest heaving, my knees buckling with exhaustion. The difference now, though, was that having got this far through the course, there was no way I was going to give in.

After a quick shower, we paraded again in our civvies, now somewhat tatty. An instructor informed us that tonight we would be doing an internal recce of a pub. This raised a bit of a laugh, and we wondered whether this was the instructors' way of telling us we had the night off.

We were soon put right. 'Frankly, I suspect you wouldn't choose to drink in the sorts of pubs that you're going to visit. They're all pretty rough and there'll certainly be some drug dealing going on. If the regulars are suspicious about you, they'll think you're the police. If they think that, anything might happen, so watch out for each other and don't drink more than two pints.'

He explained that we were surreptitiously to note as many

details as we could about the interior of the bars, before returning to camp to produce accurate scale plans of the interiors. Obviously, we were to ensure that none of the punters noticed what we were up to.

We set out by minibus after supper and were dropped off in groups of three in rundown areas around the outskirts of a major town. My group quickly located our target pub. It was on a street corner at the end of a row of tatty shops, some of them boarded up, the rest protected by heavy metal security shutters. From the outside, in the orange glare of the streetlights, the pub did indeed look pretty rough. It was certainly not the sort of place I'd ever frequented before, and I doubted that they would knowingly serve an army officer!

We strolled in, ignoring the hostile stares of a group of scruffy, bomber-jacketed youths round a pool table. Although it was only just 9 p.m. it was a Thursday, so the bar was already relatively busy. It was a horrible place, with worn and stained lino on the floor and the cheapest possible furnishings. The yellow foam stuffing of the black bar stools and tacky banquettes was visible through the splits and cracks in the red vinyl which covered them, the metallic beading around their edges long since missing. They were spotted with cigarette burns. The low tables were scarred and etched with ring stains, and every surface seemed to be covered in a film of greasy dust. The atmosphere in the large room was blue with smoke and reeked of marijuana, but there were other smells as well – the vinegary stench of stale beer and an odour of cabbage soup that probably came up from the drains. The clientele was rowdy and mainly young, but there were some older men with that broken, dispirited look of the unemployed. There were no women visible at all, not even behind the bar.

I was grateful that number fifty-four, a broad-shouldered Welshman, was with us. It took a while for him to catch the barman's attention. While he did, number twenty-three – who I guessed was a Royal Marine – and I pretended to chat together as we took in the internal details of the room. Fortunately, the noise from the jukebox meant no one could eavesdrop on us, with our strange out-of-town accents.

Armed with our pints of heavy, we found a table. We took it in turns to sketch the proportions of the interior on a couple of beermats, marking the windows and doors, the position of the light switches, the types of light fittings, the location of boxed pipework, tables and stools, everything that we could see. We visited the loos in turn to check them out.

We were definitely being scrutinised by the locals, and I desperately tried to avoid eye-contact with anyone who looked remotely evil! After about thirty minutes, we were joined by an instructor who chatted briefly, then suggested we make our way back to the rendezvous with the minibus. On our way back to camp, we concluded that the only possible point to the exercise had been to test our ability to act covertly in an environment considered as fairly hostile.

For the next couple of hours we produced a large room plan, sketching all the details we had collated on to a 36-inch-square grid. We still didn't understand the significance of this skill, but we were getting quite good at it. Hopefully this will be useful one day, I thought.

As I fell into bed at about one o'clock, my head spinning with fatigue, I couldn't even remember when it was I'd last spent the night between these sheets. Was it before the icy swim or after? Whenever it was, it seemed a very long time ago.

At 6 a.m. we were roused and paraded in PT kit for another run. As we struggled round the training area, the frosted bracken whipping at our legs, I knew I was getting close to the end of my tether. We stopped from time to time and did push-ups and squat thrusts, but never long enough for me to recover my breath. A final sprint brought us back to the gymnasium, where we reformed into three ranks in the empty carpark outside, chests heaving and sweat soaking our vests. Now the chief instructor appeared, the senior officer beside him.

'When I call your number, come to attention, move over to the right and form three ranks,' he said.

The realisation that we had reached the end of the selection suddenly dawned. A hush fell over us and we stood at ease, steam rising gently from our overheated bodies in the weak morning sunlight.

'73 . . . 28 . . . 51 . . .' he began.

Christ, I thought, which group is which? I felt numb, unable to decide whether or not I wanted to hear my number called. The sky was clear, light blue, dotted with little puffs of white cloud. The atmosphere was quiet and still, and I listened to my pulse beating gently through my head.

'12 . . . 102 . . . 32 . . . 90 . . .'

The group on the right was growing fast. I could hear the faint crunch of gravel as an instructor standing beside me eased his toes inside his boots.

'27 . . . 51 . . . 16 . . .'

On and on the chief instructor intoned, and I caught myself holding my breath. Then there was a silence. I glanced at him, standing in front of us. He was scanning his clipboard.

Suddenly an instructor behind the new group called them to attention, turned them to the right and they doubled away. All who remained stood waiting, swaying gently, our breathing under control now. There were fewer than half of us left.

The chief instructor continued to leaf through the pages attached to his clipboard. Suddenly he stopped, looked up quickly and glared at us. 'Well done, you lot, you're through.'

Chapter Three

We were ushered into the lecture theatre, where we sat dopey with fatigue. Craning around to see just who was left I spotted two women and over in the corner I could see forty-two, the officer with whom I'd shared the misery of the OP exercise. Just in front of me was the young Geordie who'd slunk around the darkened village with me. It didn't seem possible that these things had happened only within the last few days; I felt as if I'd known the people in this room for years.

The chief instructor entered and stood in front of us, scanning our tired faces. For once his permanent scowl seemed to have evaporated.

'Congratulations. You've passed the first hurdle. We have judged you suitable to undergo further basic training for a very specialised counter-terrorist role in Northern Ireland. If you pass that, you will move on to advanced training. Some of you will not be able to master the essential skills, and some of you will find yourselves temperamentally unsuited to the activities required of you.

'Shortly, you'll be moving to a secret training location. For reasons which will become obvious, the security of this unit and the individuals within it is paramount. Therefore, you will still not exchange any personal details with each other or with the instructors at any time. If you have a welfare or pay problem visit the chief clerk – he is the only person authorised to know your real identity and parent unit. Do not communicate directly with anyone from your own unit. Your commanding officers and respective pay offices are being informed today of your future movements. If you are single, your personal belongings will be boxed up, ready to be sent to you if you pass the course.

'You will of course have to explain your absence to your parents, wives or lovers. Think about this now – but for the next month I suggest you say that you are on an adventure training course.' He smiled. 'It's not that far from the truth, as it happens. I'll discuss this subject again with those of you who pass the next stage.

'I warn you now that we operate a strict need-to-know policy. Don't speculate about the bigger picture – just concentrate on what we're teaching you and everything will eventually fall into place.'

Next we were invited to choose a false Christian name, our sole identity from here on in. Officers kept their real names, because of the chance of meeting fellow officers in the green army whom we might already know. It would clearly be ridiculous and counter-productive to insist that someone we already knew should call us by a new name. I was delighted to remain as James. I suspected that I would have quite enough to contend with without having to get used to a new name as well.

It was now Friday, and we were given a long weekend to recover from the trials of selection. A coach, we were informed, would be waiting for us at 6 p.m. on Monday at a particular main-line railway station.

I drove back to my parents' house, where I wallowed in the bath, then slept late into Saturday morning.

Twice I tried to call my girlfriend Alison at home, but there was no answer. At about six o'clock I tried again and this time got an engaged tone. I kept trying every few minutes, but the line stayed busy. Her housemate, a vivacious girl called Kirsty, was always on the phone to someone. Sod it, I thought, this could go on all night. I'll drive over and surprise her, she's only an hour away. I asked my mother to call to tell her I was on my way.

As I drove through the darkened countryside, I wondered if it was a good idea to drop in on Alison at such short notice. During my time in Germany, we had seemed to communicate less and less frequently. About twice a year she'd come over as my partner to some regimental function, and she seemed to enjoy herself and would always share my bed – but recently, when we'd talked on the phone, I'd felt that she sounded a bit distracted. She had said she was fine, then quickly added that she wouldn't be able to come over for the next Guest Night in the mess because she couldn't take two days off work at this time of year. Not to worry, I'd said, I'm over on a two-week course, I'd give her a ring then. Fat chance of that, as it transpired!

I stopped off at an off-licence and bought a bottle of champagne and some chocolates. It was nearly eight when I pulled up outside Alison's flat. She occupied the ground floor of a Victorian semi in a pleasant suburb. At least the lights were on and her car was there. I pressed the bell and heard it shrill down the narrow hallway. Within seconds a blurred figure approached through the frosted glass set into the door and I heard Ali's voice.

'He's here, he's here!' she called excitedly up the stairs to Kirsty. I breathed a sigh of relief. Thank goodness Mum had got through; it could have been really embarrassing if she hadn't wanted to see me after all. With a rattle of chains the door squeaked open and I beamed at Ali, who looked as slim and delicious as ever, standing barefoot and draped in a white bathrobe.

The look of horror on her face stopped me in my tracks and I felt as if I'd been punched in the solar plexus. She jerked one hand over her mouth and let out a short gasp. 'We . . . I . . . er . . . thought you were the pizza boy,' she stammered, then glanced quickly over her shoulder and tried to pull the door to behind her.

I tried to grin but it didn't work. Stupidly I held out the wine and chocolates, more to indicate my intentions than to pass them over.

She looked down and stared at them in my hands. 'Oh God, you should have rung. Why didn't you ring?' She bit her lip. 'I'm sorry, James, if you'd rung I could have . . . er . . . .' Her voice trailed off miserably. Someone was approaching the door behind her and a young male voice said, 'Hey, d'you need some change?' A mop of blond hair and a bare chest appeared and gazed blankly at me over her shoulder.

'Oh shit, Ali,' I said. 'I'm sorry. I know I should have called – actually I did try just now. But I've been pretty busy. Look, sorry to break up your evening. Forget it. Give me a ring sometime. I'm over here for the next few weeks at least. See you around.'

The lump in my throat was threatening to rupture. On an impulse, I bent down and left the champagne and chocolates on the step at her feet before turning to go. Then, on another impulse, I turned back and retrieved the bottle. Might as well salvage something from the débâcle! I smiled ruefully at her as she stood watching me, her lover's hand resting lightly on her shoulder, then walked back to the car. Should I have punched him, whoever he was? I wondered as I started the car. No. She's free to choose, I realised. I should have tried harder to keep her. Huh! Loverless!

Severely depressed, I drove home and shared the fizz with my parents, an impromptu and somewhat gloomy celebration for passing the selection.

The next day I washed and repacked my kit, and on the Monday I set out in good time for the rendezvous. I dozed for most of the two-hour trip, though I took care to note the route we took – you never knew what might happen next with this lot.

It was dark, windy and drizzling when we arrived at the small camp. After we had dumped our bags in the accommodation block we were shown briefly around the area that would be our home for some time. An impressive array of training facilities were dotted around a large, partially wooded training area, and the accommodation block, classrooms, TV room, bar and canteen were all spacious, comfortable and modern. The four-man rooms were brightly decorated, and from the windows, which faced the back, I could make out amongst the trees the floodlit perimeter fence topped with the ubiquitous razor wire. The security here was intense: armed M.o.D. police regularly patrolled the area and manned the main entrance, and banks of cameras and sensors surveyed the entire training area. No part of the camp was visible from the nearby public road and, as I later discovered, it simply didn't feature on Ordnance Survey maps.

We appeared to be the only occupants.

After breakfast the next morning we gathered in civvies in the lecture room. The chief instructor took the rostrum and began to explain the regime. He was wearing a casual jacket over cords, and I guessed that he must have been about thirty-six, with short dark hair greying at the temples and a powerful physique. All the instructors here were in casual civilian clothing.

'For the next month you're going to be working pretty well flat out, seven days a week. In particular, we are going to teach you two major skills; we will then test you on them and everything else that we cover. If you fail, you're out.'

We divided into two groups. My lot made our way outside, led by the fair-haired instructor, who introduced himself as Mick. It was he who had met me out of my car on day one of the selection.

In front of a large garage block stood a number of civilian cars. I could see a Golf, a Peugeot, a Volvo – just ordinary models, nothing flash. A knot of instructors was waiting for us. As each called out three trainees' names, they were joined beside a vehicle. Jill, the brunette instructor, called mine and waved me and two others – Barry and Nick – over to a blue Astra. Nick had been number forty-two. I had guessed from the way he spoke that he was from a technical regiment. Barry, ginger-haired and stocky, I suspected to be an NCO, perhaps in the RAF – certainly not the army, anyway.

The scent of her perfume filled the interior of the car the moment she switched off the ignition, cutting out the fan. After only a few minutes' drive from camp, Jill had pulled the car over and parked in a lay-by. Barry and I were in the back, Nick in the front, and to be honest we were feeling rather self-conscious.

The only other vehicle in the lay-by was an old Honda. An elderly couple was sitting, enjoying the view over the rolling hills, and drinking something from a stumpy tartan flask. I surreptitiously nudged the window lever with my knee to open it a little to the fresh air outside. The driving seat creaked slightly as Jill released her safety belt and twisted round so she could see us all.

'OK, guys, I'm going to be your instructor in advanced driving,' she said, the faintest hint of a northern accent detectable in her voice. 'From time to time other instructors will take you, so that we all get a look at each of you. Over the next two weeks, you'll learn how to drive fast but safely. The purpose of this will become clear as the course progresses . . . that's assuming you're still with us.' She smiled sweetly and it struck me that she really was very pretty. She was quite slim, but nicely rounded, and she was wearing expensive-looking jeans and a green knitted cardigan over a white blouse. She went on, 'If you fail the driving test, or if I don't reckon you're safe to take it, I'm afraid you'll be of no use to us. Just concentrate on the techniques for now. They need to become second nature, because later you'll be too busy to think about the actual driving. We call it advanced driving, but it isn't exactly the same as your average Uncle Harry might have learnt for his advanced test.'

I glanced sideways at Barry. I could sense from his expression that he was having the same idea as me: a girl, teach me something about driving? It seemed unlikely. Of course, she couldn't know that I was something of an ace myself. My first lesson had been at the age of eleven – flogging an ancient Morris Minor at twenty miles an hour around my prep school's playing fields, pursued by a tribe of my little chums on their bicycles, whooping like Red Indians – and I'd been driving ever since. Here we were, beside a main road in rural England on a brilliant February morning. Maybe now I'd have a chance to show her a thing or two.

She started the car again and pulled out into the light traffic. We were behind a long green bus, travelling at about forty-five.

'As far as possible, keep your hands in the ten to two position, thumbs on the inside of the rim of the wheel, never locked around it. As you turn the wheel, feed it through your hands with a pushing and pulling motion. Don't turn it by leaning sideways on it.'

We snaked right into a double bend and I dutifully watched the position of Jill's hands on the wheel. This was pretty tame stuff. But as we swooped into the left-hand bend the Astra started floating out to the right, into the oncoming lane. I saw Nick stiffen and his right foot shoot out instinctively into the passenger-side footwell, pressing hard on his phantom break pedal. Barry and I tensed involuntarily – we were going round a blind bend on the wrong side of the road!

Jill continued to lecture us in her even tone. 'You can come right out into the other lane and take a good look ahead – just make sure that you've got a space to dive back into if you meet something,' she said calmly. At that very moment a blue van appeared, careering towards us, and Jill slid the wheel sharply over and touched the brake as we tucked in again behind the bus. Now we were all clutching the grab handles above our doors.

Even before the van had fully passed us, Jill swung the Astra out again into the right-hand lane, seamlessly dropping down into second gear, and the engine shrilled. The road was beginning to straighten out of the bend, and we could now see well beyond the bus. There was a stream of cars heading towards us, perhaps 250 metres away, and closing fast. There was obviously no option except to move back in. In a flash, Jill's foot went flat on the accelerator and the little Astra shot along the outside of the bus, the needle of the rev counter flickering in the red zone.

Jill raised her voice over the scream of the engine. 'If you're not redlining the revs when you're overtaking, you're not going fast enough. Always drop a gear before overtaking – double de-clutch if you've got time, because it gives you a smoother power transition and less chance of a hiccup from the driven wheels when you let the clutch out. Make sure you take a good look before committing yourself to a move, and if you have any doubts about whether you can make it, don't try it!'

I was hardly hearing her words. The front of the approaching stream of traffic was closing far too fast and I was sure that we weren't going to reach the open road in front of the bus before impact! Yet the Astra was still accelerating rapidly, now in third, and at the last second we slipped into our lane beyond the bus and roared away.

Jill continued as if nothing was amiss. 'Always set your seat well forward on its rack, with the back of the seat more upright than usual so that you feel slightly too close to the pedals. It gives you better control and vision that way. And never use fifth gear, except perhaps above a hundred and ten. Below that, it's far too sloppy.

'See how I only ever touch the gearstick very briefly? Always keep both hands on the wheel until the very second you're ready to change.'

We were still accelerating along a smooth straight, the road ahead clear, our speed now nudging ninety. Barry and I glanced at each other, shocked. A series of black and white warning chevrons appeared, the road dipping sharply to the right.

'Read the road ahead, as far as you can see. Use the line of the hedgerows, trees and telegraph poles to give you a hint at the direction it's going next. Don't brake too early or you waste speed – which means time. Bring your speed down with the brakes, not the gears – and as soon as your speed's right for the corner, drop a gear or two and then pile on the juice.'

I was certain she'd left it too late, but she jabbed so abruptly on the brakes that Barry and I were thrown forward against the seats, where we braced ourselves. I could see Nick's ears glowing brightly. He was rigid in his seat, staring in horror as the chevrons flashed past. Having viciously killed the car's speed, dropping from ninety-five to thirty-five m.p.h. in the space of about seventy metres, Jill slipped into second gear and accelerated around the bend, our nearside wheels firmly in the left-hand gutter.

'I'm hugging the nearside because, on a right-hand twist like this, it lets me see as far ahead around the bend as possible. But you have to keep an eye out for the debris and loose gravel which tends to collect in the gutter, it can spin you off the road. Don't get too close to anyone in front or you'll shut down your view forwards. Notice how I keep my hands positioned on a bend when I'm putting the power on, guys. Keep the hand that's on the inner side of the bend at about two o'clock and move the outer hand down to about eight o'clock. This gives maximum stability and leaves you ready to steer tighter if you begin to stray off.'

Still in the bend, we had hauled rapidly up behind a small red car and Jill positioned us expertly a few feet behind it, well over to the left. Sure enough, we could see a surprising distance ahead, even though the bend was tight. Before I'd even had time to notice that there was an opportunity to overtake, we screamed past the red car, still in second gear, until at about fifty she slipped into third and raced away.

'As I'm sure you can tell, the engine's much more responsive at high revs. Of course you wouldn't want to flog your own car like this – it knackers the engine and the brakes – but that's not your problem while you're here.' The road now led broadly into the distance, and we hit a hundred before smoothly overtaking several cars and a lorry. Each time it was the same. Jill would control her approach behind the vehicle, slowing gradually, timing her arrival with a gap in the oncoming stream of traffic, then pulling out wide into the other lane and dropping a gear before powering past. It was an astonishing – and heartstopping – display of skill, and she made it look so effortless.

'Keep looking as far ahead as you can see. Don't let your eyes settle on the back of the vehicle in front of you, you'll only slow down. As you approach a car to overtake, drift out wide like this . . . and look underneath it, because from a distance you'll be able to see wheels or a shadow if there is any other vehicle immediately in front of it.

'Keep looking out for escape routes in case you meet an emergency and have to leave the road altogether. Anything like a gate or a gap in the hedge will do. And keep the power on as you corner – let the engine pull you round. The traction helps to counter the centrifugal force so you stick to the road better.'

Now we entered a small town and she showed us how to nip in and out of the traffic, sometimes overtaking on the inside, but always in complete control and aware of pedestrians.

'Never trust a driver wearing a hat! I don't know why, but they always drive erratically. Same goes for anyone with fluffy dice. Give them a wide berth!'

Soon we were in open countryside again, cruising past cars and trucks. Jill resumed the lesson on high-speed control. 'Never overtake where a junction enters from the right. If someone approaches it to turn left on to your road, they'll be checking to their right. If they see it's clear and pull out without checking their left you'll meet head-on as you overtake in their lane. Same goes for petrol stations, pubs and crossroads.

'Read the road markings and signs, they're surprisingly reliable. Bend warning signs, posts and chevrons are invaluable, particularly at night. Look at these white lines in the middle of the road – hazard warning lines. They're both unbroken here; this confirms to me that there's no way I can get past this truck because I can't see over the crest of the hill. But now look. From on top here I can see the road swings right in the distance, and on our side the markings change to a broken line. So I'm closing right up on the truck, well to the left so I can see as far as possible . . . and down into second . . . and away.

'Also notice that though I'm driving fast I'm still checking in my mirrors before I do anything outrageous, and I'm indicating as normal. After all, other team members may be whizzing up on your outside to pass you – so you have to keep an eye out all around. Sure, there'll be some situations when you won't want to indicate, but we'll talk about those another day. Generally, remember that you're not supposed to behave like reckless road-hogs – you're supposed to be expert drivers, even if you are in a hell of a hurry!'

After a few more minutes driving like the wind and maintaining her running commentary, Jill swung the Astra into the back entrance of the large training area behind our camp, and along a tarmac track.

'Of course, there's more to it than just high speed,' she said. 'You've also got to be able to control skids, whether they happen by mistake – perhaps because you're cornering too fast – or when you want to use one to your advantage. Brace yourselves now and I'll show you a handbrake turn.'

The Astra was travelling at about forty on the narrow, gritty road. Jill slapped the palm of her hand flat on to the bottom centre of the steering wheel and spun it hard one and a half turns to the right. With a loud squeal of tyres, the bonnet dipped, the back of the car began to swing wide to the left and Barry cannoned into my side of the back seat. Nick was grabbing at the top of his seat belt with both hands. I gawped, eyes wide in fright, as Jill yanked up on the handbrake. Now we were travelling backwards in a screeching skid down the road, and I could still hear Jill calmly describing the manoeuvre. 'The back of the car has taken us through 180 degrees. I'm slipping into first and gunning the throttle flat down . . . handbrake off now . . . releasing the clutch . . . As the wheelspin settles and bites, you can feel our acceleration gather. Don't worry about the rubber smoke. The front-wheel drive is pulling us nicely on to our new course, dragging us forward.

'That was a handbrake turn. As you can see, it lets you go from forty miles an hour in one direction to forty in the other in the space of about seven seconds. Quite handy if you're in a hurry, or if you're being chased!'

Chased! Bloody hell. I swallowed hard and exchanged a glance with Barry.

She drove back out on to the public road, still pouring out advice and guidance, until after a couple of miles we found a lay-by with a caravan selling teas and snacks. We clambered out, feeling flushed and a bit car sick, having been thrown around for the best part of forty minutes. 'Anyone else want a bacon roll?' Jill asked. 'I'm buying. They're good here.'

'Er, no thanks. Just tea, please,' we mumbled, still queasy and now feeling a bit sheepish. Perhaps this wasn't going to be such a breeze after all.

We spent the rest of the day taking the wheel in turn, swapping every thirty minutes or so. It was surprisingly tiring, perhaps because you can't let your attention stray for so much as a second when you're haring around at high speed. And when we weren't driving, we were being thrown around in the back and trying to learn from each other's mistakes. We drove for hundred of miles over the next few days, practising the various techniques on different types of road, from rough tracks to motorways. Each day we took out a different car, and always Jill sat in the front passenger seat, coaxing us to drive faster and faster, but ready to shout a loud 'No!' the moment we attempted a manoeuvre that was reckless or beyond our reach. It was particularly disconcerting that we never seemed to be going fast enough for her.

'Come on, James, put your foot down! That Metro's being driven by a crumbly with a hat on! What are you doing in fourth! You should have passed it as we came out of the last bend!'

I could feel the sweat on my brow and my palms as I slipped back down into third and screamed past it. At seventy-five m.p.h. I moved back into fourth and powered away, entering a series of gently sweeping bends. In the distance, the road wound up a hill in front, twisting and turning.

'I think your problem is that you're not looking far enough ahead, James. I want you to concentrate on watching the furthest point you can see on the road ahead. Remember to note the position of houses and junctions, left and right, well before you approach them. Be ready for someone to pull out of a driveway unexpectedly.'

As the first of the rising bends appeared I braked savagely, still in fourth, then double de-clutched – clutch in, gearlever into neutral, clutch out, blip the acclerator to increase the revs, clutch in, straight down into second gear, clutch out again, and away. The fancy footwork ensures that the engine is revving at the right level to accept such a low gear, leaving the car travelling at the right speed to enter the bend. With a little acceleration we swept around the bend, but I could feel that the back wheels were on the point of skidding from under us.

'Keep the power on. Go for it now or you'll lose it!' urged Jill. The realisation that I had narrowly averted disaster flicked across my mind, but immediately I was concentrating on the road again, now furiously trying to measure my approach behind a tractor towing a heavily laden trailer. I kept half an ear on Jill's commentary as I balanced the need to maintain the maximum speed against passing this obstacle safely.

'Think about it. He can't be going far with a load like that; he can't see much behind him, if anything; and you can't see his indicators, even if he remembers to use them. So don't push your luck with an obstacle like this, treat it like you would a rider on horseback.' As if the tractor driver was in cahoots with Jill, the moment she finished speaking the tractor swung sharply right without any warning, filling the road, and began to bump into a field through a muddy gateway. I let my speed fall, then accelerated towards the gap that would surely open up on the left as the tractor disappeared between the hedgerows.

'No!' Jill said sharply. 'Close up to him, but don't accelerate like that or you won't be able to stop if he does something unexpected.

You can't be certain he'll clear the road quickly enough. What if he has to stop to open the gate, or slows right down because the field's soft? Your only option then would be to hit the trailer or go through the hedge. If either happens, you're out of the game. Got it?'

'Yup, I got it.' Shit, wrong again.

Now the road was clear.

'Right then, you've lost a bit of time here – not your fault – so imagine you've got to catch up with the rest of the team. Let's see some redlining!'

I launched us up the incline, and for the next twenty minutes I forced myself to push the little car to its limits, working the brakes and gearstick feverishly, swinging out wide to the right to see round left-hand bends and passing vehicle after vehicle. Each incident drew comment from Jill as gradually, the lessons began to gel.

'Well that wasn't too bad for a beginner, James . . . considering,' she said as I refilled the car with petrol at a garage. 'You need to concentrate on your road positioning and keeping your speed up. You tend to drive in fast spurts. You have to be able to drive like the wind for long periods, not just in bursts.' She strolled off to pay at the kiosk.

I wanted to ask her why it would be necessary to drive like this, but I knew what the answer would be. 'Don't worry about that now, when you need to know, we'll let you know.' And anyway it was Nick's turn behind the wheel and I was grateful to slump on to the back seat.

Nick adjusted his seat and the mirrors and pulled out into the busy traffic. He put his foot down and soon he was leap-frogging from gap to gap along the line of cars and lorries ahead. We cleared the front of the column and swooped down a low rise, picking up speed quickly, till we were doing close to a hundred on a long and wide flat. Barry and I grinned at each other – and again it struck me what a strange experience this all was.

At lunchtime we met up in a lay-by with a few of the other cars. While we ate the packed lunches that we'd brought with us and drank tea from the ubiquitous caravanette, we discussed the significance of what we were being taught. The instructors gathered together well away from us, as they always did. It seemed likely that the 'team' Jill had referred to that morning must be a surveillance team.

After lunch at the roadside, Jill gave us another demonstration to illustrate some more lessons. This time, confident of her skill, we enjoyed the sensation of being driven by an expert, as she whipped in and out of the busy traffic on the outskirts of a town.

Whenever we saw a police car, we reined back and drove sedately because it didn't make sense to draw attention to ourselves by provoking traffic police into a high-speed chase.

After each day's driving – having cleaned and refuelled the cars and reported any defects to the REME fitters who worked late every evening renewing scoured brake pads and changing oil filters – we changed for a vigorous PT session. Still the instructors seemed in better shape than us, as we panted and groaned around the training area, sprinting and relaying up and down the various woody banks and rough tracks.

Sometimes after supper we would have lessons in vehicle recognition from a red-haired instructor called Eric. He taught us how to distinguish one make of car from another by the rear light clusters, the shape of the wheel arch, the silhouette and so on, then tested what we'd learnt by flashing up slides of cars, which we had to identify, taken from odd angles.

Other evenings were spent listening to lectures on first aid, signals voice procedure, or in familiarisation with the range of Soviet, Chinese and Eastern European small arms that terrorists might have access to – such as the Tokarev and Makarov pistols, the AK47, 74 and AKM, and the most common Western systems such as the Uzi submachine gun from Israel and the American M60 machine gun. We also studied the older British service weapons, like the Bren light machine gun, the Thompson and Sten submachine guns and Webley and Smith & Wesson revolvers. We even looked at wartime German Luger pistols, which could yet be in the possession of the loyalists, before moving on to cover the RUC weaponry, such as the Ruger revolver and mini-Ruger rifle.

As the days passed and we became more and more proficient at our driving, we ventured out at night and learned the refinements that are demanded by the dark. We practised glimpsing and memorising oncoming car number-plates and makes and mastered the ability to read a plate seen in a rear view mirror. I found no easy way to remember car numbers; it just seemed to take practice. Even simple things acquired a new significance. For instance; a car is following you and you see in your mirror that it's started to indicate. But which way is it preparing to go, left or right? Of course, you're seeing a mirror image, so its direction is also reversed – or is it? It was drummed into us that we needed to get small details like that right every time.

We also visited a police skid-pan, and spent a few hours pirouetting the cars around a slalom course, learning to steer out of serious skids.

The two weeks passed in a blur as I struggled to assimilate the strange new techniques I had learnt – and all too soon I was sitting in a brown Sierra beside a pleasant, middle-aged instructor called Alan, ready to take the high-speed test. I drove carefully out of the gate and followed his instructions, which led us out into a network of narrow country lanes. We stopped in a lay-by. I was pretty nervous.

'OK, James,' Alan said quietly, 'you've just heard over the radio that a team member's in trouble at a farm ten miles away. When I say go, take me to him as fast as you can. I'll direct you which way to go well before each junction. I warn you though, if I have to intervene to stop you doing something dangerous, you'll fail automatically. Got it?'

'Right-oh!' I said. Goddamn, I'm not sure I'm ready for this, I thought.

'Go!' Alan said sharply. At once I threw the car into first gear, checking the mirror and slipping the clutch out at the same time, right foot down hard. To my horror the engine note dropped to a quiet judder and the car began to crawl forwards at about three miles an hour! Fuck! What the hell's the matter with it? I thought, frantically pumping the accelerator. The engine coughed and died. I broke out into a sweat. Perplexed, I put it into neutral and started up again.

I glanced at Alan. He was staring at me, stony-faced. 'Have you driven this Sierra before today?' he asked.

'Er, no, I haven't, as it happens,' I replied miserably.

'Thought not. Well if you try to pull away in third gear that's what happens. I grant this gearbox is a bit woolly, but you really should be able to do better than that!' He turned away and stared out of his side window for a few seconds. 'OK, we'll pretend that we haven't started yet. So . . . Go!'

This time the Sierra left a cloud of blue rubber smoke behind as she leapt away up the road, engine roaring. I launched her into the first series of bends, twisting left and right, jockeying from side to side of the lane to maximise the view ahead. As we swept round each bend we should have been on two wheels, but she clung to the road like a limpet. Now we were flat out on a long, bumpy straight, topping eighty m.p.h., the wheels leaving the ground as we leapt over a little culvert. Here came a left-hand hairpin and I waited till the last second to stamp on the brakes pumping rapidly to prevent the wheels locking in a skid, before dropping into second gear and powering round the curve, and flashing away up to the next crest.

From time to time Alan yelled directions – take the next left; go right after the next farmhouse – and we whipped around each junction, rubber screeching on the dry tarmac. Out of the corner of my eye I noticed Alan had both feet braced hard against the glove compartment. Hah, I thought, at least he won't accuse me of being too slow!

I was driving at my limit and I hardly noticed the passage of time as I fought to keep up our speed all the way. After about ten minutes Alan said, 'OK, that'll do now. You can stop driving like a loony! You've passed all right.' Then he grinned and added, 'Holy dogfuck, James! I thought we'd had it for a while back there! Look, you've got me gripping the grab-handle – I don't usually do that! For Pete's sake, take me back to camp, I need a cup of tea.'

Two of our number failed the driving test, including one of the girls, and were immediately sent back to their units. This left just one female trainee on the course – Kate, pretty and auburn-haired, who can't have been much older than twenty-two.

After lunch, the rest of us learnt about the next phase of training. We gathered at the entrance to a small complex of buildings set slightly apart from the main camp. The main door was locked, but soon a rotund, slightly balding figure shambled up and introduced himself as Tony. As he fumbled with the key, he told us he was a Royal Army Ordnance Corp photographer and would be instructing us in his art over the next two weeks.

Inside, the building was a veritable Aladdin's cave of expensive equipment and photographic stores. It consisted of a small lecture room, a couple of offices and storerooms, and a series of fully equipped darkrooms with enlarging and printing suites and a separate video room. After a brief tour led by Tony and his short, ginger-haired and pasty-faced sidekick Brian, we settled down in the lecture room.

'For the next two weeks, I'm going to teach you everything you'll ever want to know about photography. You need to master the skills so that they become second nature to you, because where you're going, you're not going to be able to check things through at your leisure. We'll start with the basics, then move on to long and short lens work, infra-red, low light, aerial, car and bag set-ups, and video. But first, you'll each need one of these.' Tony held up a basic Nikon camera body, as Brian began to hand out neat little shoulder bags full of kit.

'Open your bags and I'll take you through the contents. I suggest you take notes in the exercise books on your desk. You'll have both a written and a practical test at the end of next week, so you'll need to revise.

'OK, so take out your camera and I'll talk you through it. This is a thirty-five-mil single lens reflex or SLR model. All that really means is that you see through your viewfinder almost exactly what the lens sees and what the film will record. Look in the front where the lens should be, and when you press the shutter release notice how the little mirror flips up to expose the film. The reason that we use the SLR is that you can change lenses, which gives us the flexibility we need. Now, let's go through the various controls.'

Christ, I hadn't expected any of this. I'd never had any interest in cameras before, and so I frantically scribbled away as Tony talked about apertures and f-stops, film speeds, depth preview, ASA, DIN, ISO and focal length. From the number of automatic features built into this little camera body, it was obvious that the sodding thing had a higher IQ than I did!

Tony neatly summarised the fundamental principles of photography and explained how every different situation effectively boils down to a calculated trade-off between the three mechanical variables that we can control: the size of the lens aperture, the sensitivity of the film and the speed of the shutter. The complication that arises from this and which I'd never needed to consider when using my little beach-holiday instamatic, is that both speed and aperture settings affect other important factors. A wide aperture (letting in maximum light) creates a relatively narrow band of focus – known as depth of field – in front of and behind the object you have actually focused on. Conversely, a narrow aperture (letting in much less light) produces a broad depth of field. Of course, to photograph a moving target one needs a fast shutter speed, otherwise the object will be blurred by motion. A fast shutter speed means not much light hits the film, so you would need a wide aperture to compensate. But a wide aperture means a narrow depth of field, bad news if you don't have much time to focus on the subject. So should you set a slightly slower shutter speed, enabling you to reduce the aperture, broadening the depth of field but increasing the risk that the picture could begin to blur?

Tony explained that there was another option: we could trick the camera's internal light metre into thinking there was more background light than there actually was, by manually 'uprating' the speed (meaning sensitivity to light) of the film, therefore permitting a faster shutter speed and a smaller aperture. The downside to this was that the negative would be grainier than usual.

My head was beginning to spin.

Within an hour we were helping ourselves to film from one of the fridges in the storeroom, and roaming around outside shooting our first rolls of film with a standard 50mm lens, getting to know the controls and practising trading off one factor against another. Then Tony taught us how to develop the negatives in the darkroom and dry them off, before printing positives and enlargements.

All our photography, at least initially, was in black and white. This gave the twin advantage of producing a crisper print with greater definition and allowing us to develop and print the negatives ourselves (colour printing is a laborious exercise in an ordinary dark room). By the end of the session I felt well and truly drugged from the noxious cocktail of chemicals we had been sloshing about in deep trays all afternoon. For once, the evening PT session was a refreshing and welcome change of air.

The next morning, Tony introduced us to the various additional bits of kit that we would be using, such as the motordrive that screwed on to the base of the body and allowed continuous shooting, five frames a second. We fiddled about with camouflaged lightweight tripods – indispensable in an observation post where the act of bringing a camera up to the eye might give away the position – and remote shutter-release cables. Then we were introduced to the range of lenses that would routinely be available to us. Fifty mm was the standard, with 28mm for close work, and a variety of telephoto lenses – 135mm, 200mm, 400mm and 600mm reflectors, with a two-times convertor that could double the focal length of each lens.

We learnt that if you use a zoom, such as the variable 80mm to 200mm, the maximum aperture available reduces by two f-stops, thus requiring a slower shutter speed or better light conditions. In the right conditions a 1200mm lens can take a clear mug shot at a distance of 1,500 metres.

Soon we had settled into a routine of sorts. Each morning Tony initiated us into a different technique and we would then disperse for the day to practise it before returning in the afternoon to develop and print our films. We sat inside bushes to make sure that we could take clear pictures through the foliage. We tried wrapping the cameras in cloth and shooting through it. We shot subjects in a variety of settings – for example, through chainlink fences, in areas of deep shadow, and from deep shadow into bright sunlight. Each circumstance required a different approach, and as we experimented we began to get an instinctive feel for the right shutter speed, aperture, film speed and lens that each situation demanded. Soon we were fitting motordrives to the cameras, enabling us to take five frames a second – invaluable if you have only a brief opportunity.

Once we'd mastered the basics, Tony taught us how to photograph in low-light conditions using an image-intensifying scope attached to the back of an ordinary lens. Now we could operate from a hide and record activity twenty-four hours a day. The scope simply amplified whatever ambient star and moonlight there was. It lent a ghostly greenish glow to everything, and the quality of the prints was not very high, but you could still read off a car number plate at 200 metres. We spent many late evenings wandering about in the dark mastering this new tool.

'OK, people,' said Tony one morning. 'You're all very clever now at taking pics around the clock. But what about when there's no light at all, inside a room? How can you manage that?' he asked.

'Flash?' someone suggested.

'No chance, not where you're going – at least, not the flash you mean. The answer is IR film combined with an IR flash. Infra-red is the band of wavelengths beyond ordinary visible red light. You can't see it, but black and white IR film, with an ISO of fifty, will pick it up just as ordinary film will pick up daylight. Only first you have to supply the IR light from an IR source.'

He picked up a standard flash unit and taped a dark gelatine sheet over its face. Then he dimmed the lights until the classroom was pitch black and popped the flash several times. 'There,' he said. 'You don't see anything, but in fact the room is flooded with IR light each time. This sheet of IR jelly only allows infra-red light through it. All the white light is blocked in. Now, for IR photography set the aperture at f8 or larger, and the shutter speed at one-fifteenth of a second. But here's the rub: IR film is sensitive even to the ordinary red light in the darkroom, so you're going to have to learn to load and unload the camera in pitch darkness.

'Now, to make matters trickier, you're unlikely to be able to wave a torch around if you're inside a target building, and there probably won't be enough light for an image-intensifying scope to work. So how do you see to find the things you've come to photograph? With these,' he said triumphantly in the darkness, and he turned up the lights again. He was wearing a set of standard army-issue passive night goggles, which are like lightweight binoculars, held in position in front of one's eyes by straps around the head. 'With these and an IR torch like this one – it's an ordinary white light torch with an IR jelly strapped to the lens – you can see as clear as day.

'OK, so you can see and you can photograph and no one will be any the wiser. But you can't look through the viewfinder to focus, not with this on your head. So you have to prepare the focus in advance for a set distance. If you're after shots of an interior then focus at about twelve feet, and put a bit of tape across the focus ring so that when you've reached your target you know that the focus is right without having to check it again.'

This was definitely becoming quite interesting. I liked the thought of sneaking around in the pitch dark. Very James Bond!

'Of course, often you'll want to take IR photography of interiors and close-ups on the same roll of film. Time will always be a bit short when you're collecting IR pics, so you don't want to mess around with changing lenses. That's why we usually use a wide-angle lens – it's excellent for close work and quite acceptable for distances of up to about forty feet. Simply focus on infinity and all your interior shots should be about right.'

He passed the camera body round the room and we examined

the settings as he continued to talk. 'You'll notice that I've also taped a pencil to the side of the body. In this case, with this lens, it gives me the right distance for taking a close-up shot of a weapon serial number or a document. Of course I still need to twist the focal ring to match the shorter distance, which is why I've also taped two half matchsticks – one on to the body and one on to the focal ring – so all I've got to do is match them up in the dark and I know that I'm on the new focus. Right, go and have a fiddle with the kit, take some IR film from the fridge and have a practice in the broom cupboards out there.'

Slowly we mastered the combined use of PNGs, IR torch and IR film, until we were able to move around confidently in the pitch dark, snapping the interiors of rooms. The prints with which we emerged from the darkroom were very grey and a bit grainy, but sharp enough. We discovered that using PNGs for close-up work is a bit like watching your arms reaching down into water – all the angles seem different and your limbs appear disconcertingly elongated, making any co-ordinated activity rather difficult. Also the PNGs give off a tiny high-pitched whine, like a persistent mosquito, just loud enough to be irritating. It began to dawn on me just how much kit we might have to take in on a job with us.

The next topic we tackled was aerial photography. Tony stood in front of us one morning clutching a large black oblong camera, which he held with obvious reverence. 'This is a Hasselblad,' he breathed. 'We've only got three of them and if any of you damage one of them, I'll drown you in a vat of developer! They cost about £6,000 each, so for God's sake don't drop them out of the heli!' Tony explained that the advantage of the Hasselblad's 120mm film was that the negative, because of its large format, permitted enormous prints to be made – up to three foot square – and that these would be invaluable in planning operations and giving briefings.

'Bear in mind that you can't just overfly the target directly. That would be too obvious. You have to direct the pilot to fly a tangent, and you should be about a thousand metres to one side and at least three thousand feet up. Of course, a heli is full of vibration and cruises at about eighty knots, so you need a fast shutter speed. Don't set less than a thousandth of a second. What about aperture? Any ideas?'

'Well . . .' I volunteered, 'I suppose at that distance, the camera will be focused on infinity and depth of field won't come into it. So at a thousandth of a second, I guess you'd set the maximum aperture, say f2?'

'Ah,' replied Tony, 'but up in the air, you have so much light spilling around and down on to the target that even at a speed of a thousandth of a second you could well overexpose the film if you were on the widest aperture. So you need to be guided by the camera's integral light-metre, which you can do as you're flying along. However, here's a useful tip: before you board the heli, always aim the camera at a patch of light-coloured tarmac, then set the camera's suggested setting. The method usually works pretty well and it means you've got the ability to take a quick snap without any further preparation, if an emergency pops up.'

Later that day, we spent hours flying around in a succession of Gazelle and Lynx helicopters. This was more like it, I thought, but the session was short lived. Once we'd mastered the art of shooting, developing and printing the enormous photographs, Tony led us on to the next skill. Now we learned everything there was to know about video cameras, and practised their use in a wide variety of settings and light conditions. We mounted two complete systems in a car and then wired them into the vehicle's own electrics so that the driver could monitor 360 degrees without moving his head. We took it in turns to drive around the local towns before editing a masterpiece of a travelogue in the video suite. We also fitted a camera into a briefcase and a handbag and practised wandering about collecting covert footage of each other. This was good fun, but we soon discovered that, because video lenses tend not to have a particularly wide angle of view, it's surprisingly difficult to capture the target on tape. Until one is practised at it, it's also difficult to behave casually with the covert fit, whether it is in a bag or a briefcase. Soon I was on to my second exercise book of facts and technical data and – although I'm not technically minded – I found I rather enjoyed mastering these new skills.

I put my left hand out and reached for the door handle. In the ghostly grey-green beam of the infra-red torch, my arm appeared strangely bent, and I had to keep compensating for this as my fingers sought the key in the lock. The door opened and I carefully stepped over the threshold. Again I noticed the distracting high-pitched whine of the night goggles as I pushed the door to behind me.

On the middle shelf of a tall cabinet fixed against the far wall, I could just see the butt of a pistol protruding. Ah, so far so good, I thought. I eased the camera body gently out of its pocket in the bulky waistcoat jacket that I wore under my light civilian overcoat, its voluminous pockets carrying the tools of my new trade. I lightly clicked the heavy flash-head on to the hot-shoe attachment at the top of the camera. I briefly peeled back the black masking tape that I'd fastened over the little red LED on the top of the flash gun, checking that it was active. I aimed the camera at the pile of papers and took a stream of shots, then, still using the night goggles, I set the camera assembly down to one side. Painstakingly I began to lift off the loose sheets of paper that had been placed carelessly over the pistol.

A Webley .45 revolver – recognised it at once. Quickly I inserted a long pencil into a little socket made of masking tape that I had added to the side of the lens housing. This was my focus marker. I began to shoot a series of close-ups, capturing the precise position of the pistol on the shelf. Each time the flash popped I was startled by the flare of light that hit me through the goggles, and it took a mental effort to remind myself that it was visible only to me. For good measure, I also threw in some shots of the writing on the papers that had covered it before easing the gun over to reveal the serial number stamped into the diecast black metal, just under the revolver's chamber. Even in the full glare of the IR torch, I could barely make out the tiny string of numbers and letters, but I was reasonably confident that the focus and aperture settings I had pre-programmed would catch the necessary detail.

I reassembled the pile of papers on top of the weapon and stripped down the camera, replacing the separate parts in their respective pockets in my waistcoat. Like a surgeon closing up a body at the end of an operation, we had to be certain that we hadn't left anything behind where we had been working. By religiously sticking to the same pockets for particular items, it would be more immediately obvious if we had forgotten some part of our equipment. Satisfied with my work, I turned to open the door. There was an almighty crash. Bugger it! After all that, I had swung the body of the goggles, which protruded about six inches from my face, hard into one of the supports of the metal filing cabinet. Shit! I moved out of the room as quickly as I could, emerging into a darkened classroom, and switched off the goggles. Outside in the corridor, Tony was whistling through his teeth to himself.

He smiled brightly at me as I came out. 'Trying to demolish the place?' he asked easily. 'Don't worry, it takes a bit of getting used to. Go and develop the shots, print some blowups of the pistol and bring them to me, and then I'll give you a test paper to answer, OK?'

'Right-oh,' I said. A combination of nervous tension and the warmth of the room had caused me to start sweating heavily. Was I going to screw up on every test as we progressed through the training? There were so many strange new bits of kit to get used to – what would it be like when we had to do this for real, armed and in a hostile environment? My occasional cackhandedness worried me rather, because we'd noticed that these instructors never told you if you were failing to meet the mark. Oh well, I said to myself, *que sera, sera*!

I was relieved to learn the next day that I had passed the photography course, as had all the others with me. At this point the chief instructor informed us that 'over the water' our films would in fact be developed for us by RAOC darkroom technicians – known as brownies – since we would not usually have time to do it for ourselves.

Now at last we were on to the real business. We were all sitting in the lecture theatre. 'This morning, we are going to talk about surveillance,' began the chief instructor. 'Ernie here is the expert – well, we're all expert – but Ernie's going to take you through the basics before we head out into the local town for some practice.'

'OK, guys and girls,' said Ernie in a warm Newcastle accent, moving up to a large whiteboard and picking up a fistful of coloured marker pens. 'Let's start with a basic follow. Here's your target, often referred to as a Bravo number – B for body, right? The main target of an operation is usually Bravo 1, and he lives at Alpha 1 and drives Charlie 1, OK? We want to know what he's up to, so we stake out a place we know he's at or suspect he's soon likely to be, and then follow him where he's going – without him, or anyone else in the vicinity, being aware of us, that is.

'The most important tool you'll have is your two radios, one hidden in your car and one on your body. You'll also be carrying other kit, but don't worry about that for the moment.' He introduced us to the discreet body sets and showed us how to construct a variety of pockets and holsters to enable the sets to be worn in different positions on the body, depending on one's chosen dress. The mike could be wired into the collar or shoulder-pad of a jacket, or into the cuff of a sleeve.

Ernie demonstrated the technique of speaking without moving your lips. It was pretty much done as ventriloquists do it, keeping the teeth slightly apart, and as with ventriloquism the real trick lay in making contradictory movements of the head and hands, so that an alert observer wouldn't guess that one was speaking at all. Speaking rapidly in the coded language of surveillance, and moving one's lips as little as possible, means that it's quite difficult to make out the sense of transmissions over the radio, but as we practised, so our ears developed the ability to decipher each other's words.

Ernie issued each of us with a plastic case containing a tiny earpiece and a supply of miniature batteries. The earpiece, which plugged tightly deep into one's ear, was far too small to be noticeable even at close quarters. Once loaded with a fresh battery, the earpiece received, amplified and broadcast the transmissions from and to the body set or the car radios. Until one had become used to it it felt very strange, effectively having a loudspeaker inside one's skull, and it was difficult to be confident that no one else could hear the chatter over the radio net.

'Right, so let's start at the beginning and go through some classic stake-out options.'

Ernie began to draw on the whiteboard a series of street plans and showed us how a surveillance team would be positioned to cater for every possible circumstance. 'The key thing is that someone always has control of the target, either physically – with their sight – or electronically, with the various different widgets you'll be introduced to later, which basically achieve the same thing. Now, the key difference between surveillance over the water and what is done on the mainland – by the likes of the police, Customs and MI5 – is that over here the local population at large doesn't tend to give a monkey's cuss about what's going on in the next street. So an unmarked car can sit a short distance away from the target's house, wait for him to drive past, then pull out discreetly into the follow.

'Well, as those of you who've served in Northern Ireland will know, life ain't that simple over there. If you try to sit in your car or mooch around on foot in a staunch republican or loyalist area – even if you look like you're minding your own business – sure as eggs is eggs, someone will come out and challenge you. As like as not, if they suspect that you're up to no good, it'll be a posse of the boyos and they'll be armed. If they suspect that you're army intelligence, you'll stand a good chance of winding up dead – and for your sake I hope it's before they've had a chance to use a Black & Decker on your kneecaps. Everyone's on the lookout for something out of the ordinary, and it's not really surprising, given the number of random sectarian murders that the poor bastards have suffered over the years. They are always on their guard.'

Now Ernie moved round the room issuing us with map books containing A4-sized sections of 1:50,000 Ordnance Survey maps, a small, coloured stick-on spot marking every prominent road junction or bridge, and each spot bearing a two-digit number. As we leafed through the pages Ernie explained that we would be using the system of spots to describe the progress of the target – for example, 'Charlie 1 is mobile from Red Three Two towards Red Three Three.' In the back of the book were street plans for all the local towns. Individual streets had been colour-coded, so that, for instance, one could report 'Bravo 1 is foxtrot on Purple towards Green' – meaning that the main target is walking along Purple in the direction of Green.

'Oh, by the way, make sure you learn the positions of the spots, their numbers and the colours and locations of the streets over the next couple of weeks, will you?' Ernie said casually, as we paused for a tea break. 'You'll need to know it by heart for the advanced surveillance training.' There was an involuntary gasp of disbelief from his audience.

I flicked quickly through the fat plastic folder. 'Jesus Christ,' I said quietly to Kate, who was sitting beside me. We looked at each other in shock. 'There must be forty pages of OS map and half a dozen towns in here!'

Ernie stopped half-way out of the door and turned round. He put on a slightly puzzled expression. 'Well, it's not as if you've anything better to do while you're here, have you?'

Our first mobile surveillance exercise was a nightmare. Keith, a young blond-haired lad from south London (who I suspected was a Royal Marine, from his use of words like 'Heads' and 'Galley', and his obvious military training), accompanied me in a Peugeot 305, with Mick the fair-haired instructor in the back. I drove and Keith did the map-reading, keeping the map-book open on his lap. Mick showed us how to operate the covert radio which was buried deep inside the car. As long as we were inside the car our tiny covert earpieces could pick up the radio traffic. The microphones were located inside the sun visors.

We split into three teams and my team had the task of staking out a pub car park near the centre of a small town. We immediately discovered how difficult it is to follow another vehicle through busy traffic while transmitting an accurate running commentary of its precise location and likely intentions, at the same time not drawing attention to oneself. Since only one car should be within sight of the target at any time, and since it's necessary to switch the car that has control of the target frequently, so the target doesn't realise he is being followed, those cars in the team that don't have the target must constantly be trying to get in a position from which they can take over or cover a possible escape route for the target. Thus, most of the time is spent struggling on parallel roads to catch up with or pull ahead of the target and the car that has it in its sights. So it became clear to us why a prerequisite was that we had to be able to drive like demons. If you couldn't drive like the wind and progress up a line of ordinary traffic, you'd never catch up with the follow. The trick is to be able to do it without making it look too obvious or outrageous.

We had been very surprised to learn that in a rural area a target vehicle can be most successfully 'followed' from in front, rather than from behind, and we understood that there are few surveillance agencies in the world that could match us in this. This works particularly well if you have an inkling of where the target is likely to be heading. It is extremely difficult for the subject to identify the surveillance cars in this circumstance, because as often as not the individual team cars and the target will actually be passing each other head on, or the target may even be overtaking the team one by one from behind.

Ernie's instruction in surveillance skills also included advice about what to wear and what to avoid, and how to tailor items of clothing to permit a quick change of appearance. We had already been forbidden to cut our hair and were by now looking distinctly unmilitary. Ernie pointed out that, initially, every serviceman's idea of how to look like a civilian invariably boiled down to donning a pair of skin-tight blue jeans, white trainers and a bomber jacket, and to have footballer-style collar-length hair. He demonstrated the SAS trooper's favourite droopy Mexican moustache, always a giveaway when worn by service personnel, and went on to advise us individually about the suitability of our wardrobe.

We had been incarcerated in this camp for the last five weeks now, and were looking forward to our first weekend's leave. Ernie told us to visit our local charity shops to purchase the right kind of gear – it was better to have second-hand shoes, boots and clothing – ensuring that we had appropriate sets for different types of environment. Clothes suitable for an operation in a working-class housing estate might differ significantly from those appropriate for a business district in a city centre, which would differ again from a middle-class neighbourhood. In addition, for covert work at night we would need some black outfits: jeans, shirts, sweatshirts, woollen hats, gloves and rustle-free black jackets.

'Oh, and while you're at it, buy a decent leather belt that'll take the weight of your pistol and magazines when you get them.'

We were dropped off at the local station and I travelled home by train. Although there had been some coin-operated phones in our accommodation block, we had been warned that the phone lines were not secure so we must be careful what we said over them. There was little enough to share with outsiders anyway. Our conversations within the camp had been pretty limited, since so much of what one generally talks about in normal conversation refers to one's background – and anyway, now that Alison and I seemed to have parted ways, I had no one to talk to other than my parents.

Over the weekend, I took stock of my personal position. This was the first time in three years that I hadn't had someone else to discuss things with. The job I was training for was clearly going to be difficult and stressful, so maybe it was better that way. Yet I thought that perhaps that wasn't right; if I was going to be under pressure for long periods and basically operating individually, then I should have an external supporter, to help me keep things in perspective. Otherwise I could slowly go mad without realising it! Also, I couldn't stand the thought of having nowhere – other than my parents' house – to spend my leave periods.

I rang around the few unattached girls I knew, trying to find someone to brighten up the weekend, but, as I might have guessed, at such short notice they were all tied up already or not about. I sat at home on the Saturday night, idly flicking through a copy of *Private Eye*, when I noticed a section at the back, entitled 'Eye-Love'. There were hundreds of adverts from people looking for partners. I glanced down the female columns. The girls' messages seemed genuine and it dawned on me that maybe I should put in an advert myself. Why not? It was surely as good a way as any to meet some new people. Let's face it, I thought, if I was introduced to an attractive girl at a cocktail party I wouldn't hesitate to ask her out for supper. By advertising somewhere like this, I felt certain that the girls I met would at least be game for a dinner date.

On the Sunday evening, after many drafts, I posted off my advertisement and a cheque for £30. 'Attractive, professional graduate, 24, often away from home, seeks friendly female for occasional dinner, theatre and country walks.' Well, I thought, it's perhaps a bit twee, but it might do the trick. At the same time I posted a reply, offering my services on an alternating basis, to a desperate ad from 'two females, 32, medium build, south-west London, seeking two males, any age, for damn good rogering'! Their honesty appealed to me and I wasn't in the least bit surprised that I didn't ever hear back from them. I presumed that they would have been swamped by replies!

The weekend was over in a flash. Back in isolation at camp, we spent the next ten days practising our somewhat rudimentary surveillance, endlessly careering around the countryside in pursuit of different instructors. When the target cruised around in a small town, as it often did, our amateur surveillance teams wheeled and swooped around it like Spitfires after a German bomber, the radio net a constant gabble of excited voices as we tried to keep control of the situation.

'Tango has Charlie 1 going left on to Green, now towards . . .' began a typical call.

In the background, we would hear Jill's voice interrupting him: 'That's not Green, you numbskull, that's Yellow!'

'Er . . . cancel that. Er . . . now on Yellow . . . and intending to go right on to Brown!'

However, as the days passed we became more and more expert at tailing the target. What surprised me was that a surveillance team acts more or less without any central control station or higher authority directing each operation or task, there being almost no role for a control station other than to record the overall situation and repeat certain transmissions. The start of almost every surveillance task was a stake out, waiting to pick up the target – perhaps from his local newsagent, his place of work, his girlfriend's house or simply a road junction he is likely to use. On first arrival at the scene of the stake out, each team member uses his own initiative to work out the most effective position to occupy. Only members of the team actually on the ground can determine this, and it would be dangerous folly to try to impose positions from the operations room. The moment that the target becomes mobile, it's up to the individuals in the team to take the initiative, constrained only by the guidelines and rules that we had learned.

At the end of each session, we would gather again in the classroom for a full and frank debrief, and would have to listen to the litany of errors we had made, which had been noted by the eagle-eyed instructors travelling in the back of each car:

'James, when the target passed you in Church Street, you swivelled in your seat to watch him – not very subtle; you should have used your mirrors – and you then hesitated a couple of seconds before coming on the air to give his new direction. That's no good. If you'd reported it the moment you saw it, my car could have gone right and nipped through the bus station to head it off. As it was, by the time you'd given the key information, we were committed to the one-way circuit and were out of it for a while, OK? And Phil, your navigation was all right, but the moment you were unsure of your location, you were waving your maps around like a tic-tac man.'

Soon though, our skills began to gel, and as we got into the routine of staking out a location and following a target we became more and more proficient, until we were going out in pairs without an instructor, who instead would drive around independently, observing us. However, as with every skill we had learned so far, the moment we mastered one level we were introduced to the next stage, which was always a daunting prospect. It had been difficult enough concentrating on the navigation and radio or the driving. Now, for the first time, we would each have to do all three simultaneously. Now it became apparent why we had needed to learn the town plans and road spots.

This was the first time that we had operated solo, and it proved an interesting test of one's own integrity. Connected to the rest of the team only by the radio traffic coming over the tiny earpiece, and relying entirely on our mental knowledge of the map or plan of the area, we all knew exactly what was required – and it was up to each individual to get on and do it. There were always a thousand reasons that one could have used to excuse an incorrect radio call or a missed target – when you are working alone no one can gainsay you – but now we were engaged in a new and obviously important business.

The instructors had earned our respect for their skills, and we aspired to match their professionalism. We realised that in the future we would likely be relying on each other in unpredictable and dangerous situations, and that there was therefore no room for passengers. We became totally – brutally perhaps – frank with ourselves and one another during debriefs, winkling out every lesson that arose from our errors and our successes. Gradually, a distinctive attitude was developing around us, this peculiar band of strangers, and although the instructors were still deliberately distant from us, more and more we began to resemble them in our assured mastery of the different techniques.

The daily grind of physical training continued as before. We were now seriously fit, and had no difficulty sprinting 300 metres at full tilt – at this level of fitness our heart-rates recovered within thirty seconds. But the routines were also becoming more specific in their application. Frequently the instructors would set up an indoor assault course in the gymnasium and demonstrate different techniques for rolling and falling. Now in scruffy civilian clothes rather than PT kit, we practised diving through wooden frames representing windows and doorways. The point was to be able to make a sudden flying entrance or exit, head tucked into one's chest, shoulder bunched, falling effortlessly into a forward or backward roll, then springing up and continuing a forward rush. I was only glad that we never actually had to try crashing through plate glass – I couldn't help thinking that one would end up pretty seriously injured. I decided that I would definitely hold that particular trick in absolute reserve! We also ran at high speed along narrow beams and rolled under low ones, developing spectacular speed and agility. It was an immensely satisfying feeling, knowing that one could deal effortlessly with any physical obstacle that might present itself.

The seriousness of the situations that we might find ourselves in was brought home to us when Sandy – a lanky, balding and good-humoured instructor – lined us up in the gym at the start of one evening's PT session.

'Today, we're going to cover some basic unarmed combat,' he said, strolling up and down in front of us. 'Imagine that you're by yourself and you've been pinged by the opposition for what you are. One of them strolls up to you, whips out a pistol and tells you to put your hands in the air. What do you do?'

He signalled for Barry to come forward and stand no more than two feet in front of him. Sandy pulled out a Browning pistol from his waistband and handed it to Barry – sliding back the topcover as he did so to prove that it was unloaded – and instructed him to cover him with it.

Barry held the gun at his side, pointing directly at Sandy, who continued to talk to us.

'Obviously, if he squeezes the trigger, he's going to hit me – at this range, anyway. But if he's holding you up like this, he clearly doesn't intend to execute you on the spot. So you have a short space of time in which to do something like this . . .' Almost faster than the eye could register, Sandy shot out one arm and twisted the body of the pistol to the outside, away from his body. At the same time, his other hand reached out and raked down Barry's face, momentarily blinding him. 'Notice that I gripped hard round the body of the weapon. It's a semi-automatic pistol, so applying downward pressure on to the working parts will cause the gun to malfunction and it'll jam after the first shot. If it had been a revolver, I'd have gripped it round the chamber and he couldn't have fired even one round.'

He took the pistol from Barry, who was nursing his bruised fingers, and continued. 'An alternative would have been to stick my thumb in front of the pistol's hammer, preventing it from striking the round in the chamber in the first place. As I reached forward, I turned sideways on to the threat, thus extending my reach and reducing his target at the same time. As I dragged my fingers down his face, I would have been aiming to scratch at his eyes. Now pair yourselves off and practise this move until you've got it off pat.'

In the course of the next few lessons on unarmed combat, Sandy showed us how to disarm a gunman in a wide variety of scenarios, and how to break free of the threat long enough either to disable the enemy or to draw our own concealed weapon. We practised hitting out at and kicking clear of the threat, bringing our assailant down in a tumble of legs and arms, grappling for that split-second's advantage that would allow our weapon to come into play or to disable our opponent.

At the start of every session, Sandy would lead us through a series of stretching and bending exercises, sometimes even reaching behind his neck with his feet. As he demonstrated a particularly unlikely stretch one evening I heard Carl, a likeable young Welshman who was standing beside me, mutter, 'Fucking hell, I reckon this one's a bleeding Ninja! Tie you in a knot as soon as look at you!' I certainly wouldn't want to meet him in a dark alley. Sandy went on to show us a range of disabling strokes and control grips. He demonstrated that almost any everyday item that you might have in your pocket – a comb, a pen, even a coin – can be applied mercilessly to a pressure point with astonishing results. For example, if you were to grip your opponent's ear firmly between your thumb and a hard item, like the barrel of a pen, and if you're quick enough and hit the right spot, you can incapacitate him completely.

We learned a dozen different improvised ways of achieving the same end, and I fervently hoped I would never need to use any of them for real!

At last we reached the training that I had been looking forward to.

One morning, we were divided again into two groups, and my party was dispatched to one of the classrooms, where Sandy and another instructor, a barrel-chested and weather-beaten Scot called Jock, began to hand out 9mm Browning pistols, each with a covert waistband holster and a double magazine holster containing two spare magazines.

'Today we start CQB training – standing for close-quarter battle,' Sandy informed us. 'And from this day on, each of you will carry a pistol in your waistband, so that you get used to the feel of it and the discipline it imposes.

'From now on you'll keep your pistol on you or with you, but out of sight, at all times. When you're asleep or in the shower, leave it under your pillow. Your pistol will always be made ready with a blank round in the chamber, unless we're on the range, in which case it'll be live ammunition.'

Jock roamed round, handing each of us a single blank 9mm round and helping us to position the covert holsters on our belts. I slipped the cut-away body of the holster inside my waistband, so that the muzzle rested against my right buttock and the butt against my right kidney. I passed my belt through the overhanging loop of the holster, then attached the twin spare magazine holder to my other hip.

'You can experiment to find the best position to carry your pistol when we're on the range over the next couple of weeks. Try it at the front, the rear and in the shoulder holster.

'Now for the pistol itself. It's a Browning 9mm High-Power. We use it because it's the most reliable 9mm available. There are two major advantages to 9mm ammunition: firstly it has the right amount of stopping power, and secondly our preferred sub-machine gun, the Heckler & Koch MP5K, takes the same ammunition.'

It was a strange feeling, wandering around in civilian clothes with a loaded pistol concealed under my jersey, and it took a little while to get used to the unaccustomed weight. In the regular army, we had always been taught never to load a round into the chamber until a target had presented itself – and now here I was with a loaded pistol down my trousers, with only the small safety catch to prevent me from blowing my backside off!

We climbed into a minibus and drove down to the range complex. Sandy and Jock led us into a large amphitheatre, against the back of which stood a row of man-sized targets. So began the first lesson, Sandy demonstrating the correct stance for firing, known as the Weaver position. Unlike the typical police marksman stance – both feet square to the target, weapon held directly in front of the chest, head slightly lowered – the Weaver puts the weight on to the forward foot, the right arm extended straight and the left arm slightly bent, locking the gun arm straight. The pistol is brought up to eye level, both eyes open. Sandy showed us how to adopt the Weaver swiftly and accurately from any other position. We spent the first day strolling up and down the range in a line abreast, following Sandy's barked directions, and on each whistle blast spinning around from whichever direction we happened to be walking, drawing our pistols and engaging our individual targets with a double shot, known as a double tap. As one begins the turn, weight on the balls of the feet, the gun hand closes around the pistol grip, withdrawing the weapon from the holster, at the same time thrusting it forward towards the target, the right thumb slipping the safety catch from safe to fire. Keeping both eyes open as the barrel rises to meet the line from eye to target, the first round is squeezed off, followed instantly by the second.

Because the correct position of the hands and arms – right arm locked straight out, left hand cupped under the magazine housing, it's fingers clasped around the right hand – inevitably forces the weapon into the correct position, our shots were remarkably accurate – and soon, at a range of twenty metres, there was little more than three inches separating the two-shot groups.

By the end of the first day our fingers were sore from constantly recharging our thirteen-round magazines, but at least our accuracy and speed of drawing had improved noticeably. We also became utterly confident handling our pistols, and learnt to trust the safety catch implicitly. Soon it would feel odd on the rare occasions that I didn't have the heavy bulk of a pistol hidden beneath my clothing.

Once we'd mastered the basic stance and had achieved the level of accuracy necessary to hit a target in the chest or head with two rounds from up to twenty-five metres away, Sandy moved us on to more difficult techniques. We practised changing magazines until we were so slick that we could do it blindfold in under two and a half seconds. The aim was never to let the pistol run out of ammunition altogether, since this left the empty working parts cocked open, leaving one temporarily defenceless. Thus it was necessary to keep a mental count of the rounds as we fired, double-tapping through twelve rounds, leaving the final round in the chamber as a last resort, in case the reload was interrupted. The drill was to drop to one knee, thumbing the magazine ejection button beneath the safety catch, which causes the empty magazine to jump a little way downwards out of its housing in the pistol grip. The left hand grips the bottom of the mag between the little finger and the palm, pulling it clear and, in the same movement, whips behind and under one's jersey or jacket to collect the fresh mag, held between thumb and first two fingers, from the holder concealed on one's belt. This is then pushed home inside the pistol grip, and the moment it clicks into place firing resumes.

We practised clearing stoppages and jammed rounds while running forward, tried firing left-handed, and learned how to load, unload and clear the weapon one-handed by gripping it in the fold of a knee or catching the topcover slide against the heel of a shoe. So reliable is the Browning pistol that we had to cause artificial stoppages in the weapon for training purposes by randomly loading the odd inert drill round into our magazines. Soon my pistol felt like a natural extension to my arm, and I was quite happy to carry it on my belt or in a shoulder holster.

As the days became warmer and longer I increasingly enjoyed the range practices out in the open air. In the course of those first ten days' instruction in basic weapon handling, we each fired about twelve thousand rounds – a profligacy unheard of in the regular army!

Time and again, in order to emphasise a particular point or to highlight a new technique, Jock and Sandy (and occasionally some of the other instructors) would treat us to a display of their mastery of the weapons. One morning, while we were milling around at the range having what would have been termed in the regular army a smoke-break, but was simply a tea-break here since not one of us smoked, Jill and Sally appeared and asked Sandy if they could have a quick refresher with their personal weapons. Chatting together, they charged their magazines, loaded and holstered their pistols beneath their sweaters and strolled down to set up a target. They chose a man-sized figure of a civilian, set it into a stand and began to amble back towards us.

'I know,' said Sally, glancing casually at us as they approached our group, which was now watching them with interest, 'let's shoot his balls off!' Pulling on her ear-defenders, she grinned at us and most of us involuntarily crossed our legs where we stood. 'Now,' she said quietly, and in a blur of arms and legs she and Jill span round, drawing their pistols in one fluid movement, and opened fire. The plywood panel to which the target was glued shook and rattled frantically as a hail of bullets tore through it, kicking up a shower of sand from the bank behind. The area around the crotch of the male figure disintegrated as they emptied two magazines each into an area the size of a saucer.

We let out a great cheer when almost the last round that they fired splintered the shaft that held the target vertical, and the figure dipped slowly forward and fell, with a puff of dust, on his face.

After the break, we learned how to take cover in an urban environment, lying flat and firing over the edge of a pavement, represented on the range by a line of baulks of timber. We practised rolling to the left and right using the edge of the pavement as cover, and we set up a variety of wooden door and window frames, and then spent hours leaping through them, sometimes adding a forward roll and engaging targets as they appeared. We also learned to fight off an attacker with one hand while drawing and then shooting from the waist with the other. This was the only time we fired one-handed. The Hollywood directors who ordain that it's feasible to snap-shoot accurately one-handed with a pistol over any distance greater than about five paces have clearly never tried to do it for real.

Having pretty well mastered the basic skills, we could now begin to combine them by practising fire and movement around the range, first in pairs, and then in teams of four, rehearsing the scenario of walking into an ambush.

By the end of the CQB phase, my fingers were stained with gun oil and spotted with blood blisters – it is very easy to nip the flesh of one's fingers in the various working parts of a pistol. Each evening we stripped and carefully cleaned our weapons, easing the springs in the magazine. I had always considered this routine a chore in the past, but now, knowing how much I might rely on it in the future, I enjoyed looking after my pistol. I am left-handed, and at the start of the CQB training I had toyed with the notion of converting the pistol grip to a left-handed format – the standard army-issue Browning comes as a right-handed model with the all-important safety catch located on the left side of the breech casing, to be operated by a flick of the right thumb. However, since many of the drills we learned and practised were broadly designed for right-handers I decided to change my shooting hand. In fact this was a simple transition, because one keeps both eyes open in CQB – so it was irrelevant which was my master eye. As it happened, by the end of the training I had almost forgotten that I had shot left-handed for the whole of my previous army career.

At the end of the CQB phase, Sandy and Jock set up a complex test of our newly acquired skills. We still felt intimidated by the constant testing. Having briefly glimpsed this peculiar unmilitary world full of interesting skills and individuals that we were still aspiring to join, the thought of having to return, unsuccessful, to our own units filled us with dread. As we sat outside the range, awaiting our turn to be put through our paces, we heard an intense crackle of pistol shots in the distance followed by an almighty explosion. It seemed to go on for ages – but then there was a lull.

The radio connecting us to the range came alive and I heard Sandy's voice: 'James next, please!'

Once there, Sandy called me into the range hut. In a corner, Jock was debriefing Barry while chalking scores on to the blackboard.

'Take four charged mags from the table. OK, when you're ready, go to the back of the range, make sure your ear defenders are on, and walk naturally down the range on my signal. When an armed target appears, draw and fire two double taps immediately, then run to the nearest cover and squeeze off another double tap. When the target falls or disappears, reholster your weapon and continue to advance down the range. Remember, the natives are hostile, but not all of them are armed – shoot a civilian by mistake and you're off the course before lunch!'

My heart should have been thoroughly used to the pre-test pounding that always began about now, but as usual it made me feel very uncomfortable. I swallowed hard and looked left and right down the range. There were a series of obstacles – doorways, window frames, pavements, parked cars – set out along its length, and a few unarmed civilian target figures stood around, doubtless minding their own business.

'Advance!'

I began to stroll forward. Trying to appear cool and calm, I put my right hand into the pocket of my trousers, but bunched my fingers up so that I could extract it in a flash. I was desperately scanning the scene in front and to the sides. Suddenly I heard it – a faint juddering sound followed by a quiet slap – and out of the corner of my eye I spotted a head appearing over the top of a low wall. As my eyes struggled in a fraction of a second to analyse whether this face posed a threat, I found that I was spinning into the Weaver stance, my drawn pistol punching out to the front. As the bulk of the weapon settled in line with the target, I knew there was no doubt: the little black patch to the left of the face was a weapon of some sort. Even as this thought broke, I heard the double report and felt the pistol make its regular leaps in my hand. Now I was sprinting forward to the edge of a piece of raised pavement and hurling myself down, lying as flat as I could in its lee, arms extended. I squeezed off another two rounds and the target fell.

Scrambling to my feet, I noticed that I was barely out of breath, despite the sudden burst of adrenalin – I must be quite fit after all. I replaced my pistol and continued slowly forward, running my left hand lightly over my spare magazine holder to check I hadn't lost any mags. The rest of the practice passed in a blur of fast draws, sprints and frantic reloads, and twice my pistol jammed after the first shot of a double tap, caused by the inclusion of a drill round in the magazine. By the time I had reached the end of my last mag, I was drenched with sweat and the side of my thumb felt raw from continually flicking the safety catch on and off – but at least I was fairly sure that I'd hit every terrorist and spared every civilian!

'Pretty good, James,' Jock muttered as he chalked my scores on the board. 'You've got nothing to worry about here.'

Once everyone had been through the test, we drove back to camp, our spirits soaring. It seemed that we had all passed this initial CQB training. For the first time, I really began to believe that I could indeed have a place in this unit.

After lunch we all gathered in the lecture theatre to be briefed on our next task.

The chief instructor took the rostrum. 'For the next seven days . . .', he began, and my heart sank at once. I'd been hoping that we would be given some time off after the CQB package. I was impatient to know whether I'd received any replies to my ad in *Private Eye*. He continued, '. . . . Dick and Billy are going to teach you some basic reconnaissance skills. You'll learn how to conduct a close-target reconnaissance, known as a CTR – sometimes in uniform, sometimes in civvies – and they'll teach you about setting up covert observation posts, known as OPs. Those of you with infantry experience will already know a bit about all this, but we have our own way of doing some things, so it's still important.'

That afternoon Dick took us through the planning stages of a typical CTR, starting with the initial tasking. For the first time, it was made clear that we would always be working under the direction of the Royal Ulster Constabulary's Special Branch. I had always expected that this would be the case – the current security policy in Northern Ireland was one of police primacy in terms of operational decision-making – but in the course of our training it had crossed my mind a couple of times to wonder whether this unit might, in some sense, operate above the law. We were, of course, all aware of allegations of the existence of a shoot-to-kill policy within some elements of the security forces (which had recently been investigated by John Stalker). If it had transpired that we were being trained to participate in such a conspiracy, I would have wanted no part in it. I realised that this could have left me in an awkward position, so I was somewhat relieved when Dick confirmed that we would only be deployed on an operation at the behest of the police.

We learned the different methods of gathering information about a target location, such as using the electoral register to discover how many occupants might be expected, telephone records, computerised police vehicle records, parish maps, DHSS returns, aerial photography, local police crime file and so on. Then we'd work out a plan to approach the target – usually on foot – in order to achieve the specific task we had been requested to undertake. Inevitably, as with every military activity, each operation would require a detailed set of orders to be delivered by the team commander.

In addition to the actual CTR team that went on to target there would always be drop-off vehicles and an emergency back-up team to be briefed on the overall plan, as well as the operations officer monitoring the radio net throughout the operation. Invariably, Dick informed us, tasks would need to be completed yesterday, and there would never be enough time to sort everything out to one's final satisfaction. Therefore we were to practise following a standard planning routine that at least ensured every eventuality and circumstance had been considered, and a suitable reaction discussed.

We spent the next few days preparing and executing a variety of CTRs, all at such short notice that we ended up working all night to complete each task. Then we'd grab a few hours' sleep before being briefed on the next exercise. We marvelled at the ease with which we could now summon up helicopters from a distant Army Air Corps base to carry out our photo-reconnaissance missions. Here we were, a small band of increasingly long-haired and scruffy individuals, hopping in and out of Gazelle and Lynx choppers which would ordinarily only have been made available to senior officers. Mostly the pilots, either sergeants or officers up to the rank of captain, were very co-operative and would follow our requests to fly on particular bearings and at set heights without question; but on one occasion Dave, a tiny twenty-year-old who was probably a private soldier, found himself being flown by a pompous Army Air Corps captain who clearly resented being told exactly what to do. Eventually tiring of their lack of progress, Dave pulled his Browning from under his tatty jersey and showed it to the surprised pilot.

'Listen, matey,' he said in a thick East London accent. 'You may be a captain, and I may be just a cockney grunt, but I haven't been given this for nothing. I've got a job to do, just like you. My job's different to yours, but it's just as important and I can't do it properly without your help, so can we just get on with it, and no arguing, OK?'

Thereafter, suitably chastened, the captain was a pleasure to fly with.

There were a host of new techniques to absorb and practise – for example, how to conduct daylight reconnaissance of a target that we were going to visit in the dark; or how to plan a route up to and around a target that avoids leaving evidence of our tracks. Even simple tasks, like dropping off a party from a vehicle, needed to be learnt and rehearsed, since it was imperative that the drop-off vehicle never actually came to a complete halt, and that the doors didn't slam. Sometimes we wore uniform and sometimes black civilian dress topped by a black balaclava, depending on whether it was practicable to masquerade as an ordinary green army foot patrol if we were rumbled on target. It was satisfying to discover how we were putting all our new skills together – driving drop-off, pick-up and back-up vehicles, taking rolls of photographs on target, and using our physical fitness and agility to scale walls and rooftops and overcome obstacles.

After a few days of CTR exercises, Billy introduced us to the procedures for planning, setting up and running covert observation posts, concentrating initially on rural scenarios. Again, we discovered that attention to detail was crucial. If the battery in your night-sight fails unexpectedly and you don't have a spare one, you can't complete your task; or, if you spend the hours of darkness creating a perfect hide only to discover at daybreak that you can't properly view the target, ditto. Although I'd had plenty of experience of setting up battlefield OPs, the difference here was the level of care we had to take to avoid detection – because now the enemy might be literally walking past our noses, and unless we were explicitly threatened, there was little we could do if we were discovered other than to withdraw.

After a lecture on the theory of constructing OPs in bushes and hedgerows, Billy led us on to the training area and up to a stunted hawthorn tree, about three feet high, which was surrounded by a tangle of briars, the whole bush measuring about ten feet in diameter and indistinguishable from others dotted about on the gentle grassy bank.

'OK, guys, have a scout around this bush for a brief while and tell me whether it would be suitable for a long-term OP, and if you think it is, how you'd go about constructing one in it.'

There were better, thicker bushes further up the slope, and it was obvious to me that this one was hopeless. You could see almost straight through it, the briar stalks not yet being in leaf.

After a couple of minutes, Billy asked for ideas.

'No. It's no good, this one,' I said confidently. 'Cover's too thin. I'd ignore it and go further up the slope.' There were murmurs of agreement all around me.

Billy looked surprised. 'Haven't you seen them then?' he asked.

'Seen who?' I replied, wary now.

'The OP team in this little bush. Everyone have another look. I reckon they stand out like a pair of dog's bollocks, but maybe I'm a perfectionist!'

We all stood around the rim of the bush, peering into its heart. Was he joking, or what? We couldn't see anything resembling a two-man OP.

'OK, you bunch of duffers, time's up! Sally, shake your left leg – and Mick do the same!'

From inside the bush came a faint vibration. As we stared I slowly began to discern the shape of their bodies lying flat on the ground. They were wearing camouflage uniform and they blended almost perfectly into the bush.

'Mick, show us how you get in and out without leaving any sign, will you?'

For about thirty seconds there were slight shifts and quakings amongst the briar fronds, and then Mick's head and torso began to emerge slowly, rising up out of the left-hand end of the bush. Once he was standing waist-deep, he drew up a short stick and, using it to push the barbed strands aside, he swiftly took three enormous strides, the last stepping him neatly out on to the smooth turf. He then took us round the back of the bush, where he pulled back some foliage to reveal a narrow tunnel leading into its heart, which he'd cut so that we could take it in turns to crawl inside and examine the OP's construction.

Lying on my side next to Sally, I listened as she described how they'd used small strips of green-and-brown-painted chicken wire to lift the bramble roof up from inside, being careful to use the secateurs as little as possible: it wouldn't matter much at this time of year, but if you cut the stems in high summer the exterior of the bush might begin to wilt visibly. She reminded me that in Ireland the farms tend to be pretty small, and it's quite common for a farmer to walk every one of his fields every day, probably with his dog. Either of them would notice something out of the ordinary at once, and there would always be a good chance that a dog would smell an OP's occupants.

They'd partially buried the bergen which held their kit in a rabbit hole, putting the spare earth down into a second hole. A camera with a powerful lens stood on a tiny tripod. Squinting through the viewfinder, I found that it was trained on a doorway in the camp, back across the valley. The whole camera assembly was surrounded by a light chicken-wire frame that had been expertly camouflaged, leaving clear only a narrow aperture through which the lens pointed out. I knew from our earlier course in photography that the few fronds which hung down in front of the lens, looking as if they might obscure the image, would not affect the picture quality as long as the depth of field was kept to a minimum.

When Sally had finished showing me the way they had stowed their kit inside the hide, I kitten-crawled gingerly backwards out into the sunlight. Mick was describing the typical OP routine, of hourly radio checks with the base station, the cold food and drink regime, and the bottles to collect urine and freezer bags for defecation. The thought of peeing into a bottle was fine, but defecating into a plastic bag? Sod that, I said to myself. I'd go for ten days without a crap if I had to!

Nick asked innocently, 'How does Sally manage to pee in a bottle when she's lying flat?'

Billy opened his mouth to reply but there came a loud exclamation from behind us.

'Mind your own fucking business!' said the bush sharply, and we all roared with laughter. 'What are you, some kind of pervert?'

Nick blushed scarlet.

Pairing off, we were allocated areas in which to set up our own OPs, and after carrying out all the proper preliminaries we deployed into our positions and monitored our allocated targets for forty-eight hours. I enjoyed the routine of the covert OP, despite the frosty nights, because in a hide life becomes essentially simple – one is either on duty or asleep, and when on watch the thought of missing some action from the target or failing to get good photos fills one with sufficient dread to make staying awake and alert quite easy. Billy had explained that in Ireland the added possibility of a gunman creeping up from behind with an Armalite helps to concentrate the mind.

At the end of the OP exercise we cleaned and handed back the specialised kit we had drawn, developed our rolls of film and, after a quick shower and a meal, were told to parade outside in boots, lightweights and PT vests. We were greeted by the sight of all the instructors dressed for PT, clutching clipboards and stopwatches. Oh Christ, I thought, here we go again. My heart sank and my pulse started to thump in anticipation.

We set off in three ranks, led by Jill and Mick, doubling out to the training area along a rough tarmac track. The only sound was the staccato clumping of our boots on the hard surface and the puffing from our lungs. The pace was ferocious and, even at our level of fitness, after about a mile at this speed most of us were beginning to labour severely to keep up with the front runners. As we ran, we were constantly putting a hand on the backs of our waistbands, checking that our pistols and magazines were secure in their holsters under our flapping vests. Eventually, we drew to a halt on a smooth patch of turf near the start of the assault course, whose obstacles were strung out around a quarter-mile of circular boggy path which weaved its way through a dense wood. Occasionally our daily PT sessions had brought us to these obstacles and we knew what to expect. A grim silence settled over us as we shifted from foot to foot, hands on hips, gathering our wind.

'OK, guys and girls, it's that testing time again! When I call your name, which will be at thirty-second intervals, set off around the course and get back to the finish here as quick as you can. Do every obstacle except the twelve-foot wall. Don't waste any time helping each other – it's every man for himself now. All that matters is your individual time. So, first man, Dave . . . Go!'

Soon it is my turn and I am haring away across the open space towards the wood, heart in mouth, legs flying, pistol banging on my hip. Here is the first obstacle; run up a muddy bank, try to leap the impossibly wide ditch, sheets of water, waist-deep, mud sucking, scramble onwards. Now here's a long telegraph pole, green and slippery above a rancid pool. Sprint lightly across, daren't draw breath. Ahead, a six-foot brick wall: running jump at it, kicking one foot into it half way up, forearms scrabbling on top, squirming up, body over and then thump down to the deck, lungs rasping. Check pistol, sprint away. Next is a monkey run – swinging from hand to hand along a horizontal metal ladder. Someone's yelling beside me: 'Keep at it! Faster!' Up another ramp beneath a massive tripod; throw myself forward to grab a suspended rope. Fingers clutch round it, begin the swing, but they jerk free before it's carried me all the way and I land on my back in three feet of muddy water.

'What the fuck are you doing down there, having a bath? Get up out of it and run!'

My breathing sounds louder inside my head than the instructor's shouting voice. I clamber up the bank, snorting the filth from my nose and mouth, hand reaching instinctively again to check my pistol and magazines. Stumble on, gathering pace – crawl under a twenty-foot wire entanglement; up again and vault a wooden railing five feet high. Sprint forward, here's a duckboard suspended by chains above a ditch – run on to it, swaying wildly, nearly fall off the edge, on again, check pistol, check mags, crawl through ten feet of concrete pipe, up again and into the final straight, break out of the wood, hurtling towards the distant group . . .

'Eight minutes fifty seconds!'

Heart-rate recovering quickly, we stood, hands on hips, dripping sweat and breathing hard, shouting encouragement to the others as they came in. A minute after we were complete, we were sprinting off again along the track. After half a mile, we stopped and took turns in pairs to do as many press-ups in two minutes as we could manage, followed by one minute's break, then squat thrusts, rest again, then sit-ups. Our results were logged, and then it was a timed individual run back to camp.

'Get showered and changed and be in the lecture room in twenty minutes!' said Mick. So this is it, I thought, it's make or break time. I felt resigned to my fate, whatever it might be. I'd tried my hardest over the past weeks. If I wasn't good enough, it wasn't for want of trying – I just wasn't built that way.

We congregated in the lecture theatre, quiet now, lost in our own thoughts. Someone half-heartedly cracked a joke, but no one smiled. It seemed so tough that after all this hard work some of us were going to be binned. At least I wasn't worried about returning to my regiment – nobody there would ever be criticised for trying something and failing. As far as I was concerned, the only fault was never to try at all.

I looked around the room at the faces I seemed to know so well – Dave, Barry, Nick, Kate – and I realised that we barely knew each other at all.

The door banged open and the chief instructor strode in, his face a grim mask. He kept his head down, studying his clipboard. So quietly that we had to strain to catch his words, he began quickly: 'If I call your name, leave here and go into the classroom next door. Don't talk in here or in there.'

Pause. An early bluebottle buzzed confusedly inside a strip-light casing high above us.

'Sid . . . Carl . . . Tony . . . Dave . . .' Christ, he was rattling through them, then. ' . . . James . . . Kate . . . Martin . . . Will . . . '

In a daze I joined the exodus, face deadpan, heart fluttering. Shit, which group was which?

I took a seat in the classroom. Nobody spoke. I looked around the room. We were all anxious and tired – no surprise after the strain of the last few weeks. There weren't very many of us in here, the majority were still in the other room. Fuck. They're never going to waste that many, I thought, I'm obviously in the wrong place. Goddamn. Billy had said to me a couple of weeks before that if I failed at this point, I might be invited back to join the next course, skipping the selection. But did I really want to go through all this balls-ache again?

The chief instructor entered, looking grimly determined, and shut the door behind him. From the corridor outside came the muffled tramp of shoes as the lecture theatre emptied.

He cleared his throat. 'I hate doing that! Now, you lot, don't let your egos swell just because you've passed the basic training.

There's plenty of scope left for some serious cock-ups before we've finished with you! But well done, for now at any rate!'

Instantly we all dissolved into smiles. It was as if the lights in the room had suddenly been turned up full. Everyone was glancing around as if for the first time, to see who exactly was still here. It struck me that those who were left were generally the more stable characters, the quieter and more determined types. Looking about, I instinctively agreed with the instructors' selection. I felt certain I could trust everyone in the room.

Kate was sitting slightly in front of me to the right, beaming like a searchlight. I leant forward and touched her shoulder. 'Well done, Kate.'

She turned, smiling, to look at me, and the tear on her cheek reminded me of the washroom incident on selection. 'Thanks!' she mouthed.

Then a thought crossed my mind: I hope she doesn't live to regret that.

Chapter Four

This latest clear-out marked a major change in our training. For the next three and a half months, the chief instructor informed us, we would be learning highly specialised techniques – and he expected that all of us who had reached this point were likely to be suitable to join the unit in Ireland.

'You've now got a five-day break. I leave it up to your own judgement, but I suggest that you square away with your nearest and dearest what you're up to and where you're going. If anyone, particularly the few among you who are married, hasn't yet made a will, I strongly recommend that you do so. The chief clerk will give you the necessary forms. Also, have a read of this leaflet about insurance cover – it's an excellent scheme which the majority of us and the SAS subscribe to. And the good news is that from today you are all on Special Forces pay.' This was an unexpected bonus – worth another £2,000 a year to me.

We learned that under this new regime we could bring our own cars back after the break, and that we would at last be allowed out of camp during our free moments. On past experience, though, there weren't likely to be many of those!

We handed our pistols into the armoury for the weekend and went back to our rooms to pack. The atmosphere was gloomy – it seemed our initial euphoria had worn off. The unsuccessful volunteers were already stuffing their kit into their suitcases. There was little to be said, and so we simply swapped congratulations and condolences. After about twenty minutes Alan, the kindly middle-aged instructor, appeared and herded them into a couple of minibuses for the trip to the station.

The place felt strangely quiet once they had departed. God only knew how many had applied for the initial screening and failed, but it must have been in the hundreds. A hundred and twenty odd had been on the selection course, less than half had passed that, and two had failed the driving. Now again we had been severely reduced – at least little Kate was still with us.

On the train home my mood began to lighten as I relaxed. I felt almost as if I had been in a dream for the last two and a half months, stumbling forwards from day to day, never knowing for certain what was on the programme for the rest of the afternoon, let alone tomorrow. I had found this aspect truly frustrating until the chief instructor had explained that the point of this approach was to create the same level of uncertainty about what the future might hold as we would experience on operations. Generally speaking, in my experience of the army up until then, a solution to just about any situation that an army officer might face could be found somewhere in a training manual. Here, however, the sort of covert skills and techniques we were mastering called for a very flexible approach. So we were slowly but surely being weaned off the traditional army system.

Dave, the young cockney, was heading in the same direction as me, and I decided that as we were now on a higher rate of pay we could splash out on an InterCity lunch and a bottle of wine, preceded by a double gin each. A clear five-day break seemed like an eternity in paradise to us. Dave's plans didn't extend beyond finding a cheap hotel room to shack up in, preferably equipped with a kingsize bed, a mini-bar, a colour TV and his girlfriend. That would have done nicely for me too, but I had yet to find myself a suitable partner. I certainly had mixed feelings about the prospect of organising a string of blind dates – assuming that I had had any replies to my advert, which struck me as increasingly unlikely the more I thought about it. Goddamn, I mused alcoholically to myself, staring out of the window as the Midlands unrolled, if I hadn't been stuck away in Germany for all those years I might still have some friends left in the UK.

When I got home the house was dark and cold and my parents were out. As I padded around, turning on the lights and drawing the curtains, I flipped quickly through the pile of accumulated mail that had been left for me by the front door. Near the bottom of the stack was a large manila envelope, postmarked Central London. My heart skipped a beat as I tore it open, spilling the contents on to the hall floor. I knelt down and riffled quickly through the dozen or so envelopes it had contained, a couple of them garishly coloured. Clutching them under my arm, I made myself another gin and tonic and went upstairs to run a bath. Suddenly I was ecstatic – this was a much better response than I had dared to hope!

I set a stool beside the bath, and as I soaked I avidly read each letter in turn. What a brainwave it had been! I rapidly categorised the replies into three piles: No Way, Possible, and Contact At Once. Some of the respondents had resorted to rather crude allusions to raunchy sex, presumably in an effort to grab my attention. Any that displayed this tendency were automatically promoted to a new Contact Before The Bath Has Drained pile. Then another thought struck me – perhaps it was unwise to look gift horses in the mouth. Hastily I shuffled all the No Ways across into the Possible pile. Beggars shouldn't really be choosers after all, I reasoned.

Half an hour later, and barely dry, I stood in the hall listening to the faint clicking down the line after dialling the first telephone number on my list. I tried to imagine the phone bell resounding in the Battersea flat as I breathed nervously into the receiver. From the little Trish had said about herself, I knew she was the girl for me. 'Energetic and sporty', she'd said. I could guess that was Battersea-speak for super-charged. 'Lively' too . . . Mentally I rubbed my pistol-calloused hands. A film, perhaps dinner – then back to her place to compare pulse rates.

A loud click sounded as the ringing phone was lifted from the cradle, followed by a soft, 'Mmn, yah?'

'Hi,' I gushed nervously, 'is that Trish? This is James – James Rennie. You kindly replied to my ad in *Private Eye* for a blind date!' My imagination fuelled by gin, I pictured a short skirt, thick dark tights, blue Guernsey, pearl choker, topped with an Alice band. I couldn't quite fix the style of underwear, having less experience of this area than I would have wished. Odd, though – she didn't sound twenty-three.

Silence. Was it my ear, or did it sound like a deafening one?

'Er, hullo? Um . . . this is Trish, isn't it?'

'No, it isn't actually,' replied the voice in a crystal, icy tone. 'Trish is our nanny. I'm afraid it's quite impossible for her to speak to you. Goodbye.'

Shit! I'd blown it! Why didn't I check who I was speaking to first? It was all that bloody alcohol! I was irritated to discover that

I was blushing furiously, here in my own home. Well, at least I'd learned a lesson. I wasn't going to waste any more valuable leads that way.

I worked my way down the list. Of the ten remaining, four hadn't given phone numbers – so they were relatively long-term prospects – two phones rang and rang without an answer, and one girl frankly sounded insane on her ansaphone, on which grounds I reluctantly ruled her out and hung up. One, who sounded very promising, announced that she had just found a boyfriend. I asked light-heartedly if that meant she was off the market, which she must have taken the wrong way because she instantly hung up. However, I struck gold with the last two – and arranged to meet them for supper in London on consecutive evenings.

I was feeling pretty nervous by the time I had settled myself in the richly furnished and oak-paneled lobby of my club, near St James's Square, an identifactory copy of *Private Eye* prominent on my lap. As I sat there, dressed in my best houndstooth jacket, cavalry twill trousers and highly polished brogues, it dawned on me that maybe this setting was a tad formal and stuffy for a first date. I'd only joined a West End club because I wanted somewhere to stay in London when on leave from Germany, and to date I'd hardly had an opportunity to set foot inside the place. Too late to worry about it now, anyway.

Jennifer had described herself as quite tall with long brown hair. The trouble was, looking about now, it seemed that just about every girl who came into the club was quite tall with long brown hair. I twitched the magazine suggestively at any female who glanced in my direction. Then, to my embarrassment, I noticed one of the porters staring at me, so I put my head down and pretended to read. I was so nervous that the page might as well have been upside-down, for all the sense I could make of the words.

'Ah, is it James? Hi . . . I'm sorry I'm so late.'

I leapt to my feet, thrusting out my hand. 'Hi . . . Not at all, pleased to meet you, Jennifer!' My God, she was really attractive, slim, and very elegant too. I took her coat and we headed upstairs to the pink and gilt drawing room overlooking the Square garden. She seemed very nervous too, but once we had a drink inside us we relaxed a bit.

We went downstairs again for dinner. As we chatted incessantly about anything and everything – politics, literature, films, wine, travel – over our supper of duck breasts in a ginger sauce I realised that I had really missed this side of life. I had ordered a delicious and far too expensive bottle of 1982 Pomerol, hoping to impress her. I reflected that it had been like this with Alison – to start with at least. But I knew now that Alison lacked that most vital facet, an unbounded sense of curiosity. We would never have been happy together in the long term, which is why, I supposed, we had drifted apart. Jennifer and I discovered that we had much in common as the time sped past. I explained vaguely that I worked for the civil service in order to excuse my lack of military haircut, and learnt that she was training to become an architect. We were almost exactly the same age.

After dinner I walked her to Waterloo to catch a train home to Wimbledon. Since we weren't in any great hurry we made a long detour, arm in arm and buttoned up against the chilly damp, heading south on Horse Guards, left into Parliament Square then along Millbank and over Lambeth Bridge, so that we could turn and head north along the Albert Embankment and Jubilee Gardens, which were beautifully floodlit. The Thames slid past, sparkling with the reflected orange glow from the Houses of Parliament.

I pecked Jennifer on the cheek at the barrier and, once her train had departed, I strode back to the club where I was spending the night, my heart soaring. I tried to remember – was it Polly Garter or Mrs Organ Morgan who observed with resignation, 'Men are brutes, on the quiet'? I knew it was true, but all most of us need is the civilising influence of a sophisticated and curious woman. I resolved to cancel my second blind date as politely as I could.

By the time my brief leave was over we had met a second time, this time seeing *King Lear* at the National, followed by a jolly supper at Paradiso E Inferno on the Strand. There was no question about it – I was thoroughly smitten.

'OK, people, now that you've mastered the pistol, it's time to move on to some more specialised weapons.'

Once more we were sitting in the weapon training classroom in our scruffy work clothes, concealed pistols pressed against our waistbands. Sandy swept his hand across the weapons laid out on the table in front of him. 'Walther PPK, MP5K, HK53 and G3K.'

He picked up the tiny Walther pistol, and while he described its features Jock handed one to each of us, along with an ankle holster and the normal waistband type. The pistol was about the size of the palm of my hand. So this is what James Bond carries, I thought.

Sandy continued: 'Frankly, just about the only virtue of the Walther is its concealability. Try strapping it on to your ankle now. The twenty-two calibre is too small to guarantee stopping a man dead, though it'll certainly make his eyes water. Some of the guys, and most of the girls, carry it as a back up, or if their clothing simply can't hide the bulk of the larger Browning pistol.' He showed us how to strip and assemble the gun and we practised this for a while. With the ankle holster on, it was easy to draw the pistol when seated by reaching down as if to scratch your ankle. The eight-round magazine was not ideal compared to the thirteen in the Browning, but still I looked forward to testing it on the range.

Next was the Heckler & Koch MP5K submachine gun. Sandy explained the reasons that it had been selected for use by the unit. 'The great attraction is that, unlike almost all other submachine guns, it fires from a closed bolt. Usually the working parts of a weapon like this are held to the rear when it is fully cocked and ready for action.' He picked up a standard army Sterling submachine gun and demonstrated what he meant, pointing out the firing pin on the face of the breech block. 'Squeezing the trigger on a standard submachine gun like the Sterling releases the bolt to fly forwards towards the breech, picking up the top round from the magazine as it passes. The trouble with this is two-fold – firstly, the weight of the bolt assembly travelling forward inside the body of the weapon can disturb your aim on the target, and secondly, there is much more opportunity for the weapon to jam before a round has even been fired. By contrast, when the MP5K is made ready by cocking the action . . . like this . . . the bolt closes home into the breech, chambering the round. When the trigger is squeezed, the hammer is released, striking the firing pin which protrudes through the breechlock, which in turn strikes the percussion cap on the base of the round. This is what is meant by "firing from a closed bolt". Then, as the round begins to travel up the barrel towards the target, the blow-back from the exhaust gases given off by the burning propellant in the cartridge drives the breech block back again against its spring, ejecting the empty case through the port to the right side as it goes – and on its return it picks up the next round from the magazine, ready to fire again if you keep the pressure on the trigger. You can set the safety catch on the left-hand side to safe, single shot or automatic with a flick of your thumb. There's also a three-round burst option which is now available, but we don't need that. This is an incredibly reliable weapon.'

Jock now passed out one MP5K to each of us. It was a wonderfully compact weapon, weighing about two kilos and stretching only thirty-two centimetres from end to end. The magazine could hold up to thirty 9mm rounds – conveniently sharing ammunition with the Browning pistol – and there were some neat little clips available that allowed us to fix two full mags side by side, which would dramatically increase the speed of a mag change. The safety catch was again on the left side of the body, within easy reach of the right thumb.

Sandy again took us through the strip and assembly routine, then showed us ways of carrying the weapon slung across the chest or suspended under the armpit on a quick-release harness. He demonstrated the most effective and accurate fire position, which was to thrust out the gun straight ahead, both arms extended, left hand on the front grip, right hand wrapped around the pistol grip, elbows pressing in towards each other to lock the weapon stable. Just as with pistol shooting, the intention is always to bring the weapon up into the direct line of sight between the eyes and the target, keeping both eyes open. It should never be necessary to duck the head to see along the line of the weapon sight.

'The only time you'd fire this on automatic is in a real emergency, because, as you'll discover later, it's extremely difficult to keep the rounds on target owing to the recoil and the very short barrel. Ordinarily you'll fire this in double taps, just like the pistol. If you hit a man square on the body, with two rounds, you'll stop him dead – literally.'

Now Sandy held up the HK53. 'This is technically a submachine gun, despite its 5.56mm calibre and its relatively long length – seventy-five centimetres – which makes it difficult to conceal casually. Notice this retractable butt though, which slides into the body. It's particularly useful because it knocks twenty centimetres off its overall length. The magazine holds twenty-five 5.56mm rounds, the same calibre as the Armalite and M16. Generally we don't favour 5.56mm calibre weapons because you get neither the concealability of 9mm variants nor the stopping power of 7.62mm.

However, as compromises go, this is an excellent one, and it's extremely reliable and accurate. If you're creeping around inside a building it's a comfort to have one of these strapped to your chest, leaving your hands free for your work, and if you do have to open fire, a burst from this will rip a man's body apart. Watch while I strip it, then strip yours.'

Last was the G3K, a 7.62mm assault rifle based on the standard German army-issue weapon. Sandy told us that on some jobs we would probably want to carry one of these, because when the fire selector is switched to automatic the firepower they can put down is awesome. The amount of kinetic energy carried by a 7.62mm round means that a hit on any bone in the body would shatter it like glass, and turn the surrounding tissue and organs into a revolting jelly. Also, this round will easily penetrate a course of brickwork. Sadly the Libyans have supplied the IRA with a huge number of these rifles.

Sandy then showed us the different sight arrangements that could be fitted to all the weapons bar the pistols. A powerful and compact MagLite torch could easily be bolted along the top of the weapon, with a pressure connector to the trigger assembly. With the thin but intensely powerful torch beam zeroed to the Mean Point of Impact at a chosen range, all it took was a light touch on the trigger to activate the torch and illuminate the target – and if the target was in the beam, then he was by definition firmly in your sights and only a hair's breadth away from being shot. By converting the torch into an IR source by taping a sheet of IR jelly across the lens – as we had done with the flash gun during the photography course – only an operator wearing IR night goggles would see the light – the target would not even be aware of it. Then we looked at ordinary image-intensifying nightsights and magnifying day sights. Blimey, I thought, I've never seen so much kit freely available.

After lunch we drove across to the ranges and split into groups to try out the new weapons. We spent the rest of the afternoon and all the next day haring around, practising fast draws and firing from different positions, switching between automatic and single shot. On fully automatic, even the dainty MP5K has a tendency to rise sharply. It was obvious that in a built-up area one would have to fire on single shot, double tapping as normal, for fear of taking out innocent bystanders. Besides, on automatic one could fire off a full magazine in a couple of seconds, which was all right if you needed the shock effect, but no good for a sustained fire-fight.

Kate, because of her slender frame, had great difficulty controlling the weight of fire from her G3K, tending to spray rounds wildly into the clouds. To everyone's relief she decided to limit herself to the HK53 in future, which produced a negligible recoil or 'kick' by comparison.

The next morning a group of us were sent over to the garage block to pick up some cars for range work. Range cars were simply surveillance training cars that had reached the end of their useful life, having been flogged mercilessly for thousands of miles. That said, all four cars that we picked up today seemed to be in considerably better nick than my own Talbot Horizon. But not for long!

Back at the range Sandy organised us into teams of four and briefed us on the car drills that we were to learn. While the first team rehearsed various manoeuvres, Jill gave us individual tuition in aggressive and defensive driving on the gravelly tracks around the range complex.

'OK James,' Jill said from the passenger seat. 'Remember what I showed you on day one? Let's try a handbrake turn first. The purpose of this is to change direction by 180 degrees in an emergency. For instance, an operator might be in a fire-fight and you want to extract him. This way you can approach him at high speed, begin the turn just before you reach him and be away the moment he leaps aboard.

'So, when you're doing about forty, put your palm flat on the bottom centre of the wheel and swing it hard and fast round one and a half times. There are two of us in the car at the moment, so it's quite well balanced, but if you are by yourself you must remember to swing to the right. If you whip it suddenly to the left, your body weight on the outside of the swing might be enough to overturn the vehicle and send it into a roll, OK?'

'Yup.' I was concentrating furiously now, my palms on the wheel becoming slippery with sweat.

'So, the nose of the car will dip sharply and lunge to the right, and you'll feel the back begin to slide out to the left. At this point, still in third gear and keeping the power on, you reach down for the handbrake. As soon as the whole car is committed to the skid, snap up on the handbrake. This will whip you around even faster while reducing the length of your skid along the road. Whatever you do, don't touch the footbrake. That would simply lock all the wheels and you'll grind to a rubbery halt, sideways on, OK?'

'Got it.'

'You'll find that you're now sliding backwards down the road, decelerating rapidly. Slip into first gear, gun the engine and let the clutch out pretty quickly, because you're aiming to get your wheels spinning even before you've come to a halt, to launch you on your way at the earliest possible moment. Then simply accelerate forward in your new direction. Now give it a go.'

The first two attempts were pretty hopeless, the car either stalling or slewing sideways on. But at the third attempt I executed a perfect handbrake turn, sweeping gracefully through 180 degrees then shooting back the way I'd come in a cloud of blue rubber smoke. It was all a question of timing, and having the confidence to enter the manoeuvre at the correct speed.

'Good, not too bad. You can practise that by yourself later. Now for the J-turn. It's really just a handbrake turn while you're reversing, but without the handbrake. This is useful if you run into an ambush, say, and you need to back out, turn and drive off at high speed.

'Right. Draw up to a halt, and as you do so check your mirrors for any obstructions behind – someone may be trying to box you in. Slip into reverse, floor the accelerator and steer straight back. You get brilliant acceleration in reverse gear. Once you reach about thirty, spin the wheel as before and you'll feel the back dip and the nose begin to swing around. No need for any braking in a J-turn; the two front wheels do all the work, effectively steering the nose round for you. As you swing into line, knock her into first and accelerate away. Simple, *nicht wahr*? So let's give it a go.'

The first time I tried it I discovered how tricky it is to steer in a straight line when travelling backwards at thirty m.p.h! We swerved violently off the narrow track, engine screaming, and bumped out of control over fifty metres of rough turf, eventually glissading to a halt on the wet grass. I grinned sheepishly at Jill, who grinned back and raised her eyebrows. I manoeuvred us back on to the road for another go. This time I got it right and we skated round as if we were on ice.

'OK, Stirling, give me two handbrakes and two J-turns, one after another, just to prove you've definitely got it!' said Jill, and we roared away. Yeehah!

1. Patrolling at the junction of the Springfield Road and the Ballymurphy estate in the early morning. At any other time of day we would sprint across an open area like this because of the threat posed by terrorist snipers.

2. An RUC constable examines the rubble of a block of flats in New Barnsley. The previous evening my platoon had deployed to protect firefighters against a crowd of stone-throwing youths who had set light to the block.

3. Three Bricks prepare to go on patrol from New Barnsley police station.

4. Typical accommodation for two junior officers during an Emergency Tour in West Belfast.

5. *Left.* A show of strength by PIRA gunmen, somewhere in Belfast. They are well armed and are stopping traffic at random. Dickers will warn them if any army patrols approach.

8. *Bottom.* An improvised landmine – milk churns filled with HME – placed in a culvert under a busy road. A terrorist would have detonated it by a command wire running from a vantage point when a police or army patrol drove by.

9. *Middle.* An IRA Active Service Unit (ASU) sets up a vehicle checkpoint.

6. Such displays of weaponry are usually over quickly, the terrorists soon disappearing into the crowd, but they certainly influence the next generation of volunteers.

7. A find of home-made explosives (a potent mix of agricultural fertiliser and diesel fuel known as HME), sticks of plastic explosive and a variety of improvised timing devices made from domestic electricity meters.

10. Shows of strength serve not only to generate publicity but also to intimidate the locals.

11. Gas cylinder bombs packed with HME.

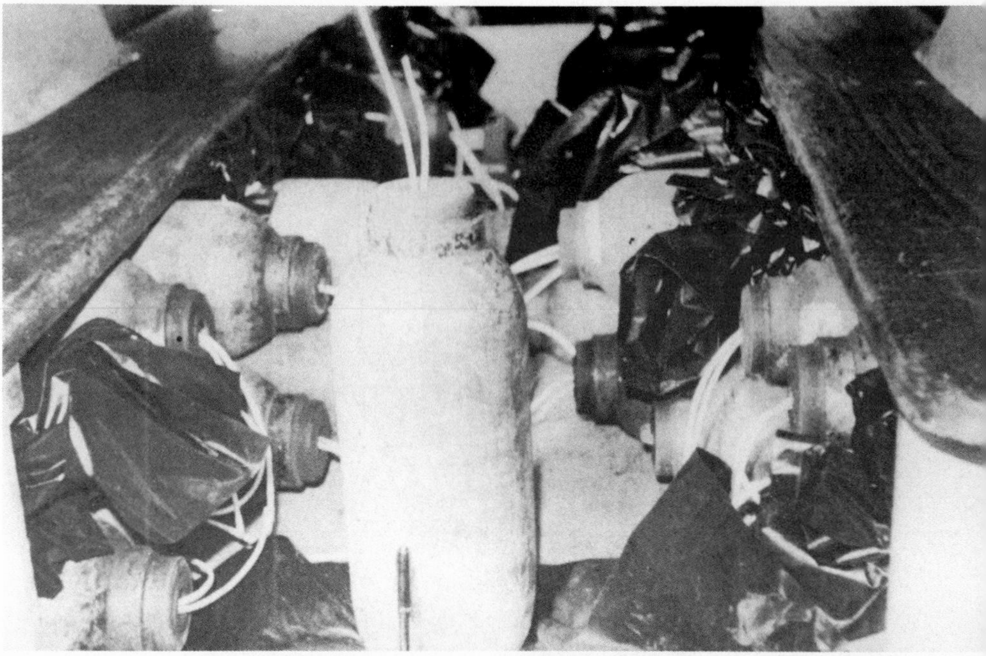

12. Cylinder bombs, linked by white detonating cord, packed into the back of a van.

13. A Thompson 9mm submachine gun in the hands of a terrorist – dated, but effective.

14. Loughgall police station from the air soon after the ambush was sprung.

15. The terrorists' Toyota van, riddled with bullet holes, still outside the police station.

16. Preparing a Nikon 35mm camera, loaded with infrared film and fitted with an infrared flashgun, for a photographic task in pitch blackness.

17. Checking and cleaning a set of Passive Night Goggles.

18. A Webley .455 revolver.

19. A Tokarev 7.62 semi-automatic pistol and a Smith & Wesson .38 revolver.

20. Taking an impression of a Chubb key in an impression pad prior to making a working copy.

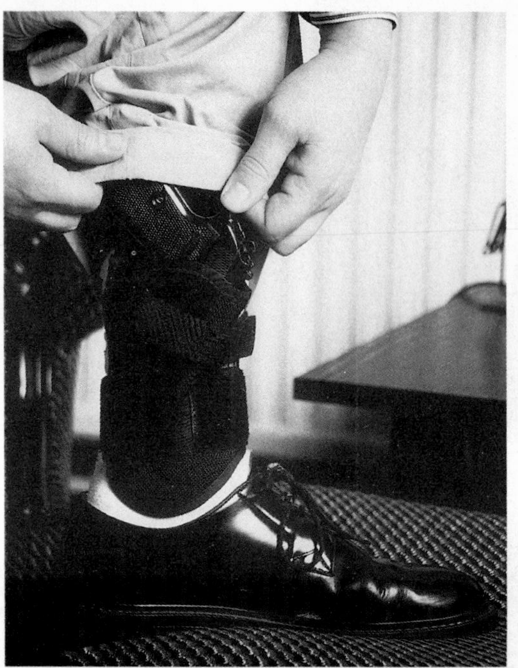

21. *Left*. Fitting a Walther PPK pistol into a covert ankle holster.

22. A Browning 9mm pistol fitted with an extended 20 round magazine.

23. Heckler & Koch MP5K 9mm submachine gun. Its small size and lightweight combined with its reliability makes it an ideal weapon for covert carriage.

24. An MP5K mounted in a briefcase. The trigger is remoted to the underside of the handle, allowing the briefcase to be fired when suspended at arms length if necessary.

25. This stun grenade is being held by a female, which emphasises its small size and concealability.

26. Female wearing an MP5K submachine gun on an underarm swivel sling suspended from a shoulder holster. She has pulled the barrel forward for the camera – normally it hangs out of sight beneath the jacket, leaving both her hands free. Under her left arm are suspended two spare magazines in a separate holster.

27. A pump action 12-bore shotgun, which is primarily carried to break down doors in an emergency.

28. Female wearing a Walther PPK in a shoulder holster.

29. Positioning a pistol beneath the thigh when driving ensures it can be reached in an emergency without making any suspicious movements.

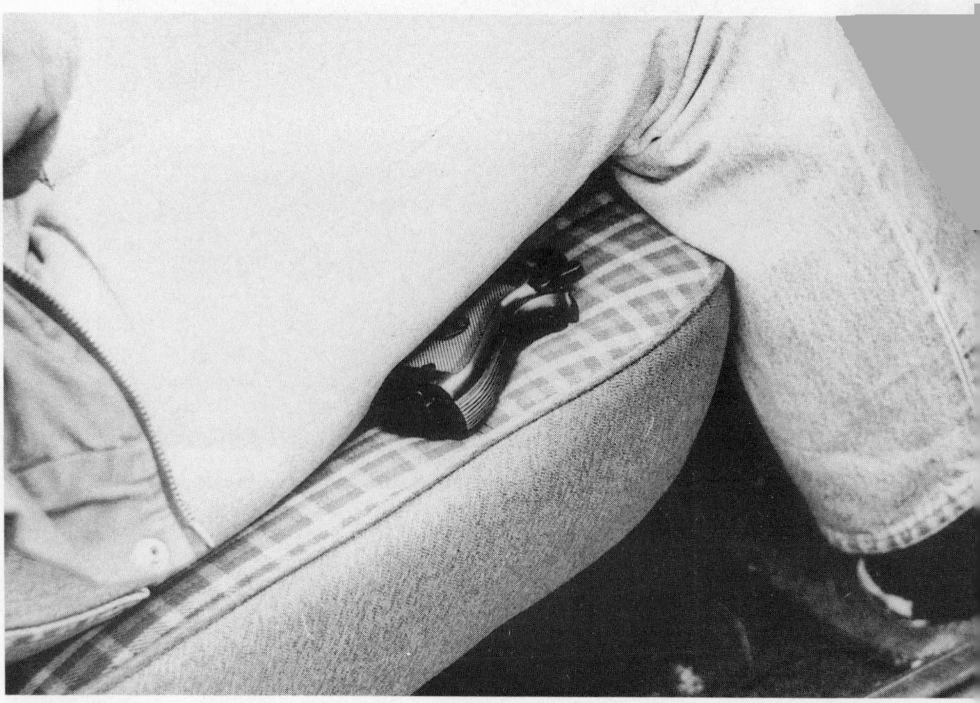

30. Rapid magazine change on a Browning pistol – pressing the magazine release button with the right thumb causes the empty magazine to jump a little way out of the butt housing. The safety catch is not applied during a magazine change, even though the last round is still in the chamber.

31. The left hand grips the base of the empty mag between the palm and little finger and draws it clear of the weapon, before reaching back for a fresh mag from the covert mag carrier on the shoulder holster or the waist belt.

32. The new mag is held between the thumb and forefinger and is pressed home into its housing.

33. As it clicks into place firing resumes, with the empty mag still held in the palm of the left hand. At the first opportunity it will be stuffed into a pocket.

34. A fine example of a nicely shaped butt.

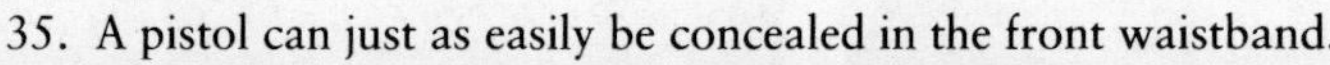

35. A pistol can just as easily be concealed in the front waistband.

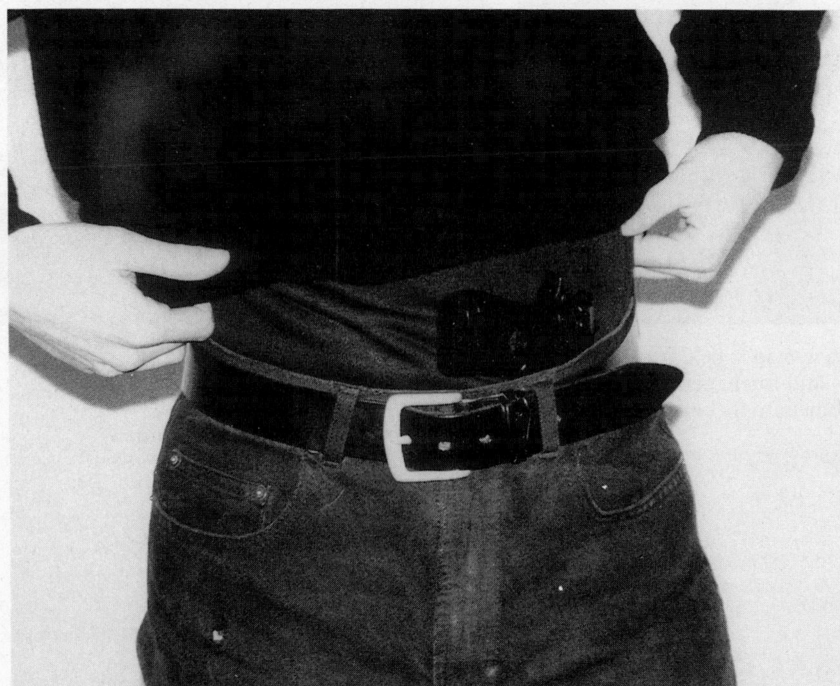

Back on the range again, we followed Sandy into the hut where he showed us a home-made video of car drills, starring what was obviously a group of instructors. We watched in silence as a car containing two operators drove into the range. Suddenly there was the flash and whump of an explosion and the vehicle was engulfed in a sheet of flame. At the same second an array of terrorist targets popped up out of the sand all around the horseshoe-shaped area and there was a loud crackling ripple of submachine-gun fire. The car jerked to a halt and the two operators rolled out of the doors and immediately began to open fire. The passenger was on automatic initially, spraying the targets with his MP5K, then switched to double taps, while the driver double tapped with his pistol, both of them firing, rolling into a new fire position, and firing again.

After a few seconds of this I noticed a high-pitched whine growing in the background. Suddenly a second car appeared, racing in towards the first. This was clearly the Seventh Cavalry come to effect a rescue. It roared towards the abandoned car and at the last moment the driver swung it into a tight handbrake turn, scattering gravel and grit in a wide arc. Even as it was sliding to a halt the passenger stepped out and engaged the targets with his MP5 on automatic, covering the retreat of the two operators who now sprinted back towards the second car. Still in his seat the driver reached back and opened both rear doors, then gunned the engine, so that as the three operators hurled themselves in the rear wheels were spinning wildly. The car leapt forward and out of the range. As it withdrew at high speed an operator knelt on the back seat and fired bursts through the rear window at the receding targets. The whole scenario hadn't taken more than about a minute and a half to unfold.

'Right,' said Sandy, 'we'll watch that again and I'll highlight some important points as we go. Then you can try the drill for yourselves.' He rewound the tape and set it running again.

'First off, notice how quickly the car responds to the ambush. The passenger instantly engages the general area of the enemy with a short burst of automatic fire to try to suppress their fire, then switches to double taps and methodically takes on individual targets. Before debussing, the driver has sent an ambush contact warning over the net to alert the rest of the team. Now they are conserving their ammunition and changing their positions regularly. Notice the slick mag changes.

'Now, the driver of the rescue vehicle has judged his approach just right so that he can handbrake turn in the space between the first car and the operators. As the passenger steps out he remains standing so that he can fire over their heads. That's why they're crouching as they run back – matey's rounds are only about eighteen inches above them. See the driver opening the doors? He's also got a pistol in his hand, but it's not his personal one, it's his car pistol. Over the water you'll be given two pistols each. You can just make out the longer twenty-round mag sticking out the bottom of the pistol grip. If the rescue car or his passenger is disabled, the driver will open up with the car pistol, but until then he'll be concentrating on a fast getaway.'

Here Sandy froze the video temporarily. 'There are only two ways to board a moving car. The most dramatic and least practical is through the window, like the CIA practise endlessly – I'm not sure why. The truth is that the window is unlikely to be open and if it is it would be dangerous to the other occupants to try and dive in with a semi-automatic weapon in your hand. The only other way is to hurl yourself through an open door, but the knack is to put your backside in first. Watch how they do it!' He set the tape in motion again and we saw that the car had definitely begun to accelerate before the operators actually arrived. 'See them turn back towards the enemy as they fall backwards on to the seats, bums in first? If you put your foot into a moving vehicle before the bulk of your weight, you'll find yourself doing the splits before you can say knife, and you'll be left behind. The other advantage of this method is that you can continue to fire more or less without any interruption.

'Right. Charge your magazines. First time round, Tony you be the driver, with Will – and James, you can drive Carl in the second car.'

So we screamed about the range, swapping roles and firing a huge amount of ammunition. Every so often the poor old range cars received a direct hit or a ricochet, but no one seemed to mind so long as the engine and the tyres remained serviceable. Now we were becoming accustomed to firing directly past each other, missing by inches. Even a simple thing like clambering swiftly from the driving seat and out of the passenger door required practice to perfect.

Then we moved on to other forms of car drill. We covered the situation of four operators in a car being ambushed and having to debus, firing past each other's shoulders. Even wearing ear defenders the noise from a pistol or a submachine gun is deafening if you are slightly in front of the muzzle and very close to the line of fire. You can also feel the hot blastwave from each report.

The car drills were interspersed with foot drills, during which we would wander about the range in our surveillance clothing, weapons concealed. Sandy and Jock would then initiate a scenario and we would have to react as a team, taking on any direct threat and ignoring any civilians. Jock manned a video camera so that we could be debriefed in detail after complex exercises.

The set-up on the range became more and more elaborate as we constructed walls, doorways, windows and pavements out of hessian sacking tacked to wooden frames, so that we could practise skirmishing around a built-up area, where vision is restricted by physical obstacles. Our weapon handling became very impressive and our confidence in each other soared.

Several times a week now we had the evening to ourselves, and a group of us would drive out into the countryside to find a quiet pub. Other evenings were spent learning advanced first aid, mugging up on our map books and town plans, or practising at night some of the skills that we'd been taught. In our first aid training we learnt how to insert drips to replace fluid loss and combat the shock of a wound. I had always been quite squeamish about inserting needles, but now we practised finding a vein – most conveniently in the inner forearm, but sometimes in the leg or back of the hand – and puncturing it with a canula, the fat but extremely sharp needle that comes in a sealed packet with each drip set, to which is attached the clear plastic tube from the drip sack. This was the life-saving technique pioneered, for use by ordinary soldiers at least, by the Israeli army during the 1973 Yom Kippur war. We learnt the priorities for treatment and how to monitor the state of a casualty. In the scenarios that we might face in Ulster, we were never likely to be more than thirty minutes' drive from a hospital (at least, not the way we drove), but the first few minutes would always be crucial. We also watched instructional videos taken by US Army medical teams at the height of the war in Vietnam. These clearly demonstrated the internal damage to tissue caused by gunshot wounds and I found the images shocking in their intensity.

We were introduced to the very ingenious 'Gladiator Anti-Shock

Trouser Suit'. This was a pair of inflatable over-trousers which could be slipped on to a casualty who had lost a lot of blood and was going into shock. Once the trousers were inflated with a foot pump they acted just like a pilot's G-suit, the pressure of air constricting the flow of blood to the casualty's legs, thus reducing the overall requirement for blood in the body, and therefore concentrating all that was still available into the vital organs. The only drawback was that to use them safely one had to monitor the blood pressure of the casualty regularly. So we also had to learn how to do this, using a stethoscope, an inflatable armband and a pressure gauge – not an easy task to perform at night in a moving car, I couldn't help reflecting! As with everything else we were taught, we were constantly being tested to ensure that we had absorbed the lessons. The value of these tests soon became apparent.

About once a month we had a four-day break, but it was impossible to plan ahead because we could rarely be certain when they would be granted. This was particularly vexing because I was spending as much of my time off as I could with Jennifer, staying with her in Wimbledon. By now I was extremely fit and I would sometimes cajole her into joining me in a run round Richmond Park, jogging past the herds of stately deer. Afterwards we would lounge together in the bath drinking wine, listening to tapes as she introduced me to a wide range of classical composers, explaining the historical context and subtleties of each.

One Tuesday morning after a long weekend we were back on the range, and I was finding it quite hard to concentrate. We were doing yet more car drills – the variations were endless because the range itself could be set out in so many different ways. This morning Carl, the stocky Welshman, was driving, I was sitting behind him with an MP5, Bob was in the front passenger seat, also with a covert MP5, and Sid was in the back on my left. As we entered the range, Carl drove carefully down a narrow alleyway, when suddenly there was an enormous explosion from directly in front of us and a blast of heat came through my slightly open window.

We burst out of the back, pouring rounds down as we engaged the terrorist targets. Despite the crackle of gunfire I became aware of a commotion behind me and glanced back. My heart missed a beat as I took in the scene. Carl was hanging forwards out of the driver's door, his pistol lying on the tarmac, and I could see a stream of blood running from his shirt and down his outstretched arm.

I shouted to the others: 'Carl's hit!' Shock registered on their faces as they stared at him, writhing in agony and groaning loudly. I swallowed hard and dashed back to him, applying the safety catch to my submachine gun. Holy fuck, he was very pale and there was blood beginning to run off the seat into the well of the car. I could feel the panic rising inside me, but I forced it down. Sid and I reached him at the same time and we dragged him from the car. During range practices we routinely carried two shell dressings taped to our belts next to our magazine holder, and now we frantically ripped at them, peeling open the sterile wrapping, our hands slick with the blood that was welling out of his back. We began to stuff the dressings on to the wound to try to stem the flow. I checked quickly across his front for any sign of an exit wound, but couldn't find one. This wasn't too surprising, since he'd been hit by a 9mm round, but I knew that it greatly increased the likelihood of severe internal damage.

Carl seemed to be slipping into shock now and Sid shouted for a drip-set. If we could get some fluid into his system and stop the flow of blood, we should be able to stabilise him temporarily. Sandy sprinted up with a large medical holdall which he thrust at me. I dug inside it and pulled out half a dozen more shell dressings and tossed the drip-set to Bob, who tore open the sealed canula pack. I was watching Carl's face and saw his eyeballs roll up into his skull. Jesus Christ! I could feel a strong pulse beneath his jaw so I bent my ear to his mouth to check that he was still breathing. If he was I couldn't detect it. I dug around again inside the bag to find a plastic airway opener – if he was becoming unconscious he'd almost certainly swallow his tongue unless I got the short tube into his throat. Sid was preparing to give him artificial respiration, but as I opened his slack mouth to insert the tube he groaned suddenly and opened his eyes wide, beginning to pant.

Sid yelled towards the range hut, 'Is an ambulance coming?' Someone shouted that it would be about three minutes. Usually there was one sitting outside the small medical centre back at camp, ready to go.

Bob had the canula into Carl's forearm and was connecting the drip bag to the protruding tube, so I stood and held the litre bag of saline solution aloft. I was glad to be a pace away from him now;

the stench of his blood was making me want to retch. Then a ghastly thought set my mind reeling. Carl was hit in the back! I'd been sitting directly behind him! Desperately I tried to picture the scene when the explosion went off. Surely I couldn't have fired a round through the back of the seat without realising it? Oh my God . . . Still holding the bag high, I edged towards the car, peering through the window to examine the back of the driver's seat. I couldn't see any marks on it. At that range the fabric would definitely have been badly scorched by the muzzle blast. In my mind's eye I tried to recreate the scene as I had skirmished forward past the bonnet.

I glanced at Sandy. He seemed strangely calm, almost as if he was enjoying all this. I looked back towards the range hut and for the first time saw Jock behind us, a video camera pressed to his face. Ghoulish bastard, I thought. Then slowly, like fog lifting, the truth began to dawn. This was another fucking exercise. I said quietly to Bob and Sid, 'Smile, chaps, we're on *Candid Camera*!' They both looked back, puzzled.

Carl let out a dying groan that turned into a sort of giggle. 'Fuck me, Bob,' he said in his deep Welsh accent, 'What do you think I am, a fucking pin cushion? It took you four stabs to get that needle into me, you bastard!'

Bob stared down at him, his freckled face still drained of colour. 'Serves you right, you stupid Welsh git. You had us going there, all right!'

'It's OK for you lot – I've got a bucketful of warm fucking sheep's blood down my back!' he said in an outraged tone. 'And it's got inside my kegs! It's fucking horrible!'

As the adrenalin rush subsided, anger at being taken for a ride flared inside me – but I instantly realised I was being unreasonable. This was an object lesson in how to conduct realistic training, and it had brilliantly achieved the aim of testing our first aid skills under real pressure.

Sandy talked us through the video that Jock had shot, commenting on our procedure. Just before the exercise he had taped a slim two-litre bag of fresh lamb's blood to Carl's lower back, instructing him to slit it with a penknife the moment the explosion was triggered, and then to play seriously injured. The only part of it that had backfired slightly was when Carl, for added realism, had rolled his eyes up into his skull. Faced with this sign of a retreat into coma, the rest of us immediately attempted to put the short plastic airway down his throat, and of course, not being actually unconscious, he would have gagged involuntarily on it. So he came back to life to avoid this unpleasantness.

The next, and final phase, of our weapon training was in some ways the most exciting. Sandy and Jock, assisted by two members of the Training Wing of 22 SAS in Hereford, took us through some improvised hostage rescue drills in our 'Killing House', as it was known. This was a three-storey construction, normal in every respect, except that the window frames held easily replaceable plastic sheets rather than glass, and every wall was covered with dark maroon sheets of thick impregnated rubber from ceiling to wainscot. The rubber sheets, hanging a couple of inches clear of each wall were designed to catch and slow the 9mm rounds that we fired in the rooms, eliminating dangerous ricochets. In addition, the building had an excellent air-conditioning system, which was necessary to draw out the smoke and fumes given off by our weapons and stun grenades.

Sandy explained that what we were about to learn was different from the set-piece hostage rescues practised by the SAS Pagoda teams – as enjoyed by millions of TV viewers at the breaking of the Iranian Embassy siege. In our case we would only ever be responding in the immediate follow-up to the snatch of an operator by terrorists. Since the ops room and back-up teams always knew the precise location of every operator on the ground, and were aware of all the local terrorists' haunts, if one of us was lifted by the opposition there would be a good chance of pinpointing him or her and launching an immediate assault. Speed is always of the essence because if an operator is snatched the opposition might torture and then execute him or her almost at once. We would have no time to plan and prepare an elaborate assault. Once we had a shrewd idea roughly where the operator was being held, Sandy and Jock showed us how to organise an improvised assault.

First they introduced us to the Remington 870 12-bore pump-action shotgun, one of which would routinely be carried concealed deep within a team vehicle, against just such an emergency as this. It took seven cartridges in its magazine, which extended forwards under the barrel. We test-fired it on the range, first using ordinary number six shot on clay pigeons, then solid shot, the purpose of which is to take down doors, either by hitting the hinges or the lock.

It was a fearsome weapon. Just for interest, Sandy demonstrated how one could use the shotgun to blow the windscreen out of a car from inside. It had been proved many times that a 9mm round's metal jacket, when fired through a car windshield, was often shredded by the toughened glass, at best reducing its accuracy dramatically and at worst destroying the slug altogether. Using a range car that was overdue for the scrap heap, Sandy and Jock drove up to the front of the range and let loose a round from the Remington. The result was spectacular: the entire windscreen leapt forward in a cascade of glittering glass as Jock opened up through the aperture with an MP5K. Jock warned us that the effect of the compression from the blast inside the car was like being kicked in the head by a mule.

Next we learnt about the tactics of entering a house and clearing it room by room. The emphasis was on speed and aggression, and maintaining the momentum of the assault once it had begun. Initially we practised room entries, using our Browning pistols and MP5s. The drill was to sprint as stealthily as possible from the front door and up the stairs to whichever floor the hostage was being held. We were now so fit that we almost flew up the broad flights, weapons at the ready. We would then race to the door of the room, first man to arrive briefly peering through the keyhole if there was one, second and third taking station left and right of the door. At a nod from the man in the centre, the right-hand man would operate the door handle, the centre man would boot in the door and we'd all pile through, guns blazing to front, left and right respectively. The room – which was always fully furnished with army cast-off furniture, curtains and so on – would contain a variety of targets representing the hostage, a number of terrorists and some women and children. The skill lies in identifying and engaging hostile targets the very moment one sets eyes on them. Usually Brian from the photographic centre would crouch in one corner wearing a helmet and a bullet-proof vest, a video camera pressed to his eye. He had an unshakeable – and, I couldn't help thinking, somewhat misplaced – faith in our ability to make snap decisions and shoot straight under extreme pressure.

We thoroughly enjoyed these sessions, and it really brought home to me just how competent we had become and how well we operated together. Here we were, rushing around, firing repeatedly straight past each other's heads, the rounds cracking past just inches from flesh and bone.

The closest we came to a mishap was when I had a rare stoppage on my MP5 just as we burst into a room. Kate was in front of me, firing straight ahead, I was covering right, and Tony was behind me, firing left. After one round my gun jammed and, instead of dropping to one knee and pulling out my pistol, I tripped and stumbled a step and a half to the left, just as Tony engaged a target. My outstretched arm crossed the line of his weapon just as he fired and the round from his pistol cracked through the gap between my arm and my chest, the muzzle blast singeing my jacket. Oddly perhaps, at the time we all thought this was a great joke.

Jock also introduced us to the use of stun grenades. I had always assumed these were very like the standard army thunderflashes, which let off a loud report and a white flash, and resemble fat twelve-inch-long cigars. Stun grenades come in a variety of shapes and sizes and with variable fuse times, but of most interest to us was the ripple flashbang model. This is somewhat taller and slightly thinner than a can of baked beans. When it detonates it scatters a large number of individual maroons around the room which then go off with consecutive bangs and flashes, hence the grenade's nickname of 'flashbang'.

Jock juggled one of them idly in his hand as he talked. 'OK, people, stand facing those targets on the other side of the room, pistols holstered. When I blow my whistle I want you to draw and engage your target with two double taps, aiming for the head. When I blow my whistle a second time, cease firing, if you haven't already finished, and holster your weapons. Piece of cake, eh? Oh, by the way, when I blow the first whistle I'm going to chuck this thing into the corner of the room. Just ignore it – it makes a wee bit of a flash and a few bangs. Ear defenders on . . . standby now!'

As his whistle shrilled we spun into the correct Weaver stance, right hands flashing back towards our holsters in unison, and I half noticed out the corner of my eye the little black object skittering across the floor. As my pistol snapped up into my line of sight, settling on the head of the target, a searing flash and an incredibly sharp report burst at my feet, followed at intervals of a split second by repeats of the same from different parts of the room. If you are not expecting it the effect is literally stunning – and I was mesmerised by the intensity of the display for the few seconds that it lasted, even with ear defenders on.

Suddenly it was over, and the whistle blew a second time. Shit, I hadn't fired a shot! I looked guiltily at the others. Kate had her left forearm pressed over the crown of her head and was grinning impishly, her unused pistol still in her right hand.

'Fuck me, people. Aren't we playing today, or what?' said Jock with a wide smile. 'Ha ha . . . don't worry, I knew it would have that effect. It always does first go. But now we'll do it once again – same practice, same grenade – and this time I want three dead gringos, OK?'

So we mentally braced ourselves, and this time we operated through the shocking barrage, ignoring the multiple reports and flashes, and we neatly drilled the targets.

The focus of our instruction moved back to furthering our surveillance skills. By now we had learned pretty well the entire mapbook and could drive through the countryside for miles around reporting our positions and that of the target from memory, by reference to the spot system. Our radio voice procedure became slick and clipped, and it required no effort to ensure that one's pistol was secure and concealed beneath one's clothing, but always ready for a fast draw. We also became completely used to operating individually in our cars, and before long it felt strange to have even one passenger in the car. It was difficult to recall how apprehensive I had felt at the prospect of driving a surveillance task solo. The fast driving itself was now something that one did not even need to think about; it just happened in response to a changing situation and we became adept at judging speed, time and distance.

We were also continually practising our photographic skills. Now, every time we deployed on a surveillance exercise, we vied to come back with the best black and white shots of the target's Alpha, Bravo or Charlie, developing and printing the pictures ourselves. We also set up camera rigs in our clothes for use in foot surveillance – more and more often our mobile chases would include the target parking up somewhere and walking off through a busy pedestrian precinct or a sprawling housing estate. Initally I felt very self-conscious strolling along among civilians, armed to the teeth and with a covert radio body set strapped to me, but it soon became second nature. We communicated over the net with each other by murmuring rapidly and quietly, lips barely stirring, into our shoulder mikes. If bystanders were within earshot, we resorted to our own code of clicks and double-clicks on the radio pressel switch, chatting to each other over the ether like a school of dolphins.

Rarely now could the instructor-target escape our web, no matter where he or she drove or walked. Every significant move made was surreptitiously recorded on 35mm black and white film or colour video. As we followed, the other instructors circled around us, noting individual incidents and mistakes, which were then discussed in detail at the debrief. Although these sessions were still extremely frank, there was plenty of praise when things went right.

Gradually we began to realise that the instructors were accepting us as new recruits to their unit, and this recognition simply increased our desire to prove ourselves individually to them. Despite the hundreds of hours of personal tuition, they still held themselves relatively distant from us, and I began to wonder whether this was a reaction to not knowing anyone's true identity. Maybe *everyone* in the unit is relatively distant from everyone else, I thought to myself. Just as well I'd found Jennifer to share myself with, or I'd go mad.

Security around us was extremely tight. It was obvious that our small and very comfortable camp had been purpose-built for the unit, and we and the instructors, plus a number of technical and support staff, were its only occupants. We had the odd visit from MI5 personnel, who used some of the specialist training features and were trained by our own instructors in certain skills. But we were forbidden from speaking to the few cleaners or kitchen staff that were to be seen around the camp, and our mail, which was forwarded under a separate cover from a different location, was shredded once we had read it. We assumed that the two payphones at our disposal (which couldn't take incoming calls) were regularly monitored, given the severity of all the other security measures.

The chief instructor frequently reminded us that terrorists were actively trying to discover the precise location of our base in the UK, and that we should be on our guard at all times. Twice I witnessed an impressive response to the arrival of stray civilian vehicles by the armed M.o.D. police contingent, who manned the main entrance. The camp itself operated under an effective cover story which neatly accounted for our strange appearance and our somewhat peculiar comings and goings at all hours.

'For the next hour or so, lady and gentlemen, we're going to have a little progress test to see just how well you're doing.' The chief instructor was standing in front of us in the lecture theatre. I groaned inwardly. We'd already had a tiring day of surveillance around a rough area of a city suburb about an hour's drive away, and I was looking forward to a gentle run, supper and an early night.

'Just complete this question paper over the next hour and a half.' He fanned through a sheaf of A4 sheets and began to pass them around. 'Oh, and you'll each need to visit the chief clerk in turn while you're doing it, because we need to sort out your travel documentation. Once you've seen him you can finish the test over a cup of tea in the dining room if you want, so take it with you.'

We all settled down to the set of questions, which seemed mainly to be about photography and weapon characteristics, and every few minutes or so he called a name. When it was my turn, I filed out to visit the admin block on the other side of the camp.

The concrete path led along the side of a classroom, parallel to the perimeter fence but screened from its chainlink and razor wire by a compact hedge about eight feet high. As I approached the point where the path swung left around the corner of the building I glimpsed out of the corner of my eye what looked like a sheet of white paper lying on the grass to my right. I started to turn my head to see what it was, when I became aware of something rushing towards me from around the corner. Swinging my head back round, my eyes almost popped from their sockets and my mouth started to fall open in shock. Two large bodies, clad entirely in black and wearing balaclavas, were about two feet away and hurtling towards me. It was plain that the impact would knock me off my feet.

Everything seemed to happen in slow motion. I leaned back and noticed with an odd detachment that my right hand was already instinctively worming its way under the cuff of my jersey and was beginning to close on the butt of the pistol in my waistband. As my fingers found it, and my left forearm came up to protect my face, I realised that there was only a single blank round in the weapon.

The front figure cannoned into my chest, thumping the wind from me. As I started to fall I was caught from behind, and vice-like fingers immediately closed around my pistol, breaking my grasp as it was twisted out of my hand. At the same moment my view was blotted out as a black cotton bag was slipped over my head. Three bodies were pressing and pummelling me to the ground. Within seconds a fat rope gag around the outside of the hood cut harshly into my lips, forcing my mouth open, and my hands and feet were pinioned together behind my arched back.

My brain was racing wildly, trying to make sense of the crisis. The hood and gag combined with the adrenalin were making my breathing laboured, and I struggled to bring it under control, frightened of vomiting. I was thinking, who the fuck *are* these people?

'This focker's moine!' said a deep, quiet voice close to my ear. Jesus Christ! My blood ran cold – that was an Irish accent!

Already I was being carried bodily away. I tried to struggle but all that was free was my head, which I waved around. I knew I was utterly helpless – I couldn't even tell the direction we were heading. Then I felt the distinctive brush of a tree branch and realised we must be pushing through the dense hedging screen around the perimeter wire. Shit, I thought, there must be a hole in the fence!

I was seriously frightened now. Crash! My head bumped hard into something metallic and I was dropped, sideways on, into what felt like a metal box. Instantly a car boot slammed shut inches above my head, and the gentle slosh of petrol in the tank sent a shudder through me. Now the vehicle was rocking on its springs as my kidnappers clambered in and the engine roared into life. Frantically I began to test the ties that held my ankles and wrists for any weak points, but they felt like standard police plasti-cuffs, which would need heavy pliers to cut through.

Now the car was accelerating wildly, and as we bumped along I was sent bouncing up against the roof of the boot. Calm down! Calm down! Think! I yelled at myself. Surely to God this was another exercise! They'd been inside the camp in broad daylight, for Christ's sake! It couldn't be for real, could it? Come on, make a plan! I fought to keep control of myself, mentally thrusting down the rising claustrophobia that threatened to engulf me. Shit, I was already beginning to get the first warnings of cramp in my folded legs and the overpowering smell of petrol fumes was nauseating.

I was trying to keep track of the twists and turns that we went through, but after ten minutes of this I knew I was hopelessly lost. Suddenly we slowed down and turned sharply off the relatively smooth surface and on to what felt like a rutted track. After a couple of hundred metres the vehicle pulled up on to a patch of gravel and the engine died. Doors opened and heavy feet scrunched quickly around to the boot, which was immediately yanked open. Still trussed like a turkey I was bodily lifted out, carried a few feet, then dropped on to the ground from about a foot, banging my chin hard and winding me again. A dull snip sounded behind my back and at once my legs, which had been held tightly against my buttocks, sprang free, straightening painfully. My ankles were still bound together, but at least the pressure on my knees and lower back had been relieved.

Now two pairs of hands grabbed me under the armpits, dragged me a short distance and lifted me into a vertical position. Something was tied again round the cuffs on my wrists and I realised that I was being chained to an upright post. The feet moved away and I was left, still hooded, trying to make some sense of this situation. To my left I could hear someone else breathing hard, snorting almost. I guessed it was another trainee and at last I felt confident that this was an exercise. I shifted my weight from one foot to the other and back again, trying to ease the spots where the binding was cutting painfully into my ankle bones. Suddenly I heard a crunch of gravel, then a momentary silence, and then I received a hard thump on my thigh with what felt like a booted foot. Shit, that hurt! I decided to stand still. After a few minutes another vehicle drove up and pairs of feet milled around briefly, presumably pinioning another prisoner against a post.

Without warning, hands grasped me by the feet and arms, and I was lifted upwards then laid bodily on the ground face down. Someone knelt heavily on my legs, pressing my kneecaps viciously into the grit. My arms were lifted behind me and I felt cold metal against my skin, followed by the sound of a snip which severed the cuffs. My wrists were still gripped by hands. I felt my jersey being pulled violently up, over my head and away. My shirt was ripped roughly off my chest and I felt the cold gravel against my belly as my shoes and socks were snatched off. I was rolled over on to my back and other hands unclasped the leather belt at my waist, then tore my jeans down over my thighs to my knees. Another snip released my legs and one at a time my feet were handed through the leg-holes. My boxer shorts followed. Now I was lying hooded but otherwise naked on the ground, and feeling extremely vulnerable.

After a few moments I was thrust into a coarse one-piece boilersuit, my arms and legs refastened, and I was dragged backwards across a courtyard and into a building.

As we moved deeper into the heart of the structure I became aware of a loud pounding sound in the distance, growing in volume as we moved towards it.

My bare heels scraped and banged against the rough concrete floor as we turned left and right along what seemed like a series of corridors. What was particularly disturbing was the wordlessness of the guards. It is strangely humiliating to be dragged about, blindfold and gagged, like a sack of rubbish.

Soon we came to a halt, and hands on my shoulders forced me down into a squatting position. The click and rasp of handcuffs confirmed that I was now attached by my wrists and ankles to the strange slatted wooden object I was sitting on. The sound of the guards' footsteps was drowned by the continuous loud roar that came from somewhere immediately behind me. It was as if I was chained to an industrial generator or air compressor, beating out a deafening rhythmic clamour. Fingers were now fiddling behind my head and at last the gag was removed – a huge relief – and I was left alone.

I took stock of my situation. Of course I knew that it's every soldier's duty to try to escape, but the time to do it is close to the point of capture. The further a prisoner passes up the handling chain the fewer opportunities for escape arise. It was perfectly obvious to me that there was going to be little opportunity to do a runner.

After a few minutes I had the feeling that there were no guards in the room with me, which I sensed to be fairly small, and very cold and damp. Inside the thick black hood my eyes could pick out no light whatsoever. I shuffled around on my behind as best I could, testing the amount of movement my shackles left me – which was very little – and all the while bracing myself in case an undetected guard was about to kick me. I soon worked out that I was chained to a large wooden pallet, of the type that a forklift truck would handle. The rough pine slats were very uncomfortable, their splintery edges biting into my backside. I found I couldn't rise above a low squat, nor could I fully straighten my back because my hands were secured at the level of my ankles. Any notion of escape from here seemed hopeless.

I settled down to wait for the next stage of the exercise, whatever that might be. The trouble was I couldn't get comfortable. Any position I adopted caused one or other part of me first to ache and then to shriek with discomfort. The incessant din from the machine was very trying, if not yet actually disturbing. I knew I should take my mind off my current predicament so I tried to think about other things, such as what Jennifer might be up to at that moment, or where I'd go on holiday – if ever I were to have any – but the noise from the bloody compressor thing was so loud that I just couldn't think straight. So I tried concentrating on the sound for a while. However I soon began to hear strange words mixed up with its steady thrum, and I thought to myself that I'd soon go mad that way.

Hours passed. Occasionally I was shaken with a spasm of fury at my predicament and I wanted to shout out that this was a fucking ridiculous waste of my and everybody else's valuable time. Then, as the droning noise continued to throb through me, my mood would change and I would become light-hearted, reasoning for a while that if this was the worst they could devise I should be laughing. Special Forces pay, and me chained to a bleeding pallet, ha, ha!

More time passed. It seemed to be getting colder and colder – perhaps because I was effectively naked, the boilersuit hanging open down the front as I strained forward against my shackles. I shifted for the thousandth time. With a suddenness that startled me an arm gripped me round the forehead from behind, forcing my neck back. Dammit, with this roar in the background it was impossible to hear any movement around me. A hand roughly lifted the hood clear of my mouth and thrust a large metal container against my lips, which I pressed tightly shut in a defiant gesture.

'Drink the water!' ordered a menacing voice I didn't recognise. Sod it, I thought, my throat is pretty dry. I gulped down what felt like a pint of lukewarm water, much of it slopping down my chin and cascading down my belly and on to my groin. Then the hood came down and I was left alone again. Christ, how long have I been here now, I wondered. It felt like several hours at least, perhaps four – but it is quite difficult to keep track of time when you're cold, uncomfortable, deafened, bored and apprehensive. And now a new concern was beginning to nag at the back of my mind: I would need a pee within the next hour or so. Bugger it, I wished I hadn't drunk the bloody water! It wasn't helped by the fact that my crotch now felt cold and damp as a result of the spillage. I ignored the thought and tried to concentrate on other things.

Suddenly, my heart skipping a beat, I was jerked out of my reverie by hands slipping firmly under my armpits. A key clicked quickly in a padlock below me and I found myself being dragged rapidly and without a word through the door and then left and right along wide corridors, the noise of the generator receding into the distance. My unshod feet, stiff and waxy with the cold, scraped along the pitted concrete and I tried my best to shuffle along on them, but the pace was too fast and the bindings around my ankles held them too close together. The top sides of my toes were rapidly losing their skin. As the guards climbed a couple of steps I hopped desperately but failed to avoid stubbing my toes. Here there was a distinct change of atmosphere. The temperature was many degrees warmer and there was that slight fugginess that suggested a roomful of warm and well-fed people. I felt like a tramp entering a Kensington coffee shop. The floor-covering changed to carpet, which actually stung my toes rather more than the concrete had done.

I was spun round and flung down backwards on to a plastic chair. Someone yanked my arms over the back of it and clasped a chained padlock between my wrists, pulling my arms down towards the feet of the chair and forcing me to sit up straight, arched backwards slightly – which was at least a blessed relief to the cramped muscles either side of my spine. Even through the thick black cotton of my hood I could tell that there were lights glaring at me. Someone behind me whipped the hood off and the searing intensity of the lamps directed at my face forced me to screw my eyelids together. Even with my eyes tight shut it was blinding.

'Open your eyes and look at me,' said a very cold and humourless voice. 'You'll open your eyes now and look at me if you know what's good for you.'

Carefully I relaxed my frown and squinted out. Three large angle-poise lamps, one on each side and one above in the middle, burned out at me, and in the centre was a face staring impassively from behind a pair of black-framed spectacles. As my eyes adjusted I made out the black plastic surface of the desk he was sitting behind, and the fact that he was wearing a black turtleneck sweater. I studied him for a while and he held my gaze. He looked about forty, and I'd certainly never set eyes on him before. I realised I was shaking like a leaf, shivering with a mixture of cold, humiliation and tension.

'You are our prisoner now. If you co-operate and answer our questions we will feed and clothe you properly. Now . . . what is your name?' He raised his pencil expectantly above a virgin pad of paper in front of him. I tried to place his accent. It was standard BBC, but there was a hint of something else. He definitely wasn't using his natural speaking voice. I considered his question. We hadn't been briefed on any particular line to take in any resistance to interrogation scenario – in fact to date it had never even been mentioned – so I decided to stick to the traditional Geneva Convention 'Big Four' – number, rank, name and date of birth. But for a while I'd say nothing.

He put his pencil down. 'What is your name?' He sounded more menacing now, and for the first time I noticed a two-foot length of heavy black rubber hose lying on the desk in front of him, his interlocking fingers resting lightly on it. Hmm . . . this was an exercise, of course, so it was inconceivable that he'd use that thing on me, wasn't it?

Then a thought struck me. My brother had done the army interrogation course some time before and I remembered him saying that you should always allow a long delay before answering the first question, then allow a slightly shorter delay before answering the next one and so on – the point being to wrest some slight control of the situation back from the interrogator, because he invariably begins to wait for you to answer before repeating the question. I decided to give it a go. I counted to fifteen, and just before I thought he was going to ask me again, I said, 'I can't answer that.'

'You will answer it. What is your name?'

One, two, three . . . thirteen, fourteen – then 'I'm not permitted to answer that question.'

This fruitless line of questioning went on for quite a while, until I had got down to a delay of only a few seconds before replying that I wasn't able to answer. By now my tactic seemed pretty futile, so I decided to alter my approach. Perhaps I could bargain with him.

'I need a pee,' I said.

'Tell me your name and I'll order a guard to give you a bucket.'

I hesitate a while. What would it matter if I told him my name in exchange for a bucket, since I was going to tell him eventually anyway? I wasn't sure I could hold my bladder in check much longer. Sod it!

'Rennie.'

Without warning the hood blotted out my view again, and soon I was being dragged back to my uncomfortable pallet, my feet scrabbling unsuccessfully to avoid pressure on the open sores on the tops of my toes. Left alone on my pallet once more in the throbbing din, I stretched around me as best I could – but there was no sign of any bucket. The fucking bastards! What the hell was I going to do now? This was an exercise – I couldn't just wet myself like a two year old!

I was shivering steadily now, concentrating on my bladder, shifting around constantly on the slats, trying to ease the pressure on my rather too lean buttocks. Suddenly I realised it was no good, I was going to have to let go. I relaxed my muscles, but – dammit – nothing happened! Whether it was the tension in my body or the immensely strong psychological conditioning that tells us that adults never pee in their pants voluntarily, I found it extremely difficult to get the flow started. I shuffled around again on my bottom and deliberately relaxed every muscle while trying to picture a tropical waterfall. Gradually a hot flood began to course across my thighs, running down between my buttocks and splashing on to the floor beneath me. The relief was indescribable, although within a few minutes my wet boilersuit became uncomfortably cold and clammy.

Time passed.

Again with no warning came the sudden shock of being dragged off for another interrogation session. This time it was a woman behind the desk, who sat glaring at me for a full minute, cracking and snapping her knuckles disgustingly. She looked in her late twenties and had mousy brown hair and wore no make-up, appearing deathly white in the reflected glare of the lamps. Now that I had an empty bladder I was content to bask quietly in the warmth of the lights. I glanced back over my shoulder. A guard wearing a black balaclava stood behind me, and when I turned my head he raised his fist as if to punch me, so I cowered round again to face the front.

'Tell me your name!' she snarled rather than spoke. *Crunk-crack* went her knuckles. I really wished she wouldn't do that; it was so unnecessary. I pondered the question for a brief while, then I thought, no point making a meal of this.

'Rennie,' I said for the second time.

'Liar!' she shrieked. 'Don't give me that or I'll turn really nasty!'

Ah, I thought, perhaps I'd better try a different tack. 'James,' I said.

She grunted with satisfaction and wrote on a piece of paper in front of her. Then she stopped and sniffed the air. She scrutinised me, her hooded eyes sliding down my bare chest and belly and then concentrating on my crotch. She stood up behind the desk to get a better view. She too was wearing a black turtleneck and dark cords. I tried staring at her groin to embarrass her back, but she seemed impervious to my gaze.

'You dirty pig,' she yelled. 'You've pissed yourself, haven't you! What are you, a fucking baby? Struth!' She sat down heavily and raised her pencil expectantly above the pad of paper in front of her. 'OK, James, what's your unit?' she hissed.

'I'm awfully sorry, but I'm afraid I can't –'

'No!' she screamed, banging the table hard and sending the lamps jumping. She began to advance around the table towards me. 'You shut the fuck up unless you're answering my questions properly, you no-good sack of shit, you!' Now her face was inches from mine and she was shouting directly at me, mists of spittle borne on the blasts. I caught a faint reek of garlic on her breath, and noticed her front teeth were rather higgledy-piggledy. 'You think you're very clever, but I assure you you're the stupidest fucking cunt I've ever had the misfortune to see. Fuck me, look at that!' she shrieked, roughly pulling open the front of my boilersuit. 'That's not a prick, it's a fucking cocktail sausage. Jeez, haven't you reached puberty or what? Shit, I'd be really embarrassed if I were you, you fucking twat! Now fucking shut up until I tell you to speak, then just answer the question. What is your unit?'

Blimey, I thought. 'I can't answer that quest –'

Again she was off on a tirade, bawling at the top of her voice. I guessed that she was playing the role of Mrs Nasty, while the first one had been Mr Relatively Nice. We didn't really hit it off. After we'd been through this routine a couple of times the hood was replaced and I was dragged back to my place on the pallet, which was almost a relief. On the other hand, at least these sessions broke the deadly monotony of being shackled to one spot.

I lost track of how many times I was dragged out to the warmth of the interrogation room. I guessed that there was at least an hour or more between sessions, but it was very difficult to judge. Control of the interrogations alternated between Frau Flick and Captain Mainwaring, as I had christened them. Trying to judge the passage of time, I looked carefully to see whether Flick or Manwaring had developed rings under the eyes or a five o'clock shadow, but there was no sign of either. After the first few sessions I had given out the Big Four and thrown in my religious denomination for good measure. It was always a relief to get away from that sodding sound machine and have a stretch of my cold and cramped muscles.

Twice more, back on the pallet, unseen hands poured water down my throat, which I swallowed reluctantly, and once a ball of pappy wet bread was stuffed into my mouth. As before I relieved myself where I sat, pleased and interested to have overcome this psychological barrier.

Again I was hauled up and out for the long drag through the corridors. I was now resigned to the discomfort from my toes when we did this. But this time, when the hood was lifted, sitting behind the desk was the chief instructor.

'Do you know who I am?' he asked carefully.

I guessed that he was testing my sanity, if any, before releasing my shackles. 'The chief instructor?' I replied, and he brightened up considerably.

'OK, James, you can relax now. This is the end of the exercise. I'm going to release you now, do you understand?'

I was sorely tempted to come out with something screwy like, 'I want to be known as Loretta,' but instead I just said, 'Yup, great.'

'Out of interest,' he asked, 'how long do you reckon you've been held for?'

I thought for a moment, while the padlock clicked open behind me and Ernie severed the plasti-cuffs with pliers. 'Er . . . about thirty-six hours?'

'No,' he said lightly, 'actually it was only just under twenty-four. Funny that – it's always the way. People think it's been longer than it actually is.'

I have to say it didn't strike me as particularly funny!

At last I could stand up and stretch. Phew! I reeked of stale sweat and urine. I followed the chief instructor into another room where Dave was getting dressed. We smiled at each other, and on a table I found a bundle of my clothes, shoes, holster, pistol and magazine carrier. We chatted as we dressed, and were shortly joined by Kate and Bob. She was in good spirits. We turned our backs as she got dressed.

Back in camp we showered and changed. After a gargantuan supper we were briefed on the unit's standard operational procedures for resistance to interrogation. Initially it seemed illogical to go through an exercise like this without knowing the techniques we would be expected to employ, but it was clear that it wouldn't have been possible to rehearse these techniques realistically during an exercise. The purpose of our brief ordeal was simply to attune us to the shock of capture and at the same time to give the interrogators some useful practice. The snatches had been carried out by SAS teams up from Hereford.

The whole experience was oddly disturbing. Except at the start, I hadn't been at all afraid for myself – this was an exercise, and I knew that no British organisation went in for the physical torture of prisoners, even in wartime. It was just unusual to be completely reliant on the mercy of other people in that way. But on balance I had found it a very interesting experience.

The next phase of our training covered urban operations, with the emphasis on gaining entry to buildings without detection, either to carry out a specific short-term task or to set up an observation post. This sort of activity is relatively easy for the police, Customs & Excise and MI5 to conduct on the UK mainland, because it's almost always possible to find a law-abiding person to lend the use of their front room or attic from which to observe the target. However, in the nationalist and loyalist areas of Northern Ireland this was much less likely to be the case. The very act of approaching a potential helper might blow an operation, so the insertion of a team into a building requires detailed planning and co-ordination. Again it was pointed out to us that we would only ever covertly enter private premises following a direct request from Special Branch, who would obtain the appropriate entry warrant. In no sense were we above the law, and we would be individually answerable for our actions in a court of law if necessary. I had already served under such constraints in the green army in Belfast, and frankly would have felt uneasy if this had not been the case in my new unit, being something of a libertarian at heart.

We talked through the different methods of entry (or MOE) that could be employed to gain access to a property, and the various routines that groups involved in such a task would follow. We gathered that we would be instructed further in this subject once we were over the water. Everything had to be planned to the last detail by the operation commander – who was simply whichever operator was doing the most critical part of the job. The commander had to ensure that each participant was fully briefed, from the entry team and the individuals who would walk prescribed routes to confirm that the area was clear (and who were ready to create a diversion if necessary), to the drivers of the drop-off cars and the fast response vehicles, to the ops officer who would monitor the operation over the net.

For our first exercise we used the simplest MOE – which is to borrow the real key long enough to cut a duplicate, returning the original to the keyholder before any suspicion is aroused. This requires excellent intelligence about such details as who is likely to be carrying the key, where it is routinely kept, when it is normally used and so on. Some of the information can be gleaned from informers via Special Branch, other snippets might come from MI5, and much can be obtained through classic surveillance and audacious sleight of hand.

Our task on this occasion was to set up an OP covering the main entrance to a bank in a local town. The best site for it was in a deserted storeroom on the second floor above a shoe shop in the main shopping precinct. The front of the shop was flush with its neighbours in the row opposite the bank, and it had a narrow alleyway running down one side that led to the staff entrance.

Our first task was to obtain the keys and the details of the alarm system. It takes considerable practice to open unfamiliar locks and deactivate an alarm in a hurry, particularly in the dark and when your adrenalin is pumping, so we ran through the sequence of events many times in advance. It was exciting to be doing this as a real operation: if anyone saw us they would undoubtedly call the police and we would be caught red-handed, apparently burgling a shoe shop. Although the local Special Branch office was aware of our activities, the regular beat police hadn't been informed for fear that we would have an unwelcome audience of curious policemen.

The plan was that I would drive the OP team – Tom and Will – to the vicinity of the pedestrian precinct at 12.15 on a Wednesday morning. (If we waited until the streets were absolutely deserted we would stand out more, rather than less.) Kate and Sid would be dropped off from Dave's car at one end of the precinct, while Bob, walking unsteadily and clutching a tin of cider, would be dropped off by Carl at the other. They would approach each other, checking out any loiterers and confirming over the net that all was quiet. As they neared the shoeshop I would cruise past the street behind and drop Tom and Will near the rear entrance to the alley. Kate and Sid would enter the front of the alley for a pretend snog and a quick knee-trembler, blocking it long enough for Will to open the door and neutralise the alarm. He would then lock himself and Tom inside, and they would rapidly clear the building up to the third floor.

Everything worked like clockwork, and the moment Tom reported that the shop was clear, Steve – a short, fair-haired, likeable young Scot, who was also in my car – set off down the alley carrying the holdall containing the OP kit. As he passed, Will whipped open the door and grabbed the bag. Steve then strolled on and turned right, to be picked up by Carl, while Bob was picked up a couple of streets away by Dave. Sid and Kate, the happy couple, rendezvoused with me a few minutes later, and we all sped back to camp, leaving two back-up teams in the neighbourhood as a quick-reaction force (or QRF).

We took it in turns to man the operations room back at camp and to act as mobile QRF, and during the second night I replaced Tom in the OP, more for practice in the method than out of any necessity.

It was an odd experience to have a busy shop operating all day beneath us. The owner was aware of our presence but not the staff, and consequently we were on tenterhooks every time we heard someone climbing the stairs to the first-floor storeroom. The second-floor attic we were in was bare.

In order to observe the bank entrance our camera, equipped with a long lens, had to be placed on a tripod well back from the window. So that we weren't visible to any casual observer from across the street we suspended a pale grey net curtain across the width of the room near the back wall, aiming the camera out through a tiny tear in the fabric. Whoever was on watch simply stood with his eye pressed to the viewfinder, watching the comings and goings at the bank. As the light conditions changed outside, so we had continually to update the camera's aperture and shutter-speed settings, ready for instant action. We had been provided with mugshots of two characters that we hadn't seen before, and our task was to photograph them meeting at the bank, then to guide a surveillance team on to whichever one carried away a parcel. We discovered that it takes considerable self-discipline to maintain an effective routine in such a situation; if you take your eyes off the target for a second you may well miss the action.

At about 2 p.m. on the third day Will spotted our targets approaching the bank. He shot off a roll of film while I raised the QRF and the ops room over the radio net. The rest of the guys scrambled from camp (about twenty minutes' drive away) to set up a follow. Within minutes of the Bravos' first appearance they parted outside the bank, one carrying a packet, and I triggered the QRF on to him. They had him under control long enough for the full surveillance team to arrive and take over. As Will and I packed up our kit we could hear the chase disappearing into a rural area, and eventually the target went to ground in an isolated farmhouse.

That night we extracted ourselves from the attic, making certain to remove every trace of our presence, and scattering dust back over the areas where our shoes had left patterns on the floorboards. Dealing with the alarm from the inside was more tricky than it had been from the outside, and I was grateful that this was Will's job and not mine.

Although this marked the end of the exercise, in reality we would go on to do a CTR on the farmhouse and probably insert an OP there.

We were now operating together like a well-oiled machine, slipping into gear to cover each new exercise, which was inevitably a further variation on a few well-understood themes. Having mastered the arts of surveillance using little more than the Mark One Eyeball on our CTR exercises, we were now introduced to a range of sophisticated technical aids that would refine our activities considerably, significantly increasing our capabilities without adding to our exposure. Many of the gadgets had been developed during the Cold War to combat espionage. It was a great surprise to discover that the army had access to such kit, and the ability to use and maintain it so effectively. We learnt that a designated individual from the unit used to scour the trade fairs of the world to keep abreast of any developments that could be turned to our advantage.

Now that we had assimilated the skills we had been taught, the next stage of our training was to learn how to react to the sort of situations that might arise on operations. The point of this was to ensure that a standard methodology for dealing with specific problems existed throughout the unit, so that one could guess pretty accurately just how another operator would react in a given situation, helping everyone to plan a suitable response.

Over a three-day period the instructors laid on a series of realistic and unexpected scenarios for us to cope with, sometimes individually and sometimes in teams.

'Right, you've got two minutes to sort yourselves out,' Billy the instructor said to Tony, Sid and me as we stood by a range car, checking over our weapons and radios. 'The situation is, an OP team has been compromised in a building . . . here . . .' He pointed to the location on our map. 'They've had one contact with a gunman and the last message from them was that a hostile crowd was forming. You're their QRF, so you have to go and fetch them out. There's a medpack in the boot and a fold-up stretcher. Any questions? Get going then!'

Sid drove like a demon as I directed him to the target, which was one of a group of buildings at the far side of the training area. We had blank rounds in our magazines; in addition to our pistols I carried an HK53 and Tony had an MP5K, and we each carried a stun grenade.

We swept into a narrow courtyard formed by a group of four two-storey buildings, and Sid executed an immaculate handbrake turn so that we came to rest facing the exit. Before the car had settled to a halt Tony and I were out of the doors and taking up defensive fire positions either side of the target building. The only person visible was Brian from the photographic centre, who was videoing us from a corner of the courtyard. Suddenly, from inside the house where the OP team had been operating, there came the earsplitting crash of an explosion and a great gush of orange flame and smoke billowed out of the upstairs windows. It was followed by an unearthly high-pitched screaming.

'Sid, bring the medpack and stretcher while we go and see what the damage is!' I yelled. Tony sprang up the short flight of steps under the porch and kicked in the front door. We burst into each room downstairs, covering each other left and right, then raced up the stairs. Thick acrid smoke was swirling around the landing as Tony kicked in the left-hand door and I did the same to the right.

'Yeeuuch!' slipped out involuntarily. On the floor in front of me a wounded operator was lying on his back, his right calf a bloody pulp, foot missing altogether. A steady rhythmic fountain of blood was pumping three feet into the air from the broken and mangled stump just below his knee. 'Tony,' I shouted, 'get the medpack, quick!'

Tony grinned at me and nipped back down the stairs. The casualty was groaning loudly as I ripped open the only shell dressing I had and pressed it hard down on the source of the spurting blood. Again this was real blood, warm and sticky with that very distinctive salty smell. I started to check him over for other damage, the priorities skipping through my mind – Breathing, Bleeding, Breaks and Burns. His cotton jacket was stained with blood around his midriff, and when I pressed it lightly he yelled and writhed and more blood welled up from underneath. Carefully unzipping the jacket, I was greeted by the sight of masses of raw intestines, glistening with bright red arterial blood. I quickly zipped it up again. I knew the guts didn't belong to him, but I wasn't keen on the idea of having to handle the still-warm contents of a sheep!

I suddenly became aware of a commotion outside, down by the car. I leapt to the window to see that a crowd of about fifteen people had appeared and were chucking stones and bottles at Sid and Tony, who were threatening them with their weapons, to little effect. The mob was closing in on them, so they quickly grabbed all the sensitive kit they could find in the car and legged it to the house, lobbing a stun grenade each into the crowd, then barricaded the front door behind them.

Tony ran upstairs with the medpack, and we were preparing to insert a drip when Mick appeared and called a halt to the exercise.

A few minutes later we watched humbly while Brian reran our exploits on the video and Mick gave us a ruthless critique of our handling of the situation.

'What a bunch of nancies!' he began. 'Never let a crowd get the better of you like that! If they don't back away from the stun grenades and you're certain they'll rip you apart if they get you, have the confidence to shoot one of the fuckers, no messing! You'll be within your rights so long as your life is in danger. You give them a verbal warning, then point out a ringleader and say you'll shoot him if they don't back off. If they still advance, shoot your man dead and point out another one. That should do the trick and they'll high-tail it. If they don't, it's their lookout. OK?'

It had been a well-staged exercise. I had the impression that the crowd of youths – actually a motley crew of cooks, bottle-washers and mechanics from the camp – rather relished this opportunity to give us a bit of stick. The limbless 'casualty' had simply stuck his lower leg through a hole in the floorboards and attached a bit of grisly smashed-up bone and flesh to his knee, and the contents of a concealed bag of blood were released by a little pump he squeezed in his palm. The effect had been disturbingly realistic!

Our next exercise taught us methods of countering an illegal vehicle checkpoint (or VCP). Groups of heavily armed terrorists, sometimes a dozen strong, set these up in areas where they command the support of the local community, largely as a show of strength. They stop and question the occupants of any vehicle, hoping to catch an off-duty RUC reservist or Ulster Defence Regiment soldier, whom they would murder. Since we would be operating individually in high-risk areas, it was important that we were able to shoot our way out of an illegal VCP. Inevitably we would be heavily outgunned in such a situation, so the emphasis lay on taking the initiative and getting one's retaliation in first – before withdrawing at high speed! We ought always to have the advantage of surprise on our side, thanks to the combination of our acting skills and our ability to draw a concealed weapon in the blink of an eye.

When the time came for me to practise this, Ernie briefed me to drive casually around a track on the training area, and to react appropriately to anything that might happen. As I rounded a bend in a small wood, I saw the road about forty metres ahead partially blocked by a car and a group of hooded men wearing combat jackets and carrying Armalite assault rifles. Standing in the middle of the road, a terrorist was flagging me down. I began to slow, sending a contact report over the radio and surreptitiously undoing my seat belt. I put my hand on the butt of the car pistol, which I had put in the map pocket by my right knee, and slipped the safety catch off. As I cruised to a halt, I could see in my mirrors that other men were now encircling the car and I had half a dozen rifles pointing directly at me. I smiled broadly at the terrorist, who was now at my right elbow, and casually slipped the car into first gear, holding the clutch in. The muzzle of his Armalite was resting on the door frame, aimed at my throat. My smile faded a little – even blank rounds at that range could do me an injury.

He began to speak. Quick as a flash, I whipped the pistol up, but the tip of its barrel snagged for a split second on the lip of the window. At the same time I floored the accelerator and stepped off the clutch. In an instant the terrorist squeezed the trigger and let off a long burst of blanks into the back of the car, which, after a momentary leap, stalled humiliatingly. Fuck – and I hadn't even fired a shot!

'OK, James,' said Sandy, lifting his balaclava, 'I think it's safe to say we got you that time. Step out of the car and I'll show you where you went wrong.'

We swapped places. 'First thing,' Sandy said, 'always keep your car pistol to hand. When I'm driving I usually put it under my right thigh, butt outwards. That way you don't have to bend even slightly to reach it, which saves you time.

'Secondly, as you approach, assess your situation and your options thoroughly. You were obviously going to scream away forwards just now. But look how we've placed the car across the road. There's just enough of a gap to squeeze past it, but you'd be right on the edge of that ditch – and if you're accelerating like the clappers you could well end up in it. No, in this situation you'd do better to go backwards and do a J-turn. The acceleration in reverse is much greater than in first gear, and it's perhaps a less expected manoeuvre – OK?'

'Third, if you decide to open fire – and in this instance you'd have had no option – fire straight through the door panel. Don't bring your weapon into view. Remember, until you react they don't know you're anything other than a local farm labourer going home for his lunch. The shock effect of rounds punching straight out of the bodywork will give you a great advantage.

'And finally, why not use your stun grenades? I grant that they're a bit awkward to handle loose like this – but over the water you'll have a much better system for delivering them, at the press of a button. Right, I'll show you how it can all come together. You just play my part when I drive up.'

He reversed away out of sight and then reappeared at a normal speed. I watched him carefully for any sign of his preparations, but saw nothing out of the ordinary. I flagged him down, covering him with the Armalite, and he smiled at me as he wound the window down. The car was about to halt when I took a step forward, my finger on the rifle's trigger. Suddenly a double report sounded from inside the car, the second shot almost drowned by the squeal of tyres and the shriek of the engine as Sandy flung it into reverse. In the same instant a black object rolled out of the window and fell to the ground at my feet, where it fizzed for maybe a second before exploding into a series of deafening blasts and flashes. Meanwhile Sandy was roaring backwards down the track, and spun himself into a neat J-turn before accelerating away towards the bend. I realised that I hadn't even fired a round at him, so intent was I on watching how to do it.

We were now expert at handling and thoroughly familiar with our Close Quarter Battle weapons – the pistols and submachine guns – so the final element we had to master was the use of the HK53 and G3K. For this we spent several days on a nearby army field firing range. Here we could take our cars through countryside that resembled the wilder rural parts of Ulster, and practise our anti-ambush drills using the heavy weapons to engage targets over distances of up to 300 metres. The instructors vied with one another to produce the most spectacular explosions to trigger the ambushes. Two pounds of plastic explosive taped to the back of a five-litre plastic can of petrol creates a marvellous rolling ball of orange flame. It is of course wise to keep the car windows up when driving through such a phenomenon; even then one can feel the heat from the fireball as it briefly envelops the car. Wearing ordinary army combat uniform we rehearsed conventional military patrol techniques, so that in rural areas we could patrol into a target area if need be without appearing to be anything other than local green army troops.

After a weekend's leave, we drew our personal weapons and gathered again in the lecture theatre to be briefed on the final exercise of the course. The chief instructor confirmed that, so long as we didn't mess anything up over the next seven days, we would be dispatched over the water to join our respective detachments – as they are known – of the unit.

The final exercise passed in a whirl of activity and sleepless nights, as we pulled together every element of the different skills we had learned over the last five months. For realism we moved to a forward base on the edge of a major conurbation. Here, we teamed up with local Special Branch officers to conduct a series of operations around a realistic scenario, taking us into some of the most deprived housing estates in Britain, where street crime and drug dealing are rife. It was excellent training, and it certainly set the seal on our ability to operate undercover. Had we been directing our talents against the drug dealers in the vicinity, we would have made short work of them. In fact their presence added considerably to the authenticity of our operations – local criminals are by necessity constantly on the lookout for undercover police. When we regularly escaped their notice it added to our confidence in the training.

It was the first time that we had mingled for any prolonged period with the general public, and already it was second nature to ensure that one's weapons and equipment were adequately concealed at all times, yet available for instant use. Since this was technically a military exercise, albeit conducted in civilian dress, we still carried blank ammunition in our weapons – unlike the drug dealers, I couldn't help thinking! However, we were still mindful of our normal duties as ordinary citizens. Once, when Tony and I were involved in a follow, we broke off to administer first aid when an old man collapsed with a heart attack outside a shop, staying with him until an ambulance arrived.

The exercise ended in a frantic sequence of CTRs, OPs and surveillance tasks, climaxing in the dramatic interception of our targets on a busy road by a fleet of uniformed police cars and motorcycles.

Our mission at last successfully accomplished, we packed up

our temporary accommodation and set out for the long drive back to camp, before breaking up for a weekend's leave.

Our last week in camp was devoted mainly to administration and briefings on the locations we would deploy to in Ireland. Ernie took the opportunity to cast a critical eye over our now very substantial wardrobes of second-hand clothes. As he examined my selection I showed him the pockets and slits that I'd sewn into the lining of each garment to accommodate the different bits of equipment that we needed to be able to carry concealed from view.

My hair had long since been trimmed into a casual and unmilitary style, and I was used to changing my parting or back-brushing it quickly in order to alter my appearance from time to time. I also prided myself on a rather good variable gait. Everybody has a visual signature when they are observed walking from a distance; even without being conscious of it we are all surprisingly adept at spotting individuals in a crowd by their unique motion as they walk. By subtly changing my point of balance when walking I could significantly alter both my silhouette and my gait. This, combined with a reversible casual jacket, a rough change of hairstyle and the addition of a pair of spectacles, was an excellent way to increase the amount of time I could spend within sight of a target.

We were then briefed in detail about the unit – 14 Intelligence Company – and about the police and army headquarters that tasked the separate detachments, which were responsible for operations in different areas of the province.

'Tom, Carl, James, Will and Tony,' said the chief instructor, 'you're going to South Detachment. Alan will brief you about South Det after tea.' I was very sorry to learn that Kate was going to another area. We'd grown quite close over the months and I very much admired and respected her guts and determination, and her self-deprecating sense of humour.

Alan, who had been an operator in South Det for many years, took us aside and spoke to us for a couple of hours about the different areas that we would work in. He explained that large tracts of the province were so trouble-free that the local police and Ulster Defence Regiment troops did not require our assistance. He added that the RUC's own equivalent of 14 Company – known as E4A – also operated in our area, but although they were good enough at covert operations, they were nothing like as effective as us, and did not undertake missions in the hardest republican areas.

Standing in front of a large map of the province, he gave us thumbnail sketches of the communities we would be penetrating. He spoke of places like Cookstown, Pomeroy, Dungannon, Cappagh, Armagh, Omagh, Newry, Crossmaglen, Bessbrook, Enniskillen – weaving into his talk stories of successful operations and Det characters.

The final aspect of our training was to perfect our Irish accents. To operate effectively we had to be able to hold our own in everyday conversations in the different areas that we would deploy to, and to achieve this we had been voice-coached regularly by a charming retired Irish actor and his wife. They played us tapes of the different regional accents, from the relatively soft lilt of South Armagh, with its galloping delivery, to the harsher, slightly clipped, but more measured tones of North Belfast. Now they led us in conversation classes, taking the opportunity to instruct us in certain cultural aspects of Irish life.

On the last night before we set out for a week's leave we had our end-of-course party, of which I can remember little except how awful I felt the next morning. It must have been something I ate.

The next seven days, spent with Jennifer touring Scotland, were blissful but all too short – and at 6 p.m. on the following Monday we were back at camp, climbing into the coach to take us to an RAF base. There we were driven to a corner of the airfield and, in scenes reminiscent of *Casablanca,* our small group strolled across the misty and rainswept tarmac to a waiting Andover, a small, twin-engined propellor-driven aircraft.

Sitting in the cramped and dim interior waiting for take-off, I was conscious of the drama of the scene. Young bodies, eyes and fingers betraying their nervousness, leaving the mainland by aircraft at night. I thought of the Special Operations Executive agents during the last war, volunteering to parachute into occupied Europe to help the resistance, but realised the comparison was inappropriate. We weren't in their league. They had been astonishingly brave; we were simply relatively well-paid and thoroughly trained, looking for some excitement. Watching the lights on the ground slide beneath us I reflected again how far I had come in the last six months. I'd never been fitter or more ready for a new challenge, and although I felt nervous with anticipation I was looking forward to doing the job for real for a change.

I dozed off, wrapped in the warm throb of the engines.

Chapter Five

After a bumpy hour and a half in the air, we descended into RAF Aldergrove, on the shores of Lough Neagh, and taxied to a quiet corner. Transit vans stood waiting to transport us to our respective detachments.

We said hurried goodbyes to each other in the driving rain before dispersing to our vehicles. A thickset dark-haired chap, aged about thirty, introduced himself as Phil, the ops officer of South Det, and handed around a bag of pistols and an HK53 for our protection during the drive to our base location. We chucked our luggage into the back of the van, climbed aboard, and within minutes were rattling through the darkened countryside.

If we had been driven on to the set of a James Bond movie we wouldn't have been more surprised than we were at the sight that greeted us when at last we clambered stiffly out of the back of the van at our destination. We had driven into the heart of a large warehouse-like structure on an industrial estate which housed a self-contained village of Portakabins, set out in neat rows. Along one side were two parallel sets of two-storey blocks, with some low brick buildings behind them. Ranged along the other side were rows of ordinary civilian vehicles – motorbikes, vans, saloons, hatchbacks, estates and trucks. As we unloaded our kit I saw that the place was alive with activity. Brightly lit workshops set back against the walls on each side echoed to the sound of pop music as scruffy technicians and mechanics worked under cars held aloft on hydraulic ramps. A thirty-metre pipe range (thirty metres of two-foot-diameter concrete drainage pipe set horizontally, abutting brick and sand embrasures, used to test-fire rifles in a restricted space) was reverberating to the thump of 7.62mm rounds as someone test-fired their weapon. Operators in various states of dress moved purposefully to and fro between the blocks, some carrying grips and holdalls which obviously contained weapons. High above, the roof was strung with rows of striplights, alternating with long horizontal windows, which between them provided an unchanging artificial environment, pretty well sealed from the outside world. Soon we would learn that and exit from the camp involved a complex ritual of passing through a series of gates, barriers and compounds, until at last one emerged into a network of isolated side roads.

'OK, guys, follow me and I'll show you to your bashas. We've got a couple of jobs running tonight but they won't involve you,' Phil said. As we walked he pointed out various landmarks. 'That's the cookhouse and dining room. Breakfast, lunch and supper are at the usual times, but there's always a duty cook on, so if you ever want any nosh, whatever time of day, just ask him. That's what he's there for.

'That brick building over there's our own little Killing Room, so you can keep up to date with your drills. We'll show you that tomorrow. You can hear the pipe range over there. Test-fire your longs at least once a week. That door leads to the armoury. Again, there's a duty armourer on all the time. You'll be issued with the standard weapons, but if you want anything rinky-dink for a special purpose come and ask me, all right?'

We were now passing through rows of Portakabins, each bearing a name-plate by the door – Pete, Gary, Suzy, Chris and so on. 'Security here is very tight. To keep it that way we fly the maintenance contractors in from the mainland so there's no chance of a leak to the locals. As you'll see tomorrow, from the outside none of this is visible. Right, James, this one is yours. Unpack your kit and be in the briefing room – on the top floor over there – in half an hour.'

This was more like it, I thought to myself as I wandered from room to room surveying my Portakabin. It was bright and clean and had a good-sized bedroom with a dressing room off to one side, a comfortable sitting room about ten feet square with bookshelves and standard army furniture, a little kitchen and a loo and bath with a built-in shower. On the wall somewhere in each room was an intercom box, with buttons for calling the ops room and other bashas. How civilised!

'The first priority is to get your map books made up so you can begin your familiarisation programme,' Phil began once we had all gathered in the briefing room. I groaned inwardly. Having stuck my head around the ops room door on my way here, I'd seen from the wall maps just how big the area was that we'd have to learn. He handed us each a heavy roll of Ordnance Survey maps and packets of coloured stickers. 'It shouldn't take you more than a couple of days to knock them up. For God's sake, make sure they're accurate and exactly match the one in the ops room.'

He introduced us to Colin, an experienced operator who had a warm sense of humour. He had joined 14 Company as a junior NCO many years previously, and was in charge of our induction training (which would last about three weeks). Until we had learned the ground and proved ourselves to the rest of the operators in the detachment we would not be considered available for operations. Colin was full of advice about which bits of kit to draw from the stores and how to conduct ourselves within the unit. In particular he stressed that operators should not flash their weapons or other specialised kit around inside our compound more than was absolutely necessary, because the Det didn't want to create a feeling of 'them and us' between operators and support staff, who were posted in from the regular army. So our policy was to avoid flaunting our skills and weapons openly in front of them. Obviously we could have strutted about, festooned with kit and weapons like Rambos, but this was not our style. We were on first-name terms with all the support staff, and the atmosphere in the unit was extremely friendly and relaxed.

In the morning we drew our stores, weapons and ammunition from the armoury and went across to the pipe range to zero the sights on our G3Ks and HK53s. The next stop was the Killing Room, where we check-fired our MP5Ks, personal pistols and car pistols. This room, which was about thirty feet square and draped in the usual thick rubber sheeting, also featured an excellent cine system, which projected on to the wall a variety of scenarios, such as a busy street scene, in which at some point gunmen invariably appeared. When a target was engaged, the sound of the report from the weapon would cause the film to freeze, enabling one to check the accuracy of the strike-marks on the projected figure.

Each day Colin arranged for us to drive around different areas in the company of experienced operators, who pointed out the homes and haunts of a score of terrorist suspects and related the tales of previous operations in that area. As we travelled across the length and breadth of the province we began to learn the spot codes and town plans, and at the same time got to know the other members of the detachment. Individually quite different, they all shared the same basic characteristics – friendly, extremely professional, self-confident, and not at all showy or brash or aggressive. You wouldn't pick them out of a crowded room as being anything other than office workers, farm labourers or bus conductors.

This easy ability to appear ordinary was our greatest strength. Some of the areas, particularly the border hamlets, were so aware of potential security force surveillance that we would not drive through two up (with two people in one car) unless one of them was a girl. One person alone, or one man and a woman, attract much less interest than two men together. It's usually a bit of a cliché to say that everyone knows everyone else's business in a small community, but in the border areas of Ulster it is quite literally true. In addition to terrorist activity there is widespread smuggling across the border, which is effectively unpoliced. Two men in a car, unless they are recognised, stand out as potential police or army. Again, this brought home to us all the value of female operators.

Like cabbies learning the knowledge, we memorised routes from point to point and visited all the major landmarks, so that eventually we could drive without constant reference to our bulky map books.

Phil also allocated cars to us, explaining that if ever we felt that we had been pinged or compromised – meaning identified by locals as possible security force personnel – in our vehicle while on a job, we could order a different make or model without difficulty. My first car was a scratched and grimy two-year-old Ford Fiesta. I admit that initially I was sceptical that I would be able to keep up with a follow. However, it soon became apparent that even a 1300cc engine, when driven without regard for the bearings or gearbox, can out-accelerate most conventionally driven vehicles, and ultimately I was delighted with its performance. On operations our cars were our lifelines, and each was heavily modified to satisfy the idiosyncrasies of the individual operator. I supervised the fitting out of mine with great care.

Almost all our cars carried some covert armour. For our benefit Phil described to us the merits of different arrays of armour, and I opted for plates of Kevlar in the back and base of the driving seat, inside the passenger door, and a small plate beside me in the driver's door, remembering to note its precise position so that I could still fire my car pistol through the door panel in front of the plate if I had to. Kevlar is an incredibly strong material but it is also quite heavy, so the mechanics then had to adjust my suspension to take account of the car's new weight distribution. This was crucial, because surveillance driving demands very hard cornering and any inherent instability in the vehicle would be dangerous.

Next, the vehicle-borne radio was buried deep inside the car, with a control box for switching frequency and a port for loading the secure-speech codes. These were remoted to a hidden compartment within easy reach from my driving position. Every day a new security code (or 'fill') had to be entered electronically into the car sets – an operation we called 'squirting the fill'. A team of technicians spent many hours ensuring that my tiny covert earpiece would be able to pick up transmissions from the car's radio. Miniature microphones were then buried around the interior, so that one could talk quietly anywhere within the vehicle and still be heard over the net. Endless test drives were required to tweak the radio setup and remove distortion and road noise. Finally, I experimented to find two sites for the tiny spring-loaded radio transmit switches (known as pressels), and opted for one on the floor by my left foot and one in place of the horn control. The foot pressel was to cater for the situation of being held up at gunpoint and forced to keep my hands on the wheel or above my head. All I would have to do would be to depress the button with my foot and let the ops room listen in to the situation as it unfolded. The other transmit button was operated by pressing the end of the left-hand indicator lever with the tip of my fingers. So that I could still use the horn if necessary, I had it moved to a new button hidden under the steering wheel. (Remoting the transmit button to the horn control like this worked extremely well throughout my tour except on one memorable occasion. Late one night, during a surveillance task, I was sitting in my car in a quiet suburban street with a trigger on the target's vehicle. Everything was running smoothly until the target climbed into his car and began to manoeuvre. I pressed the tip of my horn control to send a 'standby, standby', and almost fainted with shock when, instead of hearing the click over the net as I depressed the button, there sounded a loud and prolonged blast from a car horn! In fact it came from the car parked immediately behind me, coincidentally signalling to someone in a house across the street, but for the next couple of days I found I had to steel myself to use the horn pressel.)

We were also introduced to a couple of other subtleties that I wouldn't have thought of myself. Driving as a drop-off vehicle at night in a rural area, perhaps dropping a team in the vicinity of a target, it is important not to stand on the brakes at the actual drop-off point, because the extra illumination given out by the brake lights is visible for a great distance on a dark night, and even further if it's slightly misty. So we fitted a brake light cut-out switch and again hid it well out of sight but within easy reach. There was an advantage in being able to cut the engine at will, perhaps to counter a hijack attempt, and also in being able to set off the hazard warning lights from different positions within the vehicle.

Next we installed a sophisticated car alarm system – important because we would frequently have to park up in rough areas and go foxtrot for a while. Again we located hidden trips around the interior so that the alarm could be set off independently if required.

Then it was time to fit the various camera positions. I mounted several camera brackets covertly around the vehicle, so that I could take photos in all directions while driving along, and ran the shutter release cables so that they emerged under the steering wheel. Thus at the press of a button I could take a stream of photos of subjects to the left, right, in front or behind my course, perfect if I wanted to photograph someone walking along a pavement. Although it still looked completely normal, the various recesses under the dashboard of my little Fiesta were now bristling with extra buttons and switches, and it took a lot of practice to get used to their different functions. We always ensured that there was no visible trace or sign of any car-borne technical rig by asking a fellow operator to examine the car as closely as he liked from the outside. If he could tell where any kit was covertly located, that rig would be resited, until it passed the test. This level of perfectionism naturally and understandably sometimes irritated the technicians, who actually had to do the work, but they recognised that operators' lives might depend upon such attention to detail.

Next, Colin introduced us to the concept of the flashbang box.

This, as Sandy had promised all those weeks ago, was a device incorporated into the chassis of each car which permitted the instantaneous and simultaneous delivery of four stun grenades to the front, sides and rear of the vehicle. The individual grenades were propelled outwards by a small explosive charge in the centre of the cluster, and the whole thing was contained within a thin-sided metal box, which was sprayed to match the underside of the vehicle, making it invisible from a casual inspection. Colin clearly enjoyed showing us, using his own car, how to arm and fire the thing. Flicking a switch under the dashboard armed the firing circuit, and then a heavy footswitch to the left of the clutch, like the type that is sometimes fitted to change headlights from dip to full beam, actually fired the device.

'The point of this layout, guys, is that if you have to use the flashbang you can keep both hands in full view on the wheel while your foot presses the tit. It's a really good effect – listen!' He flicked a switch on the dash, which lit a small LED showing that the circuit was armed. Then, as he grinned up at us, a loud click from inside the footwell was instantly drowned by a shattering, deafening roar as the charge concealed under the car blew the stun grenades in every direction. The rippling crackle of the thirty-two subsequent flashes and bangs created a thick pall of white smoke which took an age to disperse inside our micro-climate. We were impressed.

'As you can see, you wouldn't want this to go off by mistake – so it's a good idea not to arm the circuit unless you really think you're going to have to use it.' He described the last occasion a flashbang had been used in earnest. An operator became stuck behind a broken-down bus in a narrow street in a small republican town, right outside the local Sinn Fein office, just as a party of youths poured out of the main entrance. For some reason one of them became suspicious, tapped on his window and tried to open the driver's door, which was locked. Sensing the operator's unease, and presumably guessing that he was a member of the security forces, two of the youths ran off and reappeared seconds later with a shovel from an adjacent building site. One of them swung the shovel hard at the windscreen, cracking it, and as he was about to strike again, the operator, who was still firmly stuck in the traffic behind the bus, decided that enough was enough and fired his flashbang, scattering the crowd. He then drove slowly away over the pavement and around the bus. If he hadn't had the option of using the device, he would have had little choice but to draw his pistol, seriously escalating the confrontation. I watched with interest while my box was fitted and then mentally rehearsed the sequence for firing it.

Once all these modifications had been made it was necessary to check over and thoroughly test the car's electrics, since the amount of tinkering we had been doing could affect the normal running of the electrical systems.

The Det was a hive of activity around us as we learnt the ropes as fast as we possibly could. We were very keen to join in on real operations, but accepted that first we had to learn not only the local geography but also a few other skills. So, in between spells of driving around the countryside, we were taught some technical refinements, including how to bug or disable the weapons that we would from time to time locate. It's easy enough to prevent a weapon from functioning properly, but not so easy to do it so that only a master armourer can tell why. Similarly, anyone can hide a transmitter in a weapon, but it takes considerable skill, not to say nerve, to make it indetectable. Highly sophisticated equipment would guide us on to the different bugs, enabling us to keep control of the situation. All the kit we were using here was genuinely state-of-the-art, and it transpired that the equipment that we had trained with – and marvelled at – on the mainland was far from new. With the speed of technical development so rapid, about every other month we would receive some new and more effective variant of our standard kit to add to our technical armoury.

Another skill we had to master was a rather different use for the helicopter. We had three of them on call to us at all times, specially equipped with superb sighting systems that had actually been developed for controlling air-to-ground anti-tank missiles. This type of gunsight culminated in a flexible periscope mounted just at the co-pilot's eye level, and the direction of view of the entire sight was controlled by a small joystick, operated by the thumb. So powerful was the sight that, on maximum magnification at a height of 8,000 feet and a horizontal distance of eight kilometres, it was possible to watch the front door of an individual house. The enormous advantage from our point of view was the fact that at that height and distance a hovering helicopter is inaudible and invisible to the naked eye from the ground. In fact, even if the heli was spotted with binoculars from the ground, it wouldn't have been possible to tell in which direction the sight was looking, since it could rotate almost 360 degrees and the heli always hovered nose into the wind, no matter which way it was blowing.

This specialised role for the heli gave us so great an advantage when used skilfully during surveillance operations, that it was imperative that every operator should become expert at its use. Consequently we spent many hours, feeling cold, airsick and eye-strained, sitting in the co-pilot's seat, eye glued to the sight, thumb on the joystick. All the pilot had to do was to maintain a reasonably steady hover without drifting about too much, which though it may have been seriously boring for him was not too demanding. The operator, however, had to watch the target like a hawk and, supposing it was a vehicle, trigger it away the instant it went mobile, calling its movements over the radio net. It's not hard to imagine how difficult it is to be certain exactly where the target is and in which direction it is heading – a brief glance at the mapbook on one's lap and one risks being unable to find the moving target again in the sight.

Having mastered and been thoroughly tested individually during the day, we went on to try our hand at night. Strangely enough, it is almost more effective in the dark because the resolution of car headlights and house lights seems greater, although one soon experiences a feeling of peculiar detachment, trapped in a tiny, vibrating perspex bubble. The girls always complained that the heavy flying helmets ruined their hair!

The only weather condition that could defeat this superb gunsight was heavy rain or snow, yet even as I was leaving the unit the following year it was due to be replaced with a stronger version, equipped additionally with a thermal imager that could not only see as well at night as in day, but also through cloud and rain.

Another area of training that had only been touched on to date concerned lock-picking and certain other advanced methods of entry. It had always been apparent to us that we would need to be able to enter premises through locked doors, and it seemed pretty unlikely that we would be able to use subterfuge every time to obtain a copy of the key. In one of the unit workshops Jake, an avuncular, highly respected and extremely experienced operator with many tours behind him, demonstrated how it was done. First, though, he explained in his West Country accent that officers were never trained in lock-picking, because in the nature of their promotion structure they were unlikely ever to do more than one tour as an operator, and so this rather sensitive skill would certainly be wasted. (Few officers make a career out of service with Special Forces units, simply because there are not enough senior posts available. 22 SAS Regiment is commanded by a Lieutenant Colonel, as is 14 Company. Above them is one Brigadier, commanding the Group of Special Forces. So officers tend to switch backwards and forwards between ordinary army command or staff appointments.) By contrast, other ranks could return to the detachments time and again, perhaps alternating with training jobs on the mainland.

The walls of Jake's workshop were festooned with locks, padlocks and key blanks. There was every imaginable tool and a wonderful array of electronic gadgetry to assist him with every conceivable type of lock, bolt and alarm. He showed us how to reconstruct a key from an impression in a pad, how to pick a Yale-type barrel lock, and how to manipulate a set of skeleton keys to open a multi-levered Chubb mortice lock. We learnt that there really is no such thing as an entry-proof building, and were introduced to a dazzling array of new techniques to overcome even the most sophisticated security systems.

Most surprising of all was Jake's ability to open a lock that he'd never set eyes on before, simply by filing a key there and then from a selection of blanks. The trick to this was to use a blank made out of a particular soft alloy, then each time he tried it in the lock the internal levers would leave a tiny indentation on the soft metal. Knowing the basic internal format of all locks, all he had to do was repeat this until he had filed down between the relevant indentations, and hey presto, the lock would eventually tumble. Although this was a time-consuming approach, he assured us that he had used it many times on operations. It was fascinating to watch Jake work. He insisted that there was no conventional lock he could not crack, no burglar alarm he could not disable. There were a number of operators in each detachment who were fully trained lock-picks, and Carl volunteered to attend the next training course.

Our relations with the Home Office and MI5 had never been formally discussed during our training on the mainland, but now we were fully briefed by the Det commander – a tall, fair-haired, twenty-eight-year-old captain named Tim – about the different areas of responsibility. We were introduced to our affable MI5 liaison officer, known to us as Jim to his face, and 'Bushmills' to his back. He was a jovial, middle-aged character with a fondness for the renowned Irish whiskey, which itself seemed almost a prerequisite for warm relations with Special Branch.

As in mainland Britain, MI5 in Northern Ireland relies on the police, and in particular Special Branch, to provide its executive powers. RUC Special Branch is charged directly with the fight against all forms of terrorism and is heavily assisted by both MI5 and army intelligence. MI5 still runs its own agents and informers, presumably a legacy from earlier days, and handles the bugging of target premises, for which SB hasn't the resources or expertise. Our role, in addition to classic surveillance in the hard areas that E4A (the RUC's own elite undercover force) felt unsafe to operate in, was to gather the information required by MI5 officers in the planning of their eavesdropping activities, and to lead the technicians on to the target premises. The Home Office was responsible for securing the appropriate entry warrants. The target locations were invariably exceedingly difficult and dangerous places to enter.

Tim stressed to us that, since we were now highly trained in covert surveillance and would be in daily view of known players, it was not our job to initiate ambushes on armed terrorists. He explained that anyone who opens fire in Northern Ireland is likely to have to appear in relatively open court and such public exposure would inevitably compromise a covert operator's future usefulness. We learned that Special Branch or MI5 would provide the raw intelligence from a human or electronic source, which we would then exploit either to gather evidence or to set up an arrest by uniformed police.

A few years previously the RUC had set up specially trained uniformed police squads to support covert operations carried out by E4A and 14 Company. They were known as Headquarters Mobile Support Units (or HMSUs), and travelled in unmarked but fully armoured civilian cars, with thick bulletproof windows. Although they were in uniform they toted some of the special weapons that we did, rather than the lighter Rugers that standard RUC policemen carried. They were an extremely impressive bunch, and displayed no bigotry or favour to either community. They were out to arrest murderers, and that was all. Whenever we used HMSUs in support of an operation we would, time permitting, send an operator in one of their cars to ease communications, since he could hear both radio nets at the same time.

If it was impossible to create an opportunity for an HMSU arrest, perhaps because the information received was too vague or didn't allow sufficient time, the SAS troop would be tasked to lay an ambush, the primary mission of which would be to arrest the terrorists. If armed terrorists do not surrender when challenged they are shot dead.

Each evening, operations permitting, the whole detachment would gather for 'prayers', chaired jointly by the Det commander and the ops officer, during which the forthcoming jobs were discussed and individual tasks allotted. The intensity of operations was surprising: it was an unusual evening if there was no operation going down somewhere in our area.

Soon, we trainees had completed our induction period and, after successfully passing a stiff practical test in a hard area, we hosted an extended celebration in the bar, coinciding as it did with a night of little operational activity. Our arrival had brought the Det up to full strength – it already had its full complement of girls, now that Sally, the instructor from the training course, had rejoined the Det. Many of the more experienced operators, male and female, alternated between serving in the province with a detachment and instructing at the training camp back on the mainland, thus ensuring continuity of training standards. We caroused late into the night, happy to have finally passed every hurdle. The sky was just starting to bruise into a peaceful sunrise as I stumbled back to my basha . . .

In my fuddled state I dreamt I was sitting in the cab of a helicopter which was beginning to rotate faster and faster underneath the whirring blades. With mounting certainty I became aware that I was going to be sick. I glanced at the pilot, who for some reason wasn't wearing his flying helmet. He opened his mouth and let out a very loud, piercing 'BEEP!'

Fuck. Groggily I opened my eyes. 'BEEP!' again went the intercom on the wall above my beer-infused head. I reached up and pressed the button, noticing the time on my wrist: 11.15 a.m.

'Yup?' I croaked.

'Morning, camper!' It was the duty signaller calling from the ops room. 'There's a big job on. All operators to the briefing room sharpish.' I snapped awake. What a way to start my first ever real operation, I thought. I staggered to the bathroom where I leant against the wall under a lukewarm shower, feeling ghastly.

Ten minutes later I joined the throng in the briefing room. Our resident Intelligence Corps staff sergeant, an amiable chap called Pete, who had an encyclopaedic knowledge of our patch, was pinning enormous aerial photos and map sections to the board at the front of the room. Tim, Phil and Jake were deep in conversation, peering at an OS map, and after a couple of minutes they broke up and Tim took the rostrum while Phil began to scribble away in his notebook behind him.

'Morning all. I hope we didn't wake anyone,' Tim grinned. 'We've just had Special Branch on with a hot tip from PIRA they want us to investigate. All they know is that someone is driving down from Belfast tomorrow to pick up some explosives from this farm here – they don't know who, what time, or what the kit is. They believe that the kit is stored beside some noisy machinery.

'OK, so we haven't got much to go on, but it should be enough. We're going to put an OP team on to the farm right away, with a car team supported by a heli on standby to take and identify any vehicle that leaves. Then tonight the OP team will conduct a CTR of the farm to try to locate and photograph the kit, returning to their OP position before first light. Tomorrow, if the baddies come for the kit, they'll trigger them away for the team and we'll steer them into an HMSU vehicle check point, so that it looks like a chance find and arrest in the course of a routine VCP. Phil, would you run through the jobs, please?'

The ops officer reeled off a string of names and tasks. 'Car team, make your way out there as soon as possible, on target no later than 13.30, please. First car on the scene do a drive past, then everyone scatter and stake out the options pretty loosely. The heli will hold the trigger until the OP team's on the ground. Anyone know this village well?' he asked.

'Yes,' said Colin. 'It featured once or twice in the early eighties. There are a lot of republican sympathisers, and it's technically a pretty hard area. If I recall correctly, that road along the valley is pretty exposed and we're going to stand out if we have too many cars doing passes on arrival. I suggest that the rest of the team skirts well round to the north and south, leaving that route for the first car and the OP drop-off only.'

'OK, good idea. Finally, SB say this information has come from an unexpected source – they can't tell whether this is a lucky strike or PIRA is trying to set us up for an ambush, so be careful.'

This was the real risk that we knew we ran every time we responded to 'information received'. It had been known for some time that the IRA were very keen to kill, or worse still capture, an operator. They had good reason – 14 Company operators were responsible for many of the IRA's failures – but one incident in particular had been a very public humiliation for the terrorists. The story had been recounted to us during our training, to highlight the real dangers that we would be exposed to whenever we operated alone, and to give us an opportunity to consider our actions in case a similar incident arose.

Another detachment had been asked by Special Branch to undertake a fairly routine assignment in one of the toughest areas of Londonderry. A young operator, an officer, set out by himself to conduct a casual reconnaissance of the area, which he did by driving into the vicinity, parking up and then strolling past the target, carefully noting the details that would be crucial in formulating the operational plan. As he drove through the estate which housed the target he had passed a group of IRA dickers – nothing unusual in that, but what was to prove fatal on this occasion was that they possessed a list of vehicle registration numbers that had been noted entering the approach roads to several security force bases in the city over the last few days. His car was on the list.

Although to all intents and purposes the operator looked like a local Catholic going about his business rather than an undercover soldier, the fact that the number-plate of his battered Opel Ascona appeared on the dickers' list was sufficient for them to warn the local IRA commander about his presence. Within minutes of the operator's arrival in the target area an IRA active service unit was collecting its weapons together for a little show of strength. Even if they turned out to be mistaken about the stranger's identity, there was no harm in letting the local population know who controlled the streets in that part of town. It would serve as a useful reminder of the effectiveness of the IRA as a local vigilante force, always ready to spring into action in defence of the republican community.

By the time the operator had completed his walkpast and climbed back into his car to begin the return journey to base, the terrorist gang was already hijacking a passing Ford Escort. They dragged the driver out and bundled in, two in the front, two in the back. Armed with three assault rifles and a pistol, they set out to locate the Opel. It didn't take them long.

The operator noticed the car coming up behind, but was happy to give it the benefit of the doubt. He was well armed and had little reason to suppose that his cover had been compromised. If the locals were being more cautious than usual today, he would continue to act normally and hope that he passed their appraisal. An operator's role is to remain covert as long as possible, and never to initiate a confrontation.

As the Opel slowed to approach a junction, the Escort shot past on the outside and swerved violently across the road, forcing the operator to skid to a halt, hard into the pavement. As the Escort came to rest, the doors flew open and the first two terrorists piled out, both carrying Armalite rifles. One ran straight round to the back of the Opel, from where he pointed his weapon at the back of the operator's head, while the other covered him from in front of the wing and began to advance up the car, intending to begin the questioning. If he turned out to be a member of the security forces who had wandered into this hard area, perhaps by mistake, they would execute him there and then.

Using the foot pressel hidden in the well by his feet, the operator had immediately sent a brief contact report over the net, and now he sat in the driving seat, watching the barrel of the Armalite that was aimed at his head by the approaching terrorist. He had slipped his car pistol under his thigh, with its extended twenty-round magazine (as opposed to the thirteen rounds in the pistol in his waistband), and now he calmly rolled his window down to greet his inquisitor, keeping an eye on the one behind in his mirror.

Deciding that the situation had developed far enough, the operator whipped his pistol up and, still seated, engaged the front terrorist with four rounds, killing him. Continuing the movement, he sprung the door open and rolled out. The man at the rear fired a burst at him but missed, the rounds slicing through the Opel before hitting the Escort. The operator's aim was truer, and the terrorist died in a hail of 9mm rounds. Jumping back into the driving seat, the operator again turned his attention to the Escort, firing at and wounding the next man to emerge from it. Now the fourth man opened fire at him from within the car, the rounds fortunately going slightly wide of the mark and punching holes down the side of the Opel and smashing the windows. The operator returned the fire, at the same time flinging his car into gear and reversing away into a high-speed J-turn. He was unscathed.

The tally of two dead and one wounded at the hands of one 14 Company operator was a blow to the reputation of the local IRA – at least until their next success – and so we were always alert to the possibility of being set up for an ambush by a piece of 'information received'. That particular encounter inspired the development and installation of flashbang boxes on the unit's cars, and led to an increased amount of training in how to respond to similar situations.

Now for the first time I was going to be operating solo in a hard area. I was callsign November, and my job today was to be part of the first surveillance team. I was anxious to perform well. The target area was at least forty-five minutes' fast drive away, so I'd have no time to lose. But first the Spooks, as our Intelligence Corp staff were known, briefed us on the information they had gathered in the space of the last few minutes.

Pete Spook pointed to the aerial photos. 'You can just see the farm on the edge of this shot. This blow-up's about three years old – and George has already left to get some new pics from the heli – but I doubt it's changed much. The farmer is called XXXXXXX, wife deceased. No previous PIRA activity recorded, but believed to be a Sinn Fein activist a few years back. Two boys and two girls, only one, Padraig, still living at home. Obviously we haven't got any mugshots yet, perhaps you can get some.'

'What sort of farm is it?' asked Suzy.

'Dairy. We reckon the kit is in the milking parlour somewhere; that's presumably where the noisy machinery is. We presume that the parlour is this block here, across the yard from the main gate. This little block next to it could be a dog kennel, or perhaps a chicken run. The new aerials should be able to confirm that shortly. The vehicles registered to this address and the neighbours are as per this Charlie list – take one each. The farm, the farmer senior and his car are Alpha 1, Bravo 1 and Charlie 1 respectively. XXXXXXX junior and his car are Bravo 2 and Charlie 2. We'll add to the target list as the situation develops, if need be.'

Next was the duty signaller: 'Code change at noon – don't forget to input the new secure code into your car radios. You'll be on channel four to about here . . . ' He drew a line across the map.

'... Then switch to channel three. If that doesn't work, Suzy – call-sign Tango – has a rebro set in her boot. If everything goes to rat-shit try that, and work amongst yourselves on your body sets, and let the heli relay it to us. OK?' This particular area was too far from any police station or army base for our small body sets to reach any permanent rebroadcast station, so a car in each surveillance team routinely carried a concealed rebro set. This meant that if the main radio net became unworkable, we could still communicate with each other on our body sets, as long as we were within a few kilometres of the team's mobile rebro.

'Go to it, people! I'll be on air on the ops desk from 1300,' said Phil, and turned to discuss the OP and CTR with Andy, Tom and Gary.

In the locker room, which was out of bounds to all but operators, we donned our kit. First I picked up my personal Browning – magazine in, cock a round into the chamber, apply the safety catch – and holstered it securely inside my waistband. Next my car pistol with its longer twenty-round magazine, stuffed down the front of my trousers for now. Then I put two spare pistol magazines into the covert carrier on my hip, and slipped my radio body set into the neat hidden vent in my loose cotton jacket, adjusting the microphone inside my lapel. I attached a fresh battery to it and pocketed a spare. Next I loaded my HK53 with a twin magazine, and cocked it, checking the safety catch, then put it and two spare mags into my car bag, along with a stun grenade, a couple of parachute flares and a powerful MagLite torch, in case we needed illumination in an emergency after dark. I stuffed a black balaclava and a white armband into my pocket. These last two items were for emergencies only – the balaclava would protect my identity if I was severely compromised in the operational area, and the white armband would identify operators to each other and to the HMSU if we got into a fire-fight with terrorists. The car bag already contained my map book, a pocket-sized dictaphone, a night viewing scope, a pair of binoculars and some white plasti-cuffs. As I was doing all this I was trying to memorise the registrations of Charlie 1 and 2.

Now I loaded up my car, checking quickly over the medical pack. My car had border plates – that was fine for today. If I'd needed other plates, I'd have simply used a pool vehicle with the right set on. All our sets were logged into the central police computer under various guises, so even a regular police or army patrol with a link to the VENGEFUL vehicle database computer system wouldn't be able to tell I was a member of the security forces. Then I squirted the new electronic security code into my car radio. I loaded fresh film into two cameras, screwed on their motor-drives, checked the light reading outside and set the f-stop and shutter speed, and a focal distance of about thirty feet on one and fifty feet on the other, before securing them firmly into their hidden mounts.

Lunch! I grabbed my Thermos flask and raced over to the cookhouse. The cooks had just finished cutting a pile of sandwiches and I filled a couple of bags, adding a pie and a few cold sausages and pouring fresh coffee into the flask. On the way back to my car I dropped into my basha to turn off the lights. The flutter of nerves in my stomach now sent waves of nausea through me and I spent a minute throwing up into the loo. I quickly brushed my teeth, back-combed and tousled my hair, and inserted my radio earpiece. I looked – appropriately enough – perfectly awful.

Driving fast, but carefully so as not to attract attention to ourselves, we deployed to the area. The first car on the scene was Jake – callsign Delta – who did a pass of the target and confirmed that the two Charlies were at the farm. Suzy and Steve – callsigns Tango and X-Ray – swung north behind the target as they approached, so I, as callsign November, drifted south. We spread ourselves loosely round the target area. Between us we covered an area of about nine square miles. Now Sally – callsign Whisky – arrived high above us in the heli, invisible from the ground. It felt strange being part of a team that I couldn't see, relying entirely on the radio transmissions and our training.

'Whisky has the trigger on Alpha 1. Charlie 1 and 2 static empty. Am I obvious to anyone?'

I pulled over in the narrow lane, killed the engine and rolled my window down to listen. I knew Sally was even further south than me, so if I couldn't hear the noise of the heli's engine there was no way the target could.

'November, you're fine from Red One Nine.'

Sally double-clicked her acknowledgement.

'Zero.' That was the ops desk acknowledging too.

I started up again and continued driving round the network of tiny lanes and isolated cottages, occasionally passing another vehicle. In hard rural areas even a friendly wave of the hand can have a sectarian connotation. A single finger lifted in acknowledgement as you squeeze slowly past an oncoming vehicle in a narrow lane is a predominantly Catholic gesture. The protestant equivalent is to raise the flat palm, echoing as it does the symbolism of the Red Hand of Ulster. Make the wrong sign in an area and you unnecessarily draw attention to yourself. Of course one could choose simply not to acknowledge other drivers, but in a small rural community where a strange face stands out, this too would seem a little unusual, particularly as the Irish are naturally a very warm and friendly race. It was largely for this reason that we were reluctant to drive SAS troopers around with us when we were doing joint recces for forthcoming operations – they always stared too aggressively at the locals, like angry dogs on a leash. By contrast we deliberately wore happy, smiling faces, sometimes pretending to sing along to the local commercial radio station, since this not only made us look relaxed but was also a good cover for our lip movements when transmitting on the radio or recording information on our dictaphones. When one feels very nervous inside, I found, it's surprisingly difficult not to show it through one's face and posture.

As I drove I had to keep glancing at the mapbook open on my passenger seat. I had a spare jersey thrown loosely over it and my HK53, and I checked they were out of sight each time another vehicle approached. Since few of us had worked in this particular area recently, we were all taking the opportunity to relearn the spot code as we went.

Over the net Delta was suggesting a suitable drop-off point for the OP team, from which they could approach a spinney that overlooked the farmhouse. The OP team – callsign Lima – consisted of Andy and Gary, who were now on their way out from base, being driven by Tom – callsign Hotel – in an old estate car. Under their coats they were wearing army camouflaged combat uniform, and were armed with G3Ks. The kit that they would need for the OP and the CTR was contained in a small backpack.

'Standby, standby!' Suddenly Sally broke in on the chatter on the net and my heart skipped a beat. This was the standard surveillance warning that action was imminent. 'Whisky has Charlie 1, probably one up, mobile down the track towards the main.'

Immediately a staccato ripple of acknowledgements crackled over the net.

'Delta.'

'X-Ray.'

'Tango.'

'November.'

'Zero.'

'Hotel.'

At once the surveillance cars began to close in, tightening the cordon like a drawstring closing around the neck of a purse. However, as long as Whisky kept control of the target, we wouldn't expose ourselves for fear of spooking him.

'Whisky. Charlie 1's approaching the main and intending right towards Red One Two.'

Shit, he was turning towards me. I glanced at the map again. I could parallel his road for a bit and then come in from his left, if he stayed straight.

'Delta's going for a head-on pass.' This made sense, because we needed to confirm as soon as possible who was in the vehicle.

'Zero.'

'X-Ray's to Yellow One Nine.' Steve was surging ahead, but well south – so that we maintained the loose box around the target.

'Whisky. That's at Red One Two and straight towards Red One One.'

'Hotel, Zero. Suggest you go straight to the drop-off.' Tom might as well take the opportunity to insert the OP team while Charlie 1 was away from the farm.

'Hotel.'

'Delta. That's a very probable Bravo 2 complete Charlie 1. He's about twenty-five, short black hair, denim jacket, grey jersey – and I'm unsighted, towards Red One Three.'

'Tango's Green One Three towards Green One Four.' That was Suzy driving flat out to the north, covering those options.

'Whisky. That's Charlie 1 through Red One One and towards Red One Zero.'

I put my foot down and juggled my speed to time my arrival at the next junction just right. About seventy yards short of it I saw Charlie 1 flash past. I gave him a few seconds to get clear, then pulled out behind him. He was already out of sight – which was fine by me. I'd shadow him and move forward if Sally began to lose him. But in the meantime I accelerated slightly so that I glimpsed enough of him to judge his speed. This would help the rest of the team to keep their distance.

'November's backing Whisky, trailing Charlie 1, unsighted, speed fifty, fifty-five.'

'Whisky.'

'Zero.'

'Hotel's approaching drop-off.'

'Tango's static at Green One Three.' From there I knew Suzy could take the target if he swung north.

'Zero.'

'Whisky. Charlie 1's entering the village.'

'November.'

'Whisky. That's a stop, stop, stop! Charlie 1 static on the left, I'm temporarily unsighted.'

Shit! If the target had stopped we'd need to get eyes on him as soon as possible. My heart changed gear at the same time as my little Fiesta, and we swept up the hill through the outskirts of the village. Instinctively I reached out to touch the camera switches, reminding myself of their location, since I'd only have one chance.

'Hotel. Drop-off complete.' I could hardly hear the transmission through the mush that had suddenly developed over the radio net.

'Zero.'

The radio was crackling badly now. Fuck, I'd forgotten to change frequency! I reached across and fingered the remote control, flicking on to the new channel. 'Zero, November. Check on channel three?'

'Zero, OK. Where are you?'

'Through Red One Zero, going for a pass.'

'Roger that.'

'X-Ray's approaching Green One Seven.' That was the first crossroads to the west of the village. If I got a trigger on Charlie 1, Steve could come in from ahead and keep track of Bravo 2.

'November.'

Now I was doing thirty through the centre of the village. There on the left was Charlie 1, and Bravo 2 was striding back along the pavement towards a general store. I pressed the camera button by my knee as I approached, and felt rather than heard the whirr of the motor-drive clicking through a dozen frames.

I realised that I was frowning with concentration, so I made an effort to relax and look cheerful. 'November. That's Charlie 1 static empty, Bravo 2 foxtrot towards Murphy's Stores on the left. I'm going for a trigger on Charlie 1.' I was now a good hundred metres past, and I pulled up casually against the kerb, next to the small post office, trying to look as if I was waiting to pick someone up. Out of my left wing mirror I could see the pavement beside Charlie 1, and in my right mirror I could just see its driver's door. Keeping my eyes on it, I reached into my bag for the dictaphone and clicked it on to voice-activated mode, so that every time I spoke it would automatically record. It was always worth recording any details like car registrations or descriptions of people associating with our targets. One never knew what tiny piece of information would allow the Spooks or Special Branch to press another piece into the intelligence jigsaw.

'Zero, Lima check.' Andy and Gary were checking their comms as they carefully began to move forwards into position.

'Zero, OK.'

'X-Ray's going to go foxtrot on the main. November, is there somewhere to park up east of you?'

I studied the rear-view mirror, noticing that a greasy-looking youth had just come out of the post office and was now eyeing me. He was only a couple of feet away, so I pretended to yawn, covering my mouth with the back of my hand, and murmured quickly, 'Yeah, opposite the garage.'

Steve double-clicked an acknowledgement as he drove smoothly past me and pulled into the tiny village square. 'X-Ray's going foxtrot.'

I pulled out a two-day-old copy of the *Sun* and leafed through it desultorily, all the time checking my mirrors. The youth drifted away. As soon as Steve was foxtrot he'd be out of range of his car radio – and Suzy's rebro would still be too distant – so I surreptitiously reached into my jacket lining and switched on my body set. If I transmitted on this, only he would be close enough to hear, our two sets working one-to-one like walkie-talkies.

'X-Ray, November. Check.'

Double-click from Steve.

I watched him amble across the street and pass the store. Two minutes later he was back in his car. 'X-Ray's complete. Looks pretty domestic to me – he's buying groceries. I'm going mobile towards Red One One.'

'Zero.'

'Delta.'

'Tango.'

Suddenly, there was Bravo 2 on the pavement, then round by the driver's door, clutching a white plastic bag to his chest as he fumbled for his keys. He got in quickly and started the car up.

'November. Standby, standby. Bravo 2 complete, Charlie 1 is mobile.' The car swung around in the road. 'That's back towards Red One Zero.'

'Zero.'

'Whisky, roger. I have Charlie 1 through Red One Zero and towards Red One One.'

'Zero, Lima. I have a trigger on Alpha 1 and Charlie 2.'

'Zero.'

Again the team kicked into gear and held the target firmly in its invisible grasp, back across the rolling hills; but our target simply drove home, parked up and went inside. With Lima now in place and holding the trigger, and only domestic activity observable so far, Sally could return to base while the car team loitered in the general neighbourhood.

At 5.30 Andy and Gary, callsign Lima – who had quietly crawled forward through a patch of scrub and were now inside a bush only fifty feet from the back door of the farm – reported that the old man had appeared and gone into the milking parlour for the evening milking. At that point we lifted off and returned to base, to be replaced by a fresh car team. For the next twenty-four hours we'd have a car team permanently in the general vicinity, satelliting the area around a five-mile radius, waiting to close in if any activity developed.

On arrival back at base I refilled the car with petrol and then locked all my kit into it, so that we were ready for a fast crash-out if required. I handed the rolls of film to a technician before attending a rapid debrief. Phew! This had been a tiring day, but I was relieved to have performed well enough. It was just a pity that nothing more dramatic had gone down while I was there.

Later that night Andy and Gary crept into the milking parlour wearing night-vision goggles and searched it from top to bottom. Behind a rickety wooden panel they found a large glass jar full of a brown liquid with a distinctive smell, which they knew to be an illegal nitrogen-based substance used in the manufacture of home-made explosives. They photographed it and took a small sample, replaced the jar, and then withdrew, finally resiting the OP so that it had a better view of the entrance to the parlour and the driveway. Now that we had confirmed the presence of the kit, it was very likely that the rest of the information received – suggesting that it would be picked up the next day – was also accurate.

The next morning I was detailed to act as liaison between the HMSU, who would make the arrest, and the Det surveillance team. Since I would be travelling in the back of an armoured police Ford Sierra I had to look the part. My role was to relay the target's movements to the HMSU commander, so that he could set up a routine-looking VCP in its path. This was potentially quite dangerous for the HMSU – the courier would face a long prison sentence for being caught in possession of the substance, and might therefore try to fight his way out of capture. We didn't know whether they would be armed, but it seemed probable, so I equipped myself with a pistol and an MP5K.

I spent the day lounging with the HMSU lads in a nearby RUC station, listening to the regular checks over the net as our surveillance team mooched around the area. Sally sat with Graham, one of our dedicated heli pilots, waiting to fly out at a moment's notice. A Special Branch officer paced up and down in our ops room, chain-smoking.

At 2.15 p.m. everything came together at once.

'Zero, Lima. That's Bravo 2 foxtrot into the parlour.' A strange time to be going in there, perhaps. 'That's Bravo 2 out with a large cardboard box and in through the back door of the house.'

A couple of minutes later George – callsign Zulu, now part of the outlying surveillance team – reported a car, two up, cruising slowly along the main road.

Phil, who had just taken over running the ops desk from Jake, instantly tapped the registration into the VENGEFUL vehicle data computer terminal in the ops room. 'That should be a blue Peugeot 305, Zulu. It comes up clean but it's registered to an address in Turf Lodge.' Excellent! Turf Lodge was a hard republican estate in predominantly Catholic West Belfast, just west of the junction of the Whiterock and Springfield roads. This tied in nicely with the intelligence briefing we had received.

'Roger that. Looks like they're looking for somewhere.'

Better and better!

'November, roger.'

'Whisky.'

'Lima. That's the Peugeot turning down the track slowly towards Alpha 1.'

'Zero, roger. The blue Peugeot, registration KIJ 312D, two up, is now Charlie 3; driver and passengers are Bravos 3 and 4.'

Time to get the HMSU boys moving. We piled into the two armoured Sierras – seven HMSU, all strapping lads well over six feet tall, and me, a relatively short and skinny runt in a badly fitting uniform. Never mind – I would be staying in the back of the vehicle. As the two cars nosed out of the Fort Apache-like camp, I clamped a headset over my ears.

'November's mobile.'

'Whisky's airborne.'

'Zero.'

'Lima. Charlie 3 is now static empty, all Bravos complete Alpha 1.'

'Zero.'

'November's to Green Three Three.'

'Lima. Bravo 3 is reversing Charlie 3 into the shed beside the house, unsighted to me.'

'Zero, roger. Whisky, how long on to target?'

'Whisky. About four minutes.'

'Roger. Echo, Zulu, Papa and Mike – check.'

'Echo. Going mobile to Yellow Two One.'

'Papa. OK, static at Yellow Two Seven.' Derek had positioned himself to cover routes east.

'Zulu's to Red One One.' George was covering out to the west.

'Mike.' This was Tim our boss, out today as part of the surveillance team. It was important for both the Det commander and ops officer to operate on the ground as often as possible, in order to keep their skills and local knowledge fresh.

Studying the map earlier with Micky, the towering section sergeant of the HMSU team, he and I agreed to try to cut the couriers off where the road passes north of Lough Neagh. If they were heading for Belfast it was a natural choke point. However we couldn't go straight there, because if the target headed the other way out of the end of the valley and up towards Londonderry instead, then no amount of fast driving would catch them.

'November's to Green Two Two.' The boys in my car began to check their weapons as the souped-up RUC Sierras accelerated effortlessly through the green, rolling countryside.

'Standby, standby! Lima has Bravos 3 and 4 complete Charlie 3 and manoeuvring . . . now mobile down the track.'

'Zero, roger. Who can take it?'

'Zulu can.'

'Roger.' Zulu was timing his run from the west down the valley road so that he was well short of Charlie 3 as it emerged from the track. If it turned left to head east towards Belfast, as seemed likely, he would take it, at least until Whisky arrived on the scene in the heli. If it turned right, there was time for Mike to pull down a side road and clock it through before joining the follow. It was vital not to lose control of the target.

'Zulu. I have Charlie 3, two up, from the track towards Red One Three, speed forty.'

Now the tempo on the net was gathering pace, the speech clipped and calm.

'Zulu, Whisky. I think I have Charlie 3 at Red One Three intending right to Yellow Two Two. Is there a green van between you and him?'

'Correct. He's two up from me. I'm hitting my brake light twice . . . now.'

'Roger that. Whisky has Charlie 3 towards Yellow Two Two.'

'November.'

'Zulu's off.'

'Echo's to Red One Five.' Colin would stay a mile ahead of the target, forming the front of the invisible box.

'Papa's to Yellow One Eight from the north.'

'Zero. Mike, stay near Alpha 1, in case the other Charlies move.'

'Mike. Roger, intending static Red One Four.'

'Lima.'

'Whisky. That's Charlie 3 at Yellow Two Two and intending left towards Red Three Zero.'

'November.' So they'd taken a short-cut on to the main road. That was OK. We were about five miles ahead of them. We pulled over into a lay-by, willing them to keep going.

'November, Zero. Where are you going to set up shop?'

'Just east of Green One Seven, slightly around the bend in the trees.'

'Roger that. Papa, close up behind Charlie 3 after Green One Nine, in case he tries to reverse out.'

'Papa.'

'November.' I passed on to the boys in my car the information that Papa would be following close behind the target, and Micky relayed this on his police radio net to the second Sierra.

'Whisky. Charlie 3's through Red Three Zero and straight towards Red Two Nine.'

'OK, Micky, let's go for it!' I said, and the two police cars pulled out into the road.

'Lima has Bravo 2 foxtrot into the parlour.'

'Zero.'

Damn. That was all we needed – more suspicious activity on target when we were already committed. He was probably just tidying up. Let's hope so, I thought.

I was watching the map now as the relative positions of the HMSU cars and the suspect Peugeot drew together quickly, our paths converging on our respective roads. Four miles apart, a closing speed of 120 – that's two minutes away. We were entering the wood now, and the two police cars swung hard right on to the main road and slewed to a halt left and right across it. The constables bundled out, taking up their positions front and rear to flag down the traffic. The two cars and a van that we'd just overtaken were pulling up slowly behind us, and in front I could see another van approaching round the corner. To the locals, a snap VCP by the police was a very routine event. If they looked carefully they might have noticed that these police were rather more powerfully armed – but that would be all.

'November. VCP in position.'

'Zero.'

'Lima has Bravo 2 carrying another cardboard box foxtrot towards Charlie 2.'

'Whisky. That's Charlie 3 at Red Two Nine and straight towards Green One Nine.'

'Papa's backing Whisky.'

'Zero.'

'Lima. Standby, standby. I have Bravo 2 complete Charlie 2 mobile from Alpha 1.'

'Zero.'

Shit! Did that mean we were on to the wrong vehicle? Perhaps Bravo 2 had simply received instructions from the visitors about where to take the stuff and was now going to deliver it himself!

Instinctively, the team now split into two, covering both situations.

'Papa has Charlie 3, speed sixty, sixty-five.'

'Mike's mobile.'

'Zulu's back towards Yellow Two One.'

'Echo's backing Papa.'

'Whisky, Zero. Break off and take Charlie 2 if you can.'

'Whisky, roger. Mike, put me on.'

'Mike, roger. Wait.'

'Papa. That's Charlie 3 through Green One Nine and straight, slowing now into the tailback from the VCP. I'm two behind.'

'November.' The HMSU lads were briefly checking driving licences then waving each vehicle through, so that a steady stream of traffic was crawling past me, still in the back of the Sierra. There was Charlie 3, moving slowly in the queue towards us, and a little way behind I could see Papa's Renault. I verbally pointed them out to Micky, who was standing by the driver's door, reeling off the registration numbers into his radio, a standard procedure. He nodded, eyes narrowing, and his hand loosely touched his holstered revolver.

'Mike has Charlie 2 towards Red One One, one up, speed thirty-five.'

'Zero.'

'November. Charlie 3 is in the VCP.'

Micky and Sean had casually waved the Peugeot over between the nose and boot of the two police cars. A third constable sidled round behind them, covering the rear, idly handling his HK53. I put my hand around the trigger grip of the MP5K lying beside me on the seat.

Micky indicated to the driver to lower his window, but instead the man opened the door and put his head out. All politeness and smiles now, Micky invited the two men to step out of the car. He and Sean expertly frisked them, and were examining their documents as two other constables began methodically to search the boot and under the bonnet. Another constable stood to one side of them. Everyone looked remarkably relaxed.

'Mike, Whisky, is that Charlie 2 on the sharp left bend now, behind a white van?'

'That's him, and I'm off now towards Yellow Three One.'

'Zero.'

'Zulu's paralleling north on the Greens.'

Now Papa was being waved through by the police. Shit, these

two characters looked pretty cool if they were couriers. The rapid frisk had proved that they weren't armed. The constables were now rooting around inside the car. We really didn't want to have to have the car stripped down without a good reason; that would give away the fact that we'd been tipped off. Micky was beginning to look a little uneasy.

Suddenly, the young constable standing behind the pair, who were now casually smoking while they waited, asked the driver, 'Why will the window not roll down, sir?'

The driver shrugged his shoulders, hawked and spat into the gutter.

Micky looked up and shouted across to the two boys in the car, 'Have a wee look behind the door panels, lads! They might be smuggling cigarettes or who knows what!'

The two men began to look distinctly uncomfortable now. Within a minute one of the constables called, 'Hey, Sergeant, would you look at this!'

It had taken them only thirty seconds to prise the interior panels from the door frames. A slim plastic bottle of the liquid had been slipped inside the frame on each side and the panel loosely tacked back over it. One of the bottles must have slipped and prevented the window pane from sliding down. Thank God for that! Two constables quickly handcuffed the men and began to read them their rights, as vehicles continued to stream slowly past, the passers-by gawping at the scene.

'Zero, November. We've found the kit in Charlie 3 and arrested the Bravos.'

'Whisky. That's Charlie 2 stop, stop, stop in the village again.'

'Zulu's going for a pass.'

'Zero, roger. We've got the kit. Zulu and Mike, check this is more domestic then everyone lift off. Lima, when do you want a pick-up?'

'Pick-up in thirty, please.'

'Hotel, roger that. Mobile.'

Within two hours we were all back at base for the debrief. Even though the operation had run pretty smoothly we talked through each phase, to learn from any mistakes. By way of a small celebration we invited the HMSU team to our bar that evening for an impromptu party, and for the first time I experienced the legendary drinking power of the RUC man. By the end of the evening we were clean out of beer and Bushmills.

In truth, we had plenty to celebrate. The standard of our surveillance work was incredibly high and I doubt that any other agency in the world could beat it. This was largely the result of the iron self-discipline in the unit, but also partly due to the peculiar circumstances of peacekeeping in Northern Ireland. MI5 Watchers, as their surveillance teams are known, are doubtless first class, but they are rarely armed and could not operate covertly as we did in the most hostile of environments.

I soon settled into the lifestyle of the unit. We could never tell what the next day might bring and our plans and tasking were constantly altering, influenced by the continuous flow of intelligence from the other agencies. Almost every day I would be out as part of a surveillance team, either in my car or heli-borne, as we reacted to snippets of information. The aim was to prevent terrorist activity by finding known terrorists who were tipped to be up to some unspecified and murderous activity, and then guiding the HMSU on to them so that they could be lifted temporarily. Constrained as we all were by the laws of evidence, this was preferable to waiting for a terrorist to murder an innocent victim before shooting or arresting him. Rightly, under no circumstances would we permit a terrorist to commit murder in order to protect an intelligence source or solely to obtain sufficient evidence to convict him.

Each job was different from the last, and we were constantly refining our methods to meet each new challenge. Once we had been set a mission by Special Branch or MI5 we were left to get on with the job by any lawful means at our disposal. Our technicians were wizards at cobbling together remote cameras and other surveillance systems so that we could keep a trigger on a target in even the most awkward places. Occasionally however, lack of time on a job forced us to improvise outrageously.

One evening after supper I was in the Spooks' Cell next to the ops room, browsing through some files. We had a surveillance team on the ground that night, maintaining control of a player while he was away from home, so that a CTR team could enter his house in his absence for a particular purpose. The risk of a compromise on target was very high, because he had an extended family living in the vicinity, any one of whom could conceivably enter the house in his absence (we didn't know who else might be a keyholder).

Although the target – Bravo 1 – had gone out for a drink, it was possible that a friend or neighbour might appear while the team was still inside. We'd clocked him out for a drink on several previous occasions, and were fairly sure that we'd have the required hour undisturbed on target – but of course he could choose to return home at any moment.

The background to the operation was particularly sensitive, owing to the identity of the target, and the ultimate goal was so important that we wanted to avoid having to run him into a police roadblock at all costs. However, if he left his drinking partners earlier than expected and looked as if he was heading home, we would have no choice but to intervene that way, winning the CTR team enough time to pack up and skedaddle.

From the Spooks' Cell I could hear the traffic over the net in the ops room. Tim and Phil were running the desk between them and everything was going smoothly. Bravo 1 was in his local, about four minutes' drive from his home, and had been there for about fifteen minutes. The surveillance team – consisting of Gary, Colin, Andy and Pete, callsigns Golf, Echo, Lima and Romeo respectively – was staking out the vicinity. Travelling with Romeo was Tina, callsign Victor. Unfortunately it was too built-up an area for the heli to be of much use. Callsign X-Ray (Steve and Carl) had just entered Alpha 1 through the back door and had soundlessly begun work. Keith, callsign Oscar, was cruising around with the two HMSU vehicles, ready to intercept the target if he made for home unexpectedly, and Andy was holding the trigger on an empty Charlie 1 outside the bar.

And suddenly all hell broke loose.

'Lima. Standby, standby. I have Bravo 1 and another male complete Charlie 1, manoeuvring.'

'Zero, roger. X-Ray?'

'Roger,' Carl whispered. They would be standing in the dark, breath held, waiting to find out which way he was going to go.

I drifted into the ops room to listen to the traffic.

'Oscar's mobile on Orange towards Purple.' A large street map of the area was propped up on the map desk, the main streets colour-coded. Tim and Phil pored over it.

'Lima. That's Charlie 1 mobile to the junction and intending right on to Blue. I'm unsighted.' Well, he wasn't heading home immediately, then – maybe he was simply dropping someone off first.

'Echo. I have Charlie 1 on Blue. Bravo 1 is now the passenger; the driver is an unknown male.'

'Zero.' In the ops room we all glanced at each other. Shit, this was a potentially serious complication. Maybe he was lending the car to his friend, who was about to drop him off at home. The route they were on now wasn't heading them back home, but nor were they heading away from it particularly. Did the driver also have a key to Alpha 1? Should we abort now and extract X-Ray – or carry on and run the risk that the operation is blown?

'Echo. That's Charlie 1 left into the Crescent and intending a stop, stop, stop at the end. I'm off.'

Dammit. The Crescent was a tight little estate and, despite the fact that it had only one entrance, it would be extremely difficult to keep a trigger close enough to the target to give us sufficient warning of a move. The narrow terraced houses were crowded together and parked cars cluttered the small turning circles. It was going to be awkward to keep eyes on Charlie 1. There were a few kids yelling in the street, and a gang of youths were lounging about smoking, despite the damp evening.

'Romeo. I'm going to drop Victor off for a walk through from the far side.' So Pete was going to drop Tina at the entrance to the alleyway leading into the back of the estate, and then pick her up at the front. She'd need to be quick or she'd miss them.

'Zero, Victor. Check on body comms.' Tina was testing her small radio body set as she waved cheerio to Pete and set off through the alleyway.

'You're loud and clear, Victor,' replied Tim. At least in this urban area our body sets were within range of one of the rebroadcasters we'd installed in every police station and army camp in the province. This meant that anyone on a body set could transmit and be heard clearly on the main net. In the countryside this was only possible if we had a car with a rebro set in it as part of the team.

Tina sounded a bit breathless. 'Charlie 1 is static empty outside numbers thirty-two and thirty-four, between a green pick-up and a row of wheelie-bins. I guess they're inside one or the other, but I'm not certain. It's getting quite dark now.' In the background we could hear a youth yelling at a dog that was barking wildly in the street.

Behind me in the ops room Pete Spook was leafing through the electoral register and tapping the names of the occupants of the two houses into his computer terminal. Phil was on the phone to Special Branch to find out if they knew anything about the addresses.

'Victor, Zero. How long can you hold the trigger on Charlie 1?' This was critical. If we couldn't trigger the car away, he could be half-way home before we had time to react or X-Ray had time to pack up.

'Three minutes at most. I'm pretty obvious here.' I felt for her. It wasn't a pleasant place to loiter by yourself, but it was imperative that we keep eyes on Charlie 1.

Phil put down the handset of the green secure phone. 'Nothing on those addresses from SB.' Tim looked across at Pete Spook, who shook his head. Then Phil said, 'I reckon we're going to have to bin this one – I can't think of any other way.'

Tim nodded, then looked at me. 'How do you fancy binning it, James?'

I grinned at him. 'Sure, I'm game!' I replied, trying to sound confident.

'Good man. Quick – buzz Suzy, she can drop you off. I'd take an MP5 if I were you.'

It was a ploy we sometimes used to keep eyes on a target. Large grey metal commercial wheelie-bins were fairly commonplace around the estates. An operator would nip inside the bin, pull the lid down and peer through the narrow slit, reporting over the radio. All it required was a slick drill to disguise the method of entry. It was very effective, but because of the discomfort and the risk to the operator inside, it was only used as a last resort.

I grabbed my weapons and kit from the locker room and raced out to get ready, passing Suzy, who was sprinting up the stairs. As I prepared her car I switched the radio loudspeaker on so I could monitor the situation as it unfolded, and I heard Tim briefing the rest of the team.

'November's going into the bin opposite Charlie 1 to hold the trigger, dropped off by Tango. He'll be there in about ten minutes. Oscar, in the meantime put in an immediate HMSU VCP on the main road at the entrance to the estate. Hold the trigger until November arrives, and if Charlie 1 moves, find a reason to stop him until X-Ray's clear.'

'Oscar. roger. Mobile on Pink.'

'Victor, go complete Romeo the moment Oscar's in position.'

Double-click from Victor.

'X-Ray, check?'

'X-Ray. Roger all that. We need another forty minutes on target.'

I sat next to Suzy as she drove like the wind. About a mile short of the target she swung on to the corner of a patch of wasteground, so that I could get into the back seat unobserved. My nerves were playing up and waves of nausea swept across me. Suzy sat in the car while I vomited my supper briefly and efficiently into the shadows behind her.

'Better out here than in there, eh? Don't worry, I'll stay as close as I can,' she said kindly.

I hopped into the back and crouched down in the rear footwell. Soon we passed through Keith's HMSU VCP, Suzy showing her driving licence to one of the police lads. It was necessary to go through the usual routine in case anyone was watching her. Now we were manoeuvring in the tiny roadway of the estate and inside the car Suzy was murmuring quietly to me.

'Directly behind us is a blue Fiat. The bonnet of Charlie 1 is sticking out to the left of it as you look at it. Further left you can see two doors. The one on the left is number thirty-two, the right is thirty-four. OK?'

I double-clicked on the net, which she would hear through her earpiece. The passenger side of the car was right alongside the row of bins. She left the engine idling and as she stepped out of the driver's door I eased open the rear passenger door and slipped to the ground at the base of the bin. Suzy picked a fat black binbag from her boot, came round the side of the car and lifted the lid of the bin. She braced one leg forward, offering her knee as a makeshift step and in one easy flowing movement I launched myself lightly over the sill and slithered down into the interior, which was mercifully pretty empty. Suzy heaved the binbag in behind me, lowered the lid and turned to depart. The whole routine had taken about two and a half seconds.

Peering out through the gap I whispered into my mike, 'November has the trigger on Charlie 1 and the two doors.'

'Zero.'

'X-Ray.'

'Tango's mobile.'

'Oscar's lifting the VCP and going mobile.'

'Lima.'

'Romeo.'

'Echo.'

'Golf.'

I was having to crane my neck at an odd angle to see clearly through the slit. Those damned kids were still scuffling around the close. I was feeling the first twinges of discomfort in my legs and I desperately wanted to change position in my tin coffin, but I didn't dare in case the kids noticed the noise and fetched an adult.

Time passed and my eyes were beginning to ache from squinting sideways, when, with no warning at all there was a tremendous crash on the lid of the bin two inches above my head! Holy fuck! My heart was in my mouth and I tightened my grip on the MP5, instinctively thumbing the safety catch to fire, finger firmly on the trigger, but keeping my eye to the slit. An orangey white object skittered on to the grass to my left. I took a deep breath – it was a football which must have been given a good punt and landed square on top of me. A couple of kids tore past after it. Fucking little bastards – should be in bed, it was gone ten o'clock! They'd scared the shit out of me.

My breathing steadied, and I flicked the safety catch back to safe. Now I could feel my legs beginning to cramp and I wanted to rub my calves, but I couldn't reach them without taking my eyes from the slit. There was a great deal of coming and going between the houses; people were constantly passing within feet of me, some walking their pets.

A patch of white light grew, then narrowed and disappeared as someone slipped out of the left-hand door. A dark shape crossed in front of the house close to the wall, then moved out of my line of sight. In the shadows thrown by the orange glow of the streetlights it was impossible to see clearly who it was.

'Zero, November. That's someone foxtrot to the left out of number thirty-two, hard against the wall. Couldn't see who, but they're not towards Charlie 1.'

'Zero. Anyone in position to check?'

'Romeo's going foxtrot from the front.' This time Tina would drop Pete off for a walkpast.

Pete mooched quickly through the estate, confirming that it was just a youth who went into a house further up the close.

The minutes crawled by painfully slowly, cramp ricking my calves. I was nearing the end of my tether.

'Zero, X-Ray. We're finished, just packing up now.' Carl was whispering so quietly he was barely audible over the net. The target was in a terraced row and the walls were paper thin, so his caution was understandable.

'Roger that. Echo, drop Tango, collect November.'

'Tango roger, mobile.'

Never was I so glad to hear my callsign on the net! As the rest of the team began the exit drill to extract Steve and Carl, Suzy drove up again and we reversed the routine. She drove us quickly to a deserted lay-by so that I could get back into the front of the car. As I clambered stiffly out and took a deep breath of the foggy night air, I listened to the net as the pick-up went without a hitch, and before long the whole team was following us back to base.

The work was extremely demanding, but because it was so obviously worthwhile we were happy to work flat-out for weeks at a stretch. Every six weeks, individual operators could take a four-day break, followed by another six weeks' work, then an eight-day break – operations permitting, of course. A few operators had their pet dogs living with them, and we frequently used the dogs as cover – no one takes a second glance at someone loitering by a lamppost while a dog performs.

The SAS Troop that was on call to any of the detachments in the province were clearly envious of our constant activity and our ability to operate individually in the hardest of areas. When 14 Intelligence Company was first set up in 1974 it was initially trained by SAS instructors, but since then it had become so expert and specialised in the field of covert surveillance operations that it had developed its own unique operational methodology and, of course, supplied its own instructors. In a bid to recover some of the skills, 22 SAS decided in the mid-eighties to send a couple of troopers each year to serve with 14 Company. They were exempt from the selection course, but obviously had to complete the full training successfully. The SBS also sent the occasional member across – George, dark, curly-haired and powerfully built, was one of them, an incredibly resourceful and competent character, not at all a fish out of water.

So the months rolled on and I learned more and more about the players that we were interested in and the localities they inhabited. We ranged the length and breadth of the province, using surveillance and CTRs to locate the weapons in hides, which we would then deactivate or bug, or both. The moment the weapons were picked up for use or transit we were alerted.

From time to time information received would relate to a terrorist attack on a specific target, but without mentioning the participants. Often the target would be an off-duty policeman or UDR soldier, who would be substituted when possible with an SAS trooper. We would then jointly plan an SAS ambush, operators providing surveillance around the target location to trigger the gunmen in. If the information was too vague we would saturate the area with police and troops in the hope that we could cause the murder attempt to be aborted. We never took risks with innocent lives – other than our own.

Sometimes the difficulties we faced were so ridiculous that we would crack up, giggling hysterically at one another. One night in particular, Colin and I were dressed completely in black, including black gloves and balaclavas. We needed access to a well-known terrorist's vehicle so that we could modify it to our advantage. The problem was that the car was routinely garaged in a solid brick shed with very heavy metal shutters. The shed was right beside his house, which was on a busy side street in an extremely hard republican village, and two lamp-posts either side of the entrance, one on each side of the street, floodlit the whole area. It was the sort of place where you were more likely to bump into a heavily armed sixteen-man IRA patrol than an army one.

We had both made daylight walkpasts to formulate an entry plan. The shutters would make an unholy noise if we tried to lift them, and anyway the doorway was too exposed to risk picking the twin locks. We had considered knocking out the offending streetlamps with an air-rifle, knowing how long it would take the council to repair them, but, surprisingly perhaps in the circumstances, Special Branch wouldn't contemplate being party to criminal damage!

This left us with two choices: we could either enter through the roof, removing some of the tiles, rolling back a section of felt and dropping through the hole, replacing it all on the way out; or we could force one of the tiny windows, each about twenty inches square, which were set twelve feet up into the back wall, above a lean-to tiled roof. We had decided on the latter and spent some time rehearsing how to open a secure casement window from the outside, using long and very thin metal tools to manipulate the fittings. Fortunately, there was a low wall from the top of which we could access the roof. We would have to do it in the pitch dark and in silence because the window was in full view of the back of the house. Once the window was ajar we would slip a flexible endoscope, containing its own tiny integral light source, over the raised sill and peer around inside, so that we could see what lay immediately below and how best to climb down inside without making any noise.

We also rehearsed opening a locked vehicle, practising on a similar model. We could do this in about three seconds – all we had to do was slip a 'Slim Jim', a long thin tool with a hook on the end, down into the door cavity. Because the SJ is so thin, it slides between the rubber seal and the glass like a trickle of Guinness – then it's just a matter of flicking up the hook on its end to unlock the door. We knew for sure that we had no car alarm to contend with.

We planned to approach across dead ground to the rear of the village and then scale a wall, dropping into an alleyway that ran parallel to the road. A few metres further on we would enter the target's back garden and creep up to the wall that bisected the end of the shed. I'd leg Colin up on to it, pass him the kit and then follow him up. He'd climb on to the roof and deal with the window, while I covered him.

There was no moon on the evening we dropped off, and we both used our nightsights to pick our way across the fields. It was past one o'clock, but even so there were occasional pedestrians and cars passing on the side road – a symptom of an area with high unemployment, I supposed. Strapped to my back was a neat black knapsack containing our patrol radio, our tools and a camera, and we each carried HK53s in addition to our personal pistols, which on this occasion we carried in shoulder holsters. Even armed like this, we would almost certainly be heavily outgunned if we had a contact. We still wore our body sets and earpieces so that we could communicate one-to-one if we had to split up.

The house was in darkness as we approached it, but there were lights on in the houses either side and we could hear the sound of a TV or video playing somewhere. We pressed on, confident that once we were inside the garage we would have plenty of time to hide if someone began to unlock the steel shutters and roll them upwards. We slipped over the wall and passed noiselessly along the narrow and rutted lane, before lightly vaulting the low wall that bounded the garden. We edged forward until we were at the base of the garage and without hesitating I grabbed Colin's proffered calf and quietly hoisted him up on to the brickwork. Facing back towards the house, I shrugged the bag from my shoulders and felt Colin lift it up and away. I passed him my weapon and nimbly scaled the wall myself. Then I crouched on top of the narrow bricks, under the low eave, holding both weapons as Colin extracted the tools from the bag and eased himself gingerly on to the tiled roof. Inevitably there were a few tiny clicks and clacks from the tiles underfoot as his weight bore on them, but nothing to worry about. As I waited in the shadows I could feel the occasional bead of sweat running down my back inside my shirt. Now he was hard underneath the window about seven feet from me. He reached up and began to work on it. After a couple of minutes it eased open. He spent a moment manipulating the endoscope.

'There's a workbench immediately below the window. Looks strong enough,' he murmured softly.

He quietly heaved his frame in through the aperture. Now he was balancing on his hips in the window. Suddenly his legs stiffened and I heard a low growl come from within the shed. Shit, there was a bloody dog in there!

I could hear Colin quite distinctly. 'Good doggie. There's a good boy, be a good doggie then! Lie down now, boy, sit! Sit, boy!' The dog yapped once and growled again. 'Good doggie. Sit, boy!' It yapped again, louder this time. Colin came wriggling back out, dropped on to the tiled roof and slithered over to me. We knelt side by side in the pitch dark, almost invisible to each other in our black gear.

'That's all we need!' he said quietly. He turned and looked at me directly. 'Lend us a dog biscuit!' For some inexplicable reason – perhaps because of the anxiety and tension of the moment – this rather poor joke struck us both as the funniest one-liner we'd ever heard, and we dissolved into paroxysms of helpless mirth. I nearly fell off the wall. I had to jam my gloved hand over my mouth until I'd regained control of myself sufficiently.

After we'd wiped the tears from our eyes, Colin decided to try to make entry once again. The reception from the dog was the same, but a little more voluble this time. It was a terrier of some sort and sounded like it was chained up inside the shed. It seemed a strange place to keep a dog, but it was certainly an effective burglar alarm! We dropped off the wall and sat comfortably shoulder to shoulder, backs against the base of it.

'Why don't we just kill it?' I whispered, trying to be constructive.

'What with?'

'My penknife?'

'Blimey, don't start me off again!' Colin replied. 'Anyway, I like dogs. I couldn't kill one in cold blood. And it would be obvious that someone had been inside the garage. Maybe we could tranquillise it, if we can get hold of a dart gun.'

'Yeah, but if we miss or get compromised he's going to find little darts all over the place. Anyway, it'd probably bark its head off before the dart knocked it out,' I said.

'Hmm . . . I know – meat! That's the answer, juicy bits of meat! We could put the drug inside a nice piece of steak, tie a bit of string to it and dangle it through the window. If the little bastard won't eat it, we just pull it up and out and then abort!'

'Good idea! Let's get back into some decent cover and see if we can jack something up.'

We scuttled back across the garden and into the shadows underneath the low wall. I pressed my transmit switch. 'Zero, November. We've got a problem. There's a dog, a small terrier, inside the building, and we can't get in. Roger so far?'

'Roger. Go on.' Phil didn't sound too surprised.

'We need to stun it, knock it out or something, with a bit of doped meat and about ten feet of thin string. Do you have time to organise this and get it down to us tonight?'

'Zero. Wait, I'll check.'

As we crouched in the shadows I could imagine the scenes. Any moment now a sleepy army vet at the Dog Handling Unit in Palace Barracks just outside Belfast would be receiving a call from a senior duty officer at Headquarters Northern Ireland in Lisburn. Our own duty pilot would be squawked from his sleep and would scramble into his flying kit. The duty cook would be selecting a nice bit of silverside, wondering who the hell wants raw steak at this time of night.

It took just five minutes before Phil was back on the net with an answer. 'November, Zero. The heli with the meat and string is just leaving for Belfast to pick up the tranquillisers. It'll RV with Kilo about five miles north of you and he'll deliver it to your original drop-off point, OK?'

'November. Roger that, we're foxtrot back to the drop-off now.'

We cautiously returned across the silent fields and took cover inside a bush, settling down to wait. Fifty minutes later we heard Kilo approaching. He'd doused his brake lights, and as he glided to a halt beside us Colin stepped out of the shadows and took the package from Carl, who said, 'The vet reckons there's enough in there to put a terrier out for about six hours – says it should begin to work almost at once.'

We retraced our route for a third time, careful to take a slightly different path for fear of leaving tracks in the grass. Everything was still quiet, and once more we climbed on to the roof. This time it took Colin only seconds to open the window. As he eased himself into the aperture the growling started up again.

'Look what I've got for you, you lucky boy, then!' Putting his penlight torch between his teeth, he swung the meat to and fro a couple of times before casting it at the dog's feet. The terrier yapped once, sniffed at the neat parcel and growled.

'Good boy, eat your din dins, that's a good boy!' It sniffed again, then fell on the steak and devoured it almost whole, tugging briefly on the string. Colin retreated and we sat for ten minutes before trying again. Now the little dog was snoring heavily on an old coat beside the workbench. Colin lowered himself inside and I passed in the kit, then dropped down behind him, pressing the window shut. Quietly we set our tools on a cloth and set to work on the car.

As my experience grew I helped to run the ops desk, particularly during the winter when we were out night after night searching for weapon hides and running surveillance tasks each day. In between operations we went running or played squash, trying to keep our fitness up, and of course we regularly practised our live firing car drills on one of the isolated ranges next to the coast.

I recarpeted and painted my basha, and purchased a TV and stereo through our local NAAFI. On the odd afternoon off I rummaged around in the local junk shops to find prints and pictures for the wall. It was all so unimaginably different from life as an officer in the green army. The more I thought about it, the less I wanted to return to my regiment at the end of my tour here. But neither did I want to stay in this peculiar world for the bulk of my career. It was fun when you were young and fancy-free, but I really missed Jennifer and a normal social life.

One morning in January the commanding officer of 14 Company, a lieutenant colonel whom I knew only as John, asked to see me. By repute he was vastly experienced and a man of few words. He fixed me with a beady eye. 'James, as you know we'll have a vacancy for ops officer in South Det when Phil goes back to instruct on the next training course. I'd like you to take on the job.'

'Oh . . . right-oh, John.'

Why not? I thought.

Chapter Six

Although I felt mildly flattered to be asked to become ops officer, I had by now learnt that the real control and expertise that affects the result of an operation comes directly from the teams on the ground. In most cases the ops desk, callsign Zero, must leave the direction of the surveillance or CTR to the operators undertaking the task. The overall situation and local conditions can alter so swiftly and dramatically that it is inappropriate and often dangerous to try to impose a strategy from above on to the team on the ground. The ops officer's role is to assist the team by co-ordinating the different agencies involved and to provide an overview of the situation. There is little kudos attached to the title. The appointment is often filled by non-commissioned officers (Phil had in fact been one), and I believe that this flexible approach – using the best man or woman for the job, irrespective of rank – is the greatest strength of 14 Company.

The ops officer has to continue to operate with the teams from time to time, in order to keep his or her hand in and local knowledge up. Consequently I found that my workload doubled overnight. One tricky and time-consuming part of my responsibilities was to allocate individual operators to the teams for each task. It was important not to overexpose individuals to the same terrorist targets and locations, and this had to be balanced against the need to maintain continuity of knowledge and experience on specific long-term operations. We had an unlimited budget for respraying operators' cars or replacing ones that we felt had become compromised through overexposure to a target, and we could also alter the appearance of any individual operator who felt personally compromised – by dyeing their hair, paying for a complete new wardrobe and keeping them off the ground for a while.

The Det had complete freedom to plan operations to fulfil the missions we received from Special Branch and MI5. We were more familiar with most of the hard areas that we worked in than either of those agencies, and they would usually defer to our judgement on operational matters. Internally, our planning was pretty democratic – the longest-serving operators, or those with special knowledge of the target, would lead the discussions about how best to crack any particular nut. If a CTR or an OP was required, the senior operator in the team would decide exactly when and how he wanted to deploy, the entry methods to be used and so on. This meant that even first tour operators shouldered considerable operational responsibility. In truth we were learning from each other all the time, a process that was greatly helped by a sort of informational osmosis in the bar, where informal debriefs often took place.

The greatest pressure on the ops officer and Det commander arose through lack of time. As often as not we were required to crash out as fast as possible in response to information just received, and frequently the situation would develop even as we were deploying on to the ground, necessitating an immediate reorganisation of the teams and tasks. Since in most cases innocent lives would be at risk if we failed, the pressure on us was immense, particularly if we had been active for some days already and were therefore tired. I remember feeling close to tears of exhausted frustration on more than one occasion, as yet another urgent task demanding an instant response was telephoned to us over the secure line, when we were already fully committed.

Our targets were by no means limited to the Provisional IRA and INLA. The Ulster Defence Association and Ulster Volunteer Force, although relatively amateur by comparison to the IRA, had access to a couple of sources of high-quality weapons and were prepared to use them for indiscriminate murder. We successfully located a UDA courier's car, and at the end of one two-week operation our HMSU scooped ninety Kalashnikovs and arrested a string of terrorists. I've never understood why the British press and media continue to refer to these murderers as loyalists. As far as I could see, it was we and the RUC who were the loyalists – the terrorists on both sides of the community are simply criminals.

One drawback to being part of such a specialised unit was the unremitting stream of VIPs that arrived to be briefed on the state of play of certain sensitive operations in our patch, or to talk to the SAS troop. Officials from the Home Office, senior politicians from

Westminster and senior police and army officers were regularly smuggled in and out of our location, some going down better than others! Once, a bumptious civilian visitor, having a pre-lunch drink in our bar with some SAS troopers, rashly cast doubt on anyone's ability to hit a fifty-pence piece with two shots from a pistol at twenty paces. This was like a red rag to a saloon full of bulls, but the troopers simply smiled and offered to lay on a demonstration after lunch in our Killing Room.

The visitor was invited to spectate while one man sat on a chair in front of a blank white target screen against the far wall. Everyone donned ear defenders. Suddenly a stun grenade rolled into the middle of the room, erupting into a deafening, flashing crackle. At the same instant two troopers whipped out their pistols and loosed off thirteen rounds at the seated figure each, in the space of three and a half seconds.

As the smoke cleared the man rose, picked up the target from behind him, made his way up the range and solemnly presented it to the visitor, who was wide-eyed with amazement and admiration. Twenty-six neat holes outlined the position where the trooper had sat, each hole not more than an inch from where his frame had been.

'Hmm,' said one of the firers, scratching his jaw. 'Last couple pulled a bit to the right. Must have been that shandy I drank.'

No doubt the visitor is still regaling his friends with tales of the extraordinary shooting powers of the SAS. What he never learnt was that the holes in the paper had been made beforehand with a pencil, and that the troopers had actually fired wide of the target under the diversion of the stun grenade. They may be excellent shots, but they aren't lunatics!

On an earlier occasion a visiting senior civil servant had asked to see a surveillance demonstration, so a team was laid on for his benefit. Geoff, a wiry Yorkshireman, took him out in his car to join the team, equipping him with a spare earpiece so that he could listen in to the car's covert radio. Of course Geoff played up the nature of the area that they were driving through, giving the impression that it was extremely republican, when in fact it was exceedingly tame.

They hadn't gone far when, in the middle of a follow, Geoff got a call over the net: 'Uniform, Zero. Bad news – McGinty's escaped! We need your assistance pronto!'

'Uniform. Roger, I'm on my way!'

Geoff slammed on the brakes and spun the car around, heading back the way they had come. In his slow Yorkshire accent he said to his passenger, 'Damnation! I put him away, so I'd best go fetch him now. He'll be running fast, but I reckon I can guess where he'll be aiming for.' He put his foot down and screamed back through the narrow country lanes, the passenger clinging on for dear life and gaping nervously at this unexpected twist.

'This McGinty – he's not armed, is he?' he stammered.

Geoff looked sideways at him. 'I'd be surprised if he were.'

'Well, is he dangerous?' The car was now racing along at eighty miles an hour.

'Aye, he could be if he knew he was cornered.'

Geoff screeched round a sharp bend, swung left and bumped down a rutted farm track.

'Shouldn't we call for assistance then? I mean, there's only you and me.' Now the passenger was looking distinctly pale and timid.

'No, no, we'll manage. We can get a rope round him and put him in the boot, don't fret.'

They roared into a deserted farmyard and Geoff whipped the wheel round, sliding the car to a dramatic halt in the muddy courtyard. There was no one in sight. He switched the engine off and stepped out. 'McGINTY!' he bawled. 'SHOW YOURSELF, YOU BASTARD!'

The visitor cowered in the passenger seat, peering anxiously over the dashboard. With a rattle of flailing chains an enormous black Alsatian dog tore around the corner of the shed and bounced excitedly up and down in front of Geoff, slavering and panting.

'You bad dog, McGinty. How did you get out, then? Over the fence this time, eh? After the rabbits again were you? You bad boy!'

They drove carefully back to base, where Geoff put McGinty back into his basha. 'You're looking a bit peaky, you know,' he said to his visitor. 'Come and I'll buy you a drink.'

Late on Wednesday afternoon, Tim and I received a visit from two senior Special Branch officers, Peter and Sean. Both were immensely impressive men who had dedicated their working lives to the defeat of terrorism. The Det worked with them frequently, and we all had enormous admiration and respect for their judgement. To us, Ulster was an interesting theatre in which to spend an exciting couple of years before moving on in our careers. When we needed a break from the pressures of work we could fly home to the mainland. To them Ulster was home, and as police officers they lived with the constant threat of murder.

'Gentlemen, we've just learned of a proposed murder of a part-time UDR man.' Sean named a small town well over to the west of the province not far from the border. It was a quiet place, mainly Protestant, and we hadn't worked there for some time.

I leant over to the intercom on the office wall and buzzed the duty signaller. 'Hold the team that's about to deploy; we've got a new job coming in. And could you ask Jake and Colin to join us?' We needed the benefit of their experience.

Sean continued, 'Some player, as yet unidentified, is going to walk into this chap's local bar tomorrow and shoot him dead. We don't know the weapon, but we suppose it'll be a hand gun for ease of concealment.'

'Do we know the UDR man's name?' Tim asked.

'Oh aye, and we've spoken to him. He says the only time he goes to that bar is on Thursday lunchtimes, after he visits his ma. Every Thursday, regular as clockwork. Says he always sits at the same table, usually for about an hour, then drives home by the same route that he comes in.

'Our information is that the shoot is tomorrow or not at all. We're turning all the screws we can in that area to tie down the player, but we haven't got long, so we need to plan for the worst case. We may need the Troop as well. I've already asked the boss to come over.'

'Well, let's wait for the others to join us.' I went out to get Pete Spook's boys working on some photography and maps and to organise some coffee. When I re-entered the room I was struck by the scene. Here we were, Tim and I, both in our twenties, discussing the impending murder of someone we didn't know with two grizzled old Special Branch detectives. Who'd have believed it? Now Colin and Jake arrived, followed shortly by Matt, a burly staff sergeant from the Troop next door. Sean ran over the background again and we set about considering the options.

We could saturate the area with army and police, forcing the killer to abort the shoot, but if we did it would leave a gunman at large with a weapon. He might not try again at this particular target, but in the future he was bound to make another attempt, and maybe we wouldn't be so lucky with the tip next time. So that option wouldn't help us much.

'What's the chance that this is a come-on?' I asked. It would have been simple to plant a piece of information like this on a suspected SB informer, then put a bomb in the bar to catch us.

Peter glanced at Sean and said, 'We couldn't rule it out, but we reckon it's unlikely.'

We agreed that if the gunman could be identified by Special Branch early enough, the Det would put a team on to him and steer two Troop intercept cars in for a hard arrest. We wanted to use the Troop for this rather than HMSU, because it was most unlikely that the gunman would surrender, at least initially. The Troop were thoroughly trained for this sort of aggressive role. Anyway, the arrival in such a small town of the HMSU cars, with their thick greenish armoured-glass windows, could hardly fail to be commented on by the locals and would surely tip off the gunman.

As we talked I began to sketch out the requirements for each team. We would need four cars and a heli for starters, and we'd need to get some new aerial photos as soon as possible. An operator could go up in the standby heli right now. I jotted the grid reference on a piece of paper and passed it to Tom via the duty signaller. Matt, who had also been scribbling away, nipped out briefly to pass a warning order to the Troop ops room.

In case SB didn't manage to identify the gunman in time, we would need to control the street outside the bar and the approach roads. We crowded around the map and selected three OP positions on the outskirts of town from which operators could clock car registrations approaching. With a bit of luck a car would come up on the computer as stolen, triggering an intercept by the Troop. So that would need another three teams and two drop-off vehicles.

Now, supposing that doesn't work? Pete Spook came in with a sheaf of fairly old aerials that showed the town. We spread them out on the desk between the coffee cups. There was the bar, just visible in grainy black and white, a tiny building set slightly back from the main street.

Matt pointed at the photograph. 'A couple of snipers, one here . . . and one here . . . can cover the entrance in case he tries to fire in through the window,' he said, 'assuming we can get access to these rooftops along here.'

'One of us up there might be able to ping him in advance if he approaches on foot. We've got a sack of likely mugshots to work through,' Jake added.

Sean said, 'This street's a fairly Protestant part of the town, so I'd be surprised if there wasn't any part-time police or army living somewhere along there. We could maybe borrow a front bedroom or something. I'll get the local SB office on to it now.' He picked up the green secure phone on the desk and tapped a number. Cupping the receiver, waiting for it to answer, he added, 'If we can't get you in through the front door, these boys will be able to take you up over the back tonight.' He raised his eyebrows quizzically at me and I nodded back.

'What about the UDR man?' Tim asked. 'Is he going to bait the trap?'

'No way,' replied Sean. 'He said he would, but I wouldn't let him. He's got a wife and three kids.'

'I can put a team inside the bar,' said Matt casually, 'up to four of us, dressed smartly. If the gunman appears at the window, we'll take him from inside, if the snipers haven't already. If he comes in, then it'll be four against one.' He grinned. 'In fact that'll be odds of six to one, 'cause I'll be one of the four, and I'm worth at least two!

'We'll do a recce of the bar tonight. Ask him which table he usually sits at, what he drinks and whether he always wears the same jacket. If so, let's borrow it. One of our lot is bound to fit it and we can make him up to look reasonably similar. Can you get us a recent photo of him too?'

So that was the plan. We spent a hectic afternoon preparing for the op, and later that evening Matt did a recce of the bar and worked out where they would sit. The two snipers were escorted into position by operators just before first light, our OP teams inserted, and from mid-morning a car team staked out the vicinity.

At noon, Matt and two of the Troop entered the bar and occupied the table, armed only with pistols. They'd contemplated wearing under-shirt body armour, but rejected it on the grounds that it always looked suspiciously bulky. At 12.30 the fourth man, who was playing the target, entered and joined them and they began their vigil. We clocked every vehicle into the town and photographed every pedestrian who came near the bar, but no known players appeared. By 2.30 it was clear that the gunman wasn't going to show, so we reluctantly packed up and lifted off, the surveillance team resuming the task they had been diverted from the day before. It was a shame, but a common enough outcome, and in a situation like this we could never be sure whether our actions directly deterred a crime or whether it was just down to luck. In any event we admired the bravery of the members of the Troop.

We weren't always unlucky. The hardest blow to the IRA in recent times had been a typical 14 Company, SAS and Special Branch operation which came to a bloody climax in the pleasant and usually peaceful village of Loughgall one evening in early summer. We had become aware of a terrorist plan to attack the police station there. It seemed that two ASUs, eight men in all, would drive a JCB, carrying a large bomb in its front bucket, up to the front of the building. The main terrorist party would follow behind in a van. When the bomb was detonated they would advance through the rubble, executing any surviving policemen. This plan was remarkably similar to that used for an earlier attack against a similar police station more than a year before; it had worked well on that occasion so there was no reason to suppose it wouldn't serve them well once more.

Although we understood the outline plan, still we lacked the fine detail that would have permitted the entire operation to be intercepted by the police before the terrorists actually arrived at the scene. So South Det and E4A – Special Branch's own surveillance specialists – mounted surveillance operations over an extended period to try to fill in the blanks in the intelligence jigsaw. In the meantime a contingency plan was formulated in case we were unable to orchestrate pre-emptive arrests.

Some time before the planned attack, a thirty-man SAS ambush party was inserted into and around the little village, covering all the approaches to the police station. The size of the operation meant that SAS reinforcements from Hereford were flown in at short notice. Covert OPs were set up to trigger the terrorists in on the approach roads, and a small party of troopers, led by one of the Regiment's most experienced senior NCOs, was secreted inside the police station itself.

A few days of frantic covert surveillance activity failed to crystallise the intelligence picture sufficiently, and it became increasingly obvious that the fall-back position of a full scale ambush was the only feasible option. Thus, as the hours and minutes ticked away and the most likely time for the attack approached, the radio nets fell silent except for the regular requests for number-plate checks of vehicles approaching the target area. However, as is so often the case, the first indication on the ground of terrorist activity was unmissable. A convoy of three vehicles – a car scouting the route for police or army patrols, followed by the JCB, and behind it a Nissan van – passed through the covert outer cordon encircling the village. The van and the digger headed straight for the main street, where they eventually pulled up in front of the police station.

Some of the occupants began to debus, and all were carrying powerful automatic rifles. Two strolled to the front of the digger and calmly lit the fuse of the bucket bomb, before withdrawing a short distance. Then the terrorist leader raised his rifle and opened fire on the police station. He must have been surprised by the answering volley from the score of SAS weapons that were pointing at him. At once, some terrorists tried to get back into the van as others tried to get out, but it was impossible to escape the hail of bullets that was scything through the thin sheet metal of the vehicle – and anyway, with the driver now dead at the wheel it wasn't going anywhere.

Suddenly in the midst of this fusillade was a deafening roar as the bomb detonated, partially demolishing the police station, bringing plaster and brick dust down on the SAS team inside. The JCB was completely wrecked. As the smoke started to clear the firing began to die down. The road beside the riddled van was awash with blood.

A total of eight experienced terrorists were dead, caught in the act of attempted murder. Subsequent forensic tests on the weapons recovered from the scene proved they had been used many times in the murder of civilians and off-duty RUC and UDR members.

Day after day and week after week we were kept busy with an endless round of tasks and missions, frequently operating against the biggest names in the IRA. The jobs from which we derived the greatest long-term satisfaction were those requested by Jim, our MI5 liaison officer, which usually involved what we termed 'technical attack' on a building or an open space out of doors, but might otherwise be called bugging. We always kept a bottle of Bushmills in the drawer of Tim's desk, so that at the end of a long night we could toast another small victory on the technical front with Jim.

Bugging operations were easily the most demanding because they were always carried out in the very toughest locations. It called for ingenuity and sheer nerve on the part of the operators who went on target. The MI5 personnel we frequently escorted were technical specialists, and barely trained in the use of firearms, but we did feel that it was unfair for them not to have any weapons at all so we always lent them a spare pistol each, on the strict understanding that they weren't to fiddle with them or cock the action unless an emergency arose.

Once, when driving to the drop-off for a tech attack job, Tom heard a distinctive click-clunk of a pistol being made ready behind him. Immediately he pulled the car over and twisted around in his seat. 'Excuse me for asking,' he said politely, 'but has someone just cocked a pistol behind me?'

There was silence from the two MI5 technicians who were sitting pale-faced with nervous tension. 'Yes, I did,' one of them eventually said in a small voice.

'Give it to me now, please.' Tom took the gun and quickly made it safe, then handed it back. 'That was naughty,' he said reproachfully. 'It's my car and if there's any shooting to be done inside it, it'll be me that does it. OK?'

'Yes . . . sorry,' said the tiny voice.

It was easy to rib them, but MI5 specialists unfailingly performed in the most uncomfortable circumstances, and we respected them for their technical ability.

Gaining entry to individual terraced houses or flats called for the greatest ingenuity of all. Although we might be able to control the occupants of the target property for long enough for us to get in and out again, it was of course impossible to do anything about the neighbours. Therefore we used very elaborate diversions and deceptions in order to deflect suspicion. In this, the female operators were unsurpassed. By altering their appearance and clothes they could change from teenage bimbettes to middle-aged housewives walking the dog as each scenario required. Generally speaking, if you see a teenage couple necking in a doorway, you don't automatically assume they're armed to the teeth and picking the lock!

The SAS Troop was in fact relatively rarely tasked, going out on jobs once a fortnight at most. Consequently they were keen to help us out whenever we found ourselves short of manpower. The only problem with this was that, as Ernie had pointed out to us all those months ago, SAS troopers in plain clothes always seem to resemble SAS troopers in plain clothes. To a man they liked to dress in tight blue jeans, trainers, sweatshirts and bomber jackets; and their notion of a civilian hairstyle invariably matched that of the average professional footballer – long at the back, short at the sides and front. The whole effect was in many cases neatly pulled together by the addition of a fierce-looking, droopy Mexican moustache. We admired their guts and fighting skills, but there was no doubt about it – we were the experts at covert operations.

On one occasion I found myself briefing the Det operators and Troop members together. We were involved in the interception of an INLA gun team on their way to carry out the murder of a petrol station attendant who was a part-time soldier. We had no idea which individual terrorists were involved, nor which direction they would approach from, but we hoped to trigger the gunmen into the area, then keep control of them while three SAS teams in civilian cars carried out an intercept.

In addition to a ring of operators and SAS around the town centre, our joint plan required a party of four of the Troop to act as a cut-off group. We had agreed the particular road junction that they should cover, blocking a potential escape route. As usual time was short, so the various teams would have to deploy immediately the briefing was over.

As everyone was bustling out I noticed that the four Troopers forming the cut-off group were putting their G3Ks into a long canvas toolbag, like builders sometimes carry. This struck me as odd because they would surely remain in their car until the surveillance ring confirmed that the target was approaching them.

'Er, excuse me guys. What's the bag for?' I asked warily.

'Well, if we're going to stand on that street corner for a long time minding our own business, we need somewhere to hide the weapons, obviously,' replied one of them.

'Yeah, but the four of you can't stand about on a street corner. You'll blow what we're up to,' I said.

'No we won't, we're all in civvies!' he retorted.

I looked them up and down. Four pairs of trainers . . . four pairs of stonewashed jeans . . . three assorted bomber jackets . . . two Mexican moustaches . . . only one hairstyle! 'With the greatest respect and all that, if you guys stand on the street with your bag of guns you'll have the shopkeepers boarding up their windows before you can say knife!'

He looked a bit crestfallen. 'Well, er . . . OK then, we can take it in turns to stand there, looking in the shop windows –'

'Er . . . no. 'Fraid not. I've got a better idea. You lot stay in your car, in the car park opposite, until you see them, all right? Then you can leap out and give it rooty toot from there, as required.'

Fortunately they seemed to feel this was a reasonable compromise.

The Troop were as keen as mustard and exactly the right guys to have around when the firing began, but they were not trained in the way that we were, and therefore lacked subtlety. Some in the SAS, both officers and troopers, rather resented the existence of 14 Intelligence Company as a special forces unit, and in particular our mastery of a variety of skills that they would have wished for themselves. Their nickname for 14 Company was 'Walts', as in 'Walter Mittys'. This struck me as nothing more than evidence of their jealousy that another organisation could outperform them in a special forces task and had in some ways a more important role to play in counter-terrorism. (This sentiment may have been enlivened by the difference in our living conditions: operators lived in some style in purpose-built individual portakabins, while the Troop shared two- or four-man rooms; and although both operators and SAS earned special forces pay, each operator received £150 cash in hand each month, tax free, to cover out-of-pocket expenses while on operations.)

Since the televised assault on the Iranian Embassy Siege in 1980, the SAS had revelled in the well-deserved mystique that surrounded their every action. That was fine, but the appetite of the press is insatiable once whetted and, as more and more detail was, wittingly or otherwise, released over the years, so the silver began to tarnish and the carpets began to fray a little in their Hall of Fame. In some ways the climax of this painful decline in esteem was the disastrous (and now very fully recounted) tale of the Bravo Two Zero patrol in the Iraqi desert during the Gulf War. We Brits are very good at making a virtue out of a cock-up. Sure, accidents happen on operations – but this wasn't exactly an accident. The troopers behaved stoically and heroically, as usual, and suffered the consequences.

By contrast, most of the army hadn't heard of 14 Company, let alone the press. Our competence and professionalism in the field and on the streets day after day and year after year meant that the battle for funding within the Group of Special Forces to support our esoteric activities was a relatively easy one. Unlike the SBS and the SAS, who inevitably spend most of their time training for situations that rarely arise, or travelling abroad teaching skills to foreign forces, we were engaged full-time on real operations. For our part we were perfectly happy to share our resources with the Troop.

I also suspected that the Troop, living alongside us and witnessing us setting out on operations night and day, didn't actually appreciate the risks to which we were routinely exposed. Our style was to play down the nature of the job that we did – it would have been easy enough for us to become overconfident or complacent – but occasionally something would happen to remind us of the dangers.

One lunchtime I had just completed a surveillance briefing, and strolled into the ops room to speak to the duty signaller. As we discussed the impending frequency change he casually switched on the TV in the corner to catch the lunchtime national and local news. The TV was permanently rigged up to a video recorder, and one of his jobs was to record any news item that might be of interest to the detachment. Usually this would be a reported find of weapons or bombs, or the chance arrest of terrorists. Invariably the story would run that these were the result of RUC diligence and good fortune – which was of course partly true, but it was generally far from the whole truth. It was always satisfying to see a report on TV that represented the culmination of one of our covert operations.

As the opening theme for the news began to play, the signaller interrupted me. 'Jesus, look at that!'

I span round and saw what must have been almost live footage. A civilian car, two up, was manoeuvring wildly in amongst the funeral cortège of one of the terrorists who had been killed by the SAS in Gibraltar the previous week. We watched in horror as the crowd, composed mainly of youths, closed around the vehicle like snarling jackals, the TV camera being roughly jostled but holding the picture on the car.

'They must be Protestants having another go!' I said. At an

earlier funeral a Protestant murderer had attacked a Catholic funeral cortège in Belfast's Milltown Cemetery with hand grenades and a pistol. 'Let's try that registration number in VENGEFUL.'

Now a shot was fired from within the car, momentarily scattering the barbarous pack, but I could see that after one round the pistol had jammed, the working parts held open. The car was engulfed by the mob and the occupants were being beaten and dragged away as I entered the number into the computer terminal. Three seconds later the teleprinter clattered briefly and I gasped as I read the line of text. It gave the cover details of the green army's main headquarters in Lisburn, only a few miles from the scene! 'Shit, it's one of ours!' I grabbed the green secure handset and pressed the button for our own Headquarters ops room. A second later the duty signaller there answered. He sounded almost panic-stricken.

'This is James from South. Are you watching the news? That's an army car – get your ops officer!'

'We're watching it. I've just buzzed him.' I put the phone down. Oh Christ. There was nothing we could do from here. It was obvious from their response to the situation that the occupants of the car weren't operators – we were trained firstly never to get into such a serious situation, and secondly to handle it if it did arise. In fact it turned out to be a signaller from headquarters Northern Ireland taking his newly arrived replacement for an unauthorised tour of the hard areas of West Belfast. We presumed that they had driven by ill chance into the funeral cortège. Within minutes they were beaten, stripped and executed.

Two hours later, sitting in my basha, my mind's eye kept playing over those awful scenes. I thought of the countless times that I had wandered about among these people. I walked into the loo and threw up my lunch, retching with the sheer horror of it all. This tragic incident brought home to us once more the savagery of this civil war. On our side we were all honest, decent people. We wouldn't have hesitated to shoot to kill an armed criminal intent on murder if there was no other safe way to stop him. But beneath the hard veneer of our training and conditioning we were ordinary souls, with hopes and fears like everybody else. Our enemies, on the other hand, the terrorists on both sides of the conflict, were not normal people. They were murderous, evil people, without conscience. Only an evil person could look an innocent, unarmed man square in the face and shoot him dead in front of his wife and children, in order to make a 'political' point. Doubtless every society harbours the types capable of such depravity, ready to swell the ranks of the local Gestapo or KGB. No argument of patriotism or the greater good could ever justify terrorist atrocities.

The murder of the two corporals received very wide coverage on the national news, and so later that day I rang home on a casual pretext, just to make it clear that I was all right. I hadn't noticed that I slightly resembled one of the soldiers who died, and it was just as well that I called because both my family and Jennifer (who knew what I was doing in Ulster) had been beside themselves for a few hours for fear that I might be one of them.

Operations continued apace, my time now divided between running the ops room and participating on the ground. The usual crop of difficulties would arise as we set out night after night conducting technical attacks, or preventing terrorist outrages by frustrating their plans without their knowledge.

'Zero, Oscar. We've a wee problem.' Oh shit, I thought, here we go again. This particular job was proving a real nightmare, partly because of its tricky location – the bar of a pub – and partly because of the nocturnal comings and goings from the houses either side, which continually threatened to compromise our complex entry and exit procedure on target. Keith, whispering carefully, sounded pretty concerned.

'Zero. Go on,' I replied, slipping the headset on and glancing at Jim Bushmills and the two Special Branch detectives who were here for this job. They stopped talking in the background and craned forward to hear the crackling transmissions coming over the speakers either side of the large street map mounted in front of me. The tension was palpable.

'One of us has stepped in a patch of wet concrete inside the porch and left a deep footprint. I've tried to smooth it over, but it's not going to work.'

'Roger that. Any ideas?' Fuck. We hadn't been aware of any building work, but we wouldn't necessarily have been if it was just a small repair to the floor. I guessed from the way he phrased it that it was one of the MI5 lads who had left his mark – not that it mattered much who was to blame. There was a silence from Oscar. He would be discussing the situation with Andy, the other operator on target.

One of the SB men groaned and rubbed his forehead. Quickly we ran through the options. This was a tricky one, because by now the technical work had been completed – if we withdrew leaving such an obvious sign of our presence we would have to assume the whole operation had been blown and simply abandon the kit. It would be too dangerous to rely on it in the future, in case we were being fed false information to set us up. It had taken over an hour to install it and there was no way we could now extract it without leaving some signs of our activities.

Keith's next whispered transmission interrupted our debate. 'Oscar. We've had a look around but we can't find a cement bag here. The only way is for you to deliver us some and we'll try to match what's there.'

'Zero. Roger, we're on to it. In the meantime, finish the job. All callsigns acknowledge.'

'Mike, roger.' Tim, the Det Commander, was out with the team tonight. It was our private joke that whenever Tim was on the ground, keeping his hand in, something always went seriously wrong.

'Tango.' Tonight Suzy was out again with Pete, callsign Romeo.

'Golf.'

'X-Ray.'

The team of operators who were loitering nearby to assist with the exit procedure would individually ease out of the immediate vicinity of the target now that they knew there was going to be a delay. Damn it, was nothing ever simple? The target was a good hour's drive from base and there wasn't a suitable police station or barracks near it for the heli to get into, even if we could find some cement powder here. I called to the duty signaller to buzz our storemen to check whether we had any, though I couldn't imagine why we would.

'Zero, X-Ray. I passed a building site on Blue on the left on my way in. There's probably some bagged cement there.'

'Good idea. Tango and Romeo, how about a quick scout around in the building site, see what you can find? They'll need water and something to mix it in – and a stirrer.' It was better to let Keith and Andy mix their own cement on target.

'Oscar. I'm OK for water in here.'

'Tango. Roger all that. Mobile to Blue.'

Between them, Suzy and Pete could surely lay their hands on the rest of the kit. It made sense to send a girl and a bloke together into a building site – anyone spotting them at this time of night would simply think they'd nipped in for a quick shag or a pee.

In the ops room we studied the blow-ups and aerials of the target, taken from all sides.

'Oscar, Zero. Let's avoid a complete entry and exit procedure while we deliver the kit to you, if we can. Looks to me like the little top right side-window in the bog might do. Can you check it out?'

Double-click from Oscar.

'Mike, Zero. Can you do a walkpast through the alley now to check the bog window from the outside?'

'Roger. Mike's going foxtrot on Orange.'

As he walked along, Tim reported that even at this late hour there were occasional passers-by, many of them the worse for drink. If anyone looked like they were loitering outside the target when we needed to pass the kit in through the window, we could always use the HMSU cars which were out with us to move them on, or lift them if they turned stroppy. Generally though, we'd much rather not bring uniformed police into the vicinity because the effect in hard areas like this one could be just like sounding an air-raid siren, and would simply focus people's attention on potential security force activity.

Within minutes, Suzy and Pete had located a split sack of cement on the building site and filled a plastic container with the dry powder, collecting a short length of batten to act as a combined stirrer and makeshift trowel, and adding a small square of clean polythene. They drove back to the vicinity of the target and strolled arm in arm through the alleyway, pausing momentarily to thrust the small package up to Keith's outstretched hands.

Keith stirred water into the container of powder until the right consistency was reached and then did the best he could to fill in and smooth over the footprint. When he had finished he took some IR photos of the porch floor, so that we could all satisfy ourselves that the job had been done properly. He'd deliberately mixed the bulk of the paste so that it was a little drier than normal, then skimmed on a slightly wetter layer over it, in the hope that this would encourage the whole lot to dry faster. We had no choice now but to leave it to dry in its own time, reasoning that if someone had laid the fresh concrete not twelve hours before, they were hardly likely to step on it later today, and if they did they were even less likely to guess the truth about one damp patch. The team then left the target without any further hitch.

Nonetheless, to be on the safe side, we prepared a contingency plan: if Keith's IR photography showed that the repair was unconvincing, we'd stake the target out again and trigger the HMSU in to conduct a raid on the property, on some credible pretext, the moment the first keyholder arrived to open up later that morning. The HMSU commander could be trusted to make certain that a size thirteen RUC boot was accidentally squelched firmly over the dodgy patch.

As it happened, when the darkroom technician delivered the prints to us two hours later, we could see at once that Keith had done an immaculate job.

So it was 7 a.m. when I slumped exhausted into my bed, a small shot of Bushmills coursing through my veins. I'd been up for precisely twenty-four hours and my next briefing, for a surveillance task, was scheduled for 1 p.m. – but before that I'd need to talk through a long list of administrative points with our headquarters staff. Bugger . . . I also needed to check-fire my pistols, not having done that for a week . . . and work out the teams for tonight's CTR, so that the guys had time to prepare . . . and chase up the signallers about Tony's car radio. Oh well, only two and a half weeks to go until my next leave period. Don't even think about it, I told myself as I drifted off.

As a unit we invested enormous energy in defeating the terrorists on a day-to-day basis, always trying to keep one step ahead of them. For every shooting or bombing that occurred in the province we probably defeated or frustrated a dozen attempts. Since we knew pretty well who the major-league terrorists were and where they lived, and often kept them under surveillance, we sometimes debated internally the merits of simply shooting them dead in their beds. Surprisingly perhaps, I never once heard this course of action supported by an operator. I supposed this to be because we all believed firmly in the rule of law. That probably sounds trite, but I think it is true. I had honestly expected that the personnel in a special forces unit like this would be both bloodthirsty and ruthless, but the reality was entirely different – instead we were sober, responsible and supremely competent. For one thing, a typical operator, irrespective of his rank, seemed to me to be remarkably uninvolved with his quarry. I formed the impression that the SAS Troop, by contrast, were constantly raging away inside themselves, wanting to be let off the leash to wreak revenge. We on the other hand didn't take our successes or failures personally. I think this difference arose because we were operating in the sight of our targets on a daily basis and therefore lacked the pent-up frustration felt by the Troop, who deployed for an ambush or a hard arrest perhaps once a month, or at most once a fortnight. In any event I can say categorically that there was not, is not and never will be an official policy of assassination of known terrorists in Northern Ireland. Although one could perhaps find individual members of the SAS prepared to act as executioner, the only unit in the UK that could successfully locate every terrorist in the province is 14 Company – and I am convinced from personal experience that no 14 Company operator would obey such orders. It is a simple fact that, owing to the unremittingly difficult and dangerous nature of the job, the selection and training for service in the unit homes in on those individuals who display immense personal integrity, and discards the rest. Certainly we considered that terrorists were scum who deserved to die – but operators are intelligent enough to realise that the survival of our liberal democracy is more important than a short-term palliative. God knows, had we been rogues, we could have created absolute mayhem.

As the seasons passed they blurred into an endless stream of surveillance tasks, CTRs and OPs, sometimes thoroughly planned days in advance, more often cobbled together at the last minute. Inevitably we kept strange hours, frequently going to bed long after dawn and then deploying at lunchtime on the next job. The consequence of this routine was that while on leave all I wanted to do was relax and unwind quietly with Jennifer. I had decided almost as soon as I arrived in the province that I would resign my commission rather than return to a uniformed desk job in my parent infantry regiment at the end of my tour in Ireland. I quite fancied working in the City, hopefully making a bit of money and enjoying the comforting certainty of only having to work during weekdays. Jennifer had agreed to marry me, and between us we monitored the press for suitable job vacancies. One Saturday evening I was sitting in my basha, leafing through the most recent Appointments section in *The Independent,* when I was interrupted by a squawk from the intercom above my desk.

'Jim Bushmill's on the secure line, James. Says it's urgent. I've told him Tim's on leave.'

'OK, I'll come up.' Sod it. I put down the paper and jogged across to the ops block.

'Jim, hi. It's James.'

I listened while he explained the urgency. The scrambler on this secure line lent a strange tinny quality to his speech, as if we were talking to each other down a twenty-foot aluminium pipe, but despite this I could sense his excitement.

'Evening, James. I hope I've not dragged you from your bed. We're back on to the big one. We've had a stroke of luck, but we're going to have to work like greased lightning.' I knew immediately the target he meant. We had spent weeks preparing a technical attack against a particular place the target frequented, and where he certainly discussed and plotted his murderous activities. It would be a great coup to be able to see and hear what was going on. To date we had been hampered by lack of access to the site, it being in one of the hardest of areas. The danger of a compromise on the ground in a place like this couldn't be overstated – if the locals got an inkling of what we were up to an armed posse would be summoned faster than we could deploy the HMSU cars to help extract us. Also there was the propaganda angle to be considered: it would be highly embarrassing if any technical kit had to be openly abandoned. So we had always played this particular job very safe.

Now Jim explained that his boys had just learnt of a narrow window of opportunity. If South Det could put his technical team into the target tonight for an hour or two the whole operation would be sewn up in one go. He ended by promising to put two barrels of beer behind the Det bar if we could do it. This was pretty unusual – MI5 is not renowned for the generosity of its expense account entertaining!

'Well, in that case, of course we can do it!' I said.

The small MI5 teams always came over from London for each job, and Jim had just managed to organise a flight. I could guess that they wouldn't be very happy having their weekend ruined at no notice, but that's government service for you. Jim was just setting out from army headquarters to join us, as were two senior Special Branch officers. Meanwhile I buzzed Jake, Colin and Andy, our senior operators, and we soon settled down to discuss how we should tackle it.

The biggest snag was that we were going to have to make entry off a busy street between nine and ten on a Saturday night, and be clear by 11.30. This was going to be cutting things pretty fine. The timing couldn't have been worse for us. The streets would be alive on a Saturday evening.

Peering at our street plans and photography we set to it. We would obviously need a car team to control our man and to ensure that he did actually go where we anticipated he was going for the evening. Any unexpected change to his movements would ring alarm bells and we would be forced to abort. However, once the work had reached a certain point it would of course be impossible to do so, and we would be forced to take drastic steps to prevent him walking in on the team.

The most critical points were on the way in, and again on the way out. We would be exposed during the couple of minutes it would take Jake to open the locks, and equally vulnerable when the two-man MI5 team was shepherded into or out of the building. Since at that time of night it was extremely unlikely that the narrow streets would be deserted, we would have to be ready to take advantage of any opportunity that arose. Consequently the plan we arrived at was relatively complex, beginning with a preset pattern of movements by operators around the target in order to check that the streets were sufficiently clear of passers-by. If they weren't, we would have to make a snap judgement whether to delay or to stage a diversion to distract attention.

Two hours later, the plan fully formed, our briefing room was crowded with operators, uniformed HMSU, Jim with his MI5 technical team, plus the female MI5 case officer for this particular job, senior Special Branch figures, our signallers and Spooks. Briefings for this type of covert op broadly run along the familiar military format, sticking to the principal headings of Ground, Situation, Mission, Execution – first a general overview, then detailed tasks and responsibilities of all participants – then on to Administrative Support and lastly Communications. All officers at Sandhurst are taught the famous and worryingly accurate dictum that 'no plan survives contact with the enemy', meaning that Murphy's Law will invariably intercede. So it is always advisable to build in enough flexibility and delegated responsibility to permit those on the ground to change the plan slightly as it begins to unfold, to suit new conditions. We were experts at this sort of crisis management.

The target building was a two-storey detached affair, set into a row of buildings smack in the centre of a warren of little streets and alleys in the heart of a small town. The area was as hard as they come, and it would be a real challenge to make an entry and exit without being pinged by any passers-by, particularly because at one end of the long narrow street lay a popular sports club and at the other was a large bar. Ordinarily we would never risk an operation like this on a Saturday evening, but now not only did we have no choice, but we also had only three hours in total to plan, brief and rehearse the key moves.

Since they would form the entry team, Jake and Tina had immediately set out to conduct a walkpast of the target, to confirm that the outline plan we had formulated was viable, and to check from a quick visual inspection that the locks were the same Yale and three-lever Chubb that we had had to contend with on a previous occasion. We reckoned to check that the approach route was clear using 'walkers' – operators strolling along pre-set routes in the vicinity of the target – who would report on the positions and progress of passers-by and vehicles, so that the entry team could judge the right moment to make their move. Unfortunately the property fronted directly on to the street and there was no porch to speak of, the main door opening on to the pavement. Given the early hour that entry would have to take place and the bright street lighting there, it was obviously impractical and unrealistic for Jake and Tina to spend upwards of five minutes on the doorstep in a pretend, passionate clinch while they picked the twin locks. The back door was only accessible from the walled back yard of the property, and we were fairly certain that it would be bolted from the inside. Although we could deal with bolts from the outside, using a special contraption that looked like it might have been stolen from a medieval torture chamber, a lighted kitchen window in the busy property to the right of the target looked directly on to the back door, and the risk of compromise was therefore too great to allow us to use this approach.

Fortunately, the property to the left had no windows overlooking the target, and we had in the past identified a small landing

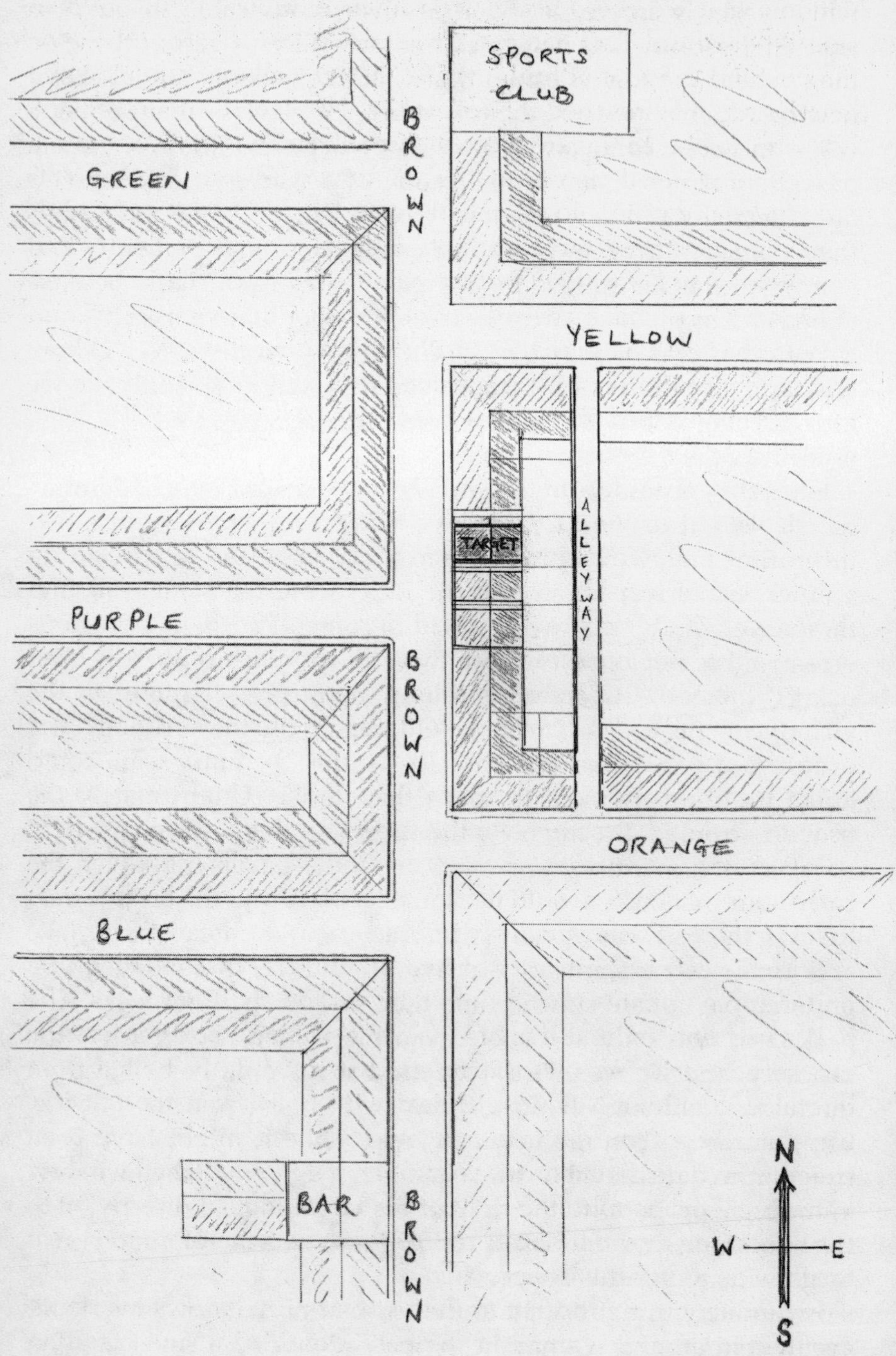
SPORTS CLUB
BROWN
GREEN
YELLOW
TARGET
ALLEYWAY
PURPLE
BROWN
ORANGE
BLUE
BAR
BROWN
N
W
E
S

window that we could access from the top of a low roof on that side. All Jake and Tina had to do was to slip into the alleyway running behind the row of buildings, scale the wall and run along its length until they reached the rear of the target, and then skirt sideways on to the corrugated asbestos roof. From here they would have unobstructed access to the landing window. They would only be briefly visible to people or vehicles passing directly in line with the side of the target, and as long as they received enough warning from the walkers, they could easily slip back into the shadows every time someone approached.

With the best will in the world there was clearly no way that the MI5 lads could safely follow the operators' route up and along the top of the wall, even if we carried their kit for them. They were neither fit nor robust enough, and the chances of a compromise occurring if one of them fell off the wall in the pitch black were too great. So we needed another route in for them. We had decided that as soon as Jake and Tina were inside the target they should secure the window again, quickly clear the building from top to bottom, and then move to the front door. Here they could pick the Chubb at leisure from the inside – of course the Yale would simply twist open as normal, this being another advantage of this approach – and receive the technicians in through the front door.

The street outside was pretty straight, with shops, small offices and houses crowding the narrow pavements either side of the road. Anyone on the target side of the street looking along it from either end at exactly the wrong moment would be able to see clearly the two MI5 men enter the darkened building through the main door. So we needed a covert approach which would neatly deliver the pair of them into the building under cover of a different and innocent activity.

We had noticed that the street narrowed slightly along the central section, and we planned to use this to our advantage. Two operators would set off along the street from south to north, walking casually a few feet apart on the same side as the target. At exactly the right moment we would drive a rickety old boxbodied van, disguised as a horsebox, and with a sliding side door, down the street from north to south, so that the side door would be on the target side. As the van approached the target it would begin to slow, indicating right down the next street. The two operators on foot would time their approach so that, as the van passed slowly by the target, they were on the pavement at either end of the vehicle, screening the view of anyone who happened to glance down the side of the van from a distance. Just here the road was narrow enough for the van to be forced to hug the left-hand kerb, even though it was intending to turn right. When it had slowed to walking pace an operator in the back would slide the door wide and bundle the technicians out. Jake would have the front door ready to swing open to receive them, securing it with the Yale the moment they were inside. The van would continue slowly around the corner and the operators would walk on up the street, leaving the team inside to set to work. Anyone seeing a horsebox on the road at this time of night would simply assume we were smuggling cattle.

So far so good. We'd done this sort of thing many times before, and were all aware that a plan that relies on strict timing often rapidly unravels if local circumstances are not ideal. It's impossible to make a contingency plan for every conceivable eventuality. If things began to go wrong we would just have to cuff it.

The next tricky part of the operation would be the extraction. The technicians could exit through the front door in a reversal of their entry process, but if Jake and Tina came out at the same time they would have to stay on the doorstep to lock the door from the outside, which would look pretty suspicious to any casual observer because they would have apparently materialised on the pavement out of thin air. A safer alternative would perhaps have been for them to retrace their steps out of the side window, along the wall and down into the alley. However, we knew this was not an option. Although one can fairly simply open a shut window from the outside, it is extremely difficult to shut it firmly from the exterior. Experience told us that as often as not the horizontal stay bar or the fastener require considerable force to secure them back into their original position, and that the required amount of leverage is very difficult to apply from the outside. The risk of inadvertently failing to restore the window to the position it had been in before we arrived was too great, and so Jake opted to exit through the front door. Relocking the three-lever mortice lock was a much simpler process than unlocking it, and of course the Yale would simply click shut. It should anyway be approaching midnight by then, a much more suitable time for a couple of minutes of tongue-wrestling on the doorstep.

Of course, the same danger from onlookers would arise on exit as it had on entry. The solution to this was to send Pete and Suzy ambling up the road, timing their progress to arrive at the target's doorstep no more than half a minute before the horsebox appeared on the scene. There they would begin a bit of heavy petting in the doorway. The van would roll slowly past, intending right again, and as it drew level Jake would propel the two MI5 lads out of the front door and in through the sliding door. Pete and Suzy would leap in behind them, and the van would pick up speed again as it began the turn. Now Jake and Tina would be standing on the doorstep, playing the original snogging couple, giving them time to relock the Chubb before apparently continuing their slow amorous meander up the road.

The surveillance team, who would have been controlling Bravo 1 several miles away during the course of this activity, would then be able to lift off, and we'd all go home to drink our two barrels of beer.

At least, that's how we'd planned the evening . . .

True to the intelligence received from Jim Bushmills, at about 9.30 p.m. the car team successfully located Charlie 1, driven by Bravo 1, and held it fast in their invisible web as he headed away to his appointment. We needed him to stay there for a good hour and three-quarters – if he left earlier and appeared to be heading back to the target we would have to make some fast decisions. At least all the decision-makers were present tonight in the ops room, I thought, which was itself a mark of the importance of the operation.

'Yankee. Am I obvious, anyone?' asked Will from 9,000 feet and seven kilometres to the north-east of the building in which Bravo 1 had gone to ground.

'Golf. You're OK from Yellow Two Seven.'

'Roger that. I have the trigger on Charlie 1 and four other vehicles.'

In the ops room, lounging on a swivel chair, I acknowledged. 'Zero.' Good. We should have plenty of notice if Charlie 1 went mobile, because he was currently parked at the end of a very long track. In the darkness it would be too much to expect Will to be able to say whether it was actually Bravo 1 driving, but we'd just inserted Carl – callsign Kilo – into the hedgerow at the junction where the track joined the minor road. He was now stalking forward into a position to clock and photograph the registrations and occupants of any vehicle that passed, so we'd soon know if Bravo 1 left, even if he was in someone else's car.

Now that Yankee had the trigger, the others in the car team were pulling back, reporting their progress and intentions so that the ops room and the rest of the team could judge how secure the stakeout box was at any particular moment.

'Quebec's to Yellow Two Two.'

I didn't need to glance at the large map in front of me to confirm that from there Steve would be covering the eastern options, but nonetheless I neatly updated his position with a fresh mark on the perspex sheet covering the map. With eighteen separate callsigns on the ground at any one time tonight, it was wise to try to keep track, at least until the pace of change became too frantic.

'Oscar's complete X-Ray at Green Two Seven.'

'Zero.' I made another alteration to the mapboard in front of me. It often made sense for two of our cars to sit side by side in one of the many popular lovers' lay-bys at night. The two operators would then sit in the front of one of the cars, reclining both front seats so that if a third party's headlights swept across the cars they would appear to be just another courting couple. Only a real pervert with his nose pressed against the window would have been able to make out that it was in fact two men! I don't know how common in-car bonking was a pastime in England, but to judge from the used condoms that littered every lay-by and beauty spot in Ulster when I was there, it should have had official recognition as an Olympic sport.

'Golf's satelliting the lanes around Yellow One Six.'

'Zero, roger. Kilo, Zero. Check.'

'Kilo. I've got eyes on the junction now.' Carl's Welsh whisper was barely audible, but at least the signal was clear and strong.

Now that we had Bravo 1 tied down it was time to clear the entry route. India, Romeo, Tango and Hotel had arrived independently in the vicinity of the town a few minutes before. Ian – callsign India – had with him his friendly jet black rottweiler, Rip, on a leash and chain – excellent cover for his perambulations. The team was well spread out in the small town, parked up in lanes and side streets, awaiting my signal to set off along their prescribed routes. But before that I needed to know that the entry team, Jake and Tina, – callsigns Delta and Victor – was cruising the area.

'Delta Victor, Zero. Where are you?'

'Static on Orange, ready when you are.'

'Zero, roger. Walkers, move in.'

'India's foxtrot.' Ian and Rip set off, their route taking them on Purple up to the junction opposite the target, then left on to the main drag, colour-coded Brown, then first right on to Yellow, before doubling back to clear down the alleyway that the entry team would use.

'Romeo's foxtrot.' Pete was starting from Orange, the first side road south of the target, turning right on to Brown, and keeping straight on for a good 150 metres past the target until he reached Tom's car. Seconds before, Tom, callsign Hotel, had gone foxtrot and was now loitering to the north-west of the target on Green, ready to emerge and turn south on Brown, crossing the paths of Romeo and India, before ambling straight down Brown until he reached Pete's car.

'Tango's foxtrot.' Suzy was strolling up from the south on Brown and would turn left on to Purple just short of the target, clearing again the route that Ian would have passed over a few moments before.

As the tempo of the operation began to pick up, the background noise in the brightly lit and now rather smoky ops room was increasing alarmingly. I swung round on my swivel stool. Two Special Branch officers were arguing about something in one corner, while behind me Jim Bushmills and the female case officer were deep in conversation over a scale plan of the interior of the target. I raised my voice over the cacophony. 'Everybody shut up or get out – I can't hear the net! If you want to talk you can use Tim's office.' Silence fell, broken only by the hiss and crackle over the net. I slipped the radio headset on again.

'Papa, zero, check.'

'Papa OK. We're static, complete at Red Two Four.' Derek was riding as liaison with the HMSU tonight. Red Two Four was equidistant between Alpha 1, our target, and Alpha 2, where the surveillance team had the trigger on Bravo 1 and Charlie 1. The HMSU were for emergencies only tonight.

'Delta, Zero. Go now.'

'Roger. We're foxtrot on Orange towards the alley.'

Suddenly Will broke in, the background clatter of the heli's blades almost drowning his speech. 'Zero, Yankee. I have movement from Alpha 2 towards the Charlies.'

'Zero,' I acknowledged, cursing inwardly. Bloody typical!

'Kilo.' Carl would clock the occupants of any vehicle moving out of the end of the track.

'Yankee. That's a Charlie manoeuvring; it's definitely not Charlie 1.'

'Oscar's complete.' That was Keith getting back to his own car, ready to move into a follow if Carl confirmed that Bravo 1 was in this unknown Charlie. It didn't seem likely, though.

'Papa.'

I switched my attention back from the mapboard to the town plan propped in front of me. The walkers were beginning to report their progress so that the entry team could time their clamber up on to the wall and then the side roof to coincide with a break in the passing traffic and pedestrians. The transmissions were rapid, low and muttered, hardly surprising since there were lots of people in the narrow streets. Although we had two signallers on duty at all times to assist with manning the various ops room radio nets, it required an operator's ear to decipher many of the calls.

'Tango's fifty short of Brown Blue.'

'Hotel's on Brown towards Yellow.'

'Romeo's at Brown Orange.'

'India's on Brown, from Purple towards Yellow.'

'Yankee. That's that Charlie mobile down the track.'

'Kilo.'

'Oscar's mobile to Yellow Three One.' Keith was moving in closer, in case we had to take this Charlie.

'Hotel, India. Watch out for that little twat in the green parka on Brown – he's drunk and looking for a fight.'

Double-click from Hotel.

'Tango. There's a car sitting two up opposite the target, looks domestic.' She gave the registration which Pete Spook tapped straight into our VENGEFUL terminal.

'Zero. That should be a grey Volvo 360. It's clean.' Or at least it wasn't registered to any known terrorist suspect or sympathiser. It was always important to confirm a car's actual description matched that of its plates, in case it had been stolen or hijacked and given false ones.

'Delta Victor's into the alleyway.'

'India's on Yellow. Alley's clear from this end.'

Double-click from Delta.

'Zero, Kilo. That's a negative Bravo 1 in that Charlie which has gone left on the main.'

'Zero.'

'Yankee.'

'Oscar's to Green Two Three.'

Now Jake and Tina would be on top of the back wall and running lightly along its length to reach the shadows against the tall building, their submachine guns strapped to their chests inside their loose black jackets. Wearing black gloves and balaclavas they would be visible only when silhouetted against the street lighting.

'Tango. The Charlie opposite the target is pulling away now, but there's a group of foxtrots approaching from Yellow. Wait till they pass in ten seconds.'

Double-click from Delta.

'Zero, roger. Romeo?'

'One foxtrot in the way, should be clear in ten.'

'Hotel, Zero. Clear?'

Double-click from Hotel. Mentally I counted down from ten.

Then Tina whispered, 'Delta's on to the roof, I need ten seconds' warning of foxtrots.' She sounded breathless. Jake would now be stretched flat out, manipulating his instruments.

'Romeo. That's a foxtrot towards you, passing in twenty.'

'Victor.'

'Romeo. Cancel that – he's gone left on Yellow.'

Double-click from Victor.

'Hotel. There's a foxtrot north on Brown. You'll be OK if he stays on your side of the road.'

'Victor.'

'Zero.'

'India. That's a bus approaching up the hill on Brown, on you in fifteen.'

Double-click.

Then, 'Delta's back on the wall.' Jake had retreated to the shadows, waiting for another gap in the traffic. He sounded incredibly cool, all things considered.

'Tango. All clear after the bus.'

'Hotel. All clear.'

'And Romeo.'

'Victor. That's Delta back at the window.'

'Zero.'

The room was silent now. Each new transmission added to the charged atmosphere. I watched the large second hand sweep half-way around the face of the ops room clock.

'Delta, Romeo. Foxtrots on you in twenty.'

Double-click. I kept my eyes on the clock. Ten seconds passed. Then, 'Delta's complete.' Jake was inside the building.

Five seconds later came the whispered call from Tina: 'Victor's complete, window shut.'

I exhaled. 'India, Tango, Romeo, Hotel – lift off, prepare for phase two.'

Acknowledgements rippled across the net.

Jake and Tina would now be sneaking quickly through every room of the target, MP5Ks at the ready, checking that it was indeed deserted before moving carefully down to the front door. This was another advantage to the side window entry – they only had to pick the Chubb lock, since the Yale would open from the inside as normal. As Jake worked silently, Tina kept a lookout from a darkened ground-floor window, warning him every time a pedestrian strolled past. Meanwhile Andy, callsign Lima, was driving the horsebox van carefully through the narrow streets, George marshalling the two MI5 lads into position by the door in the back. Simultaneously Pete and Tom, callsigns Romeo and Hotel, were walking into position to start their second pass up the main drag.

'Zero, Delta. Ready for Lima.' Jake now had the Chubb unlocked and was waiting, his hand on the Yale's mechanism, to swing the door open.

'Yankee, Zero. Check.' Best to make absolutely sure that Alpha 2 was still quiet before committing the MI5 team.

'Yankee. No movement.'

OK, so it was shit or bust. I stole a glance at Jim Bushmills behind me. He was sitting on a straight-backed chair, eyes closed, fingers steepled in front of him, lips pursed, listening to the radio traffic, no doubt, but looking almost as if in prayer.

I pressed the transmit button. 'Lima and Romeo go.'

The ops room fell silent again, except for the regular reports over the net from Lima and Romeo as their routes converged on the target. There was no mistaking their alternating calls; Romeo muttering quietly in the street, Lima with the engine whine audible in the background.

'Romeo's at Blue Brown.'

'Lima's approaching Green.'

'Romeo's at Brown Orange.'

'Lima's on Green towards Brown.'

'Romeo's ten short of the target.'

'Victor. All clear.'

'Lima's at Green Brown.'

'Romeo's five short.'

'Lima's at Brown Yellow.'

Again I watched the second hand sweep around, imagining the scene as the van slowed to turn right. By now Pete and Tom would be standing either side of its doorway, screening the three-foot breadth of pavement from view as George hustled the technicians out of the back. The van would be crawling along at about one mile an hour for about three seconds – just long enough, as long as no one stumbled or fell.

'Lima's on Purple,' cut through the tense silence.

'Delta. That's everyone complete, door shut.'

'Romeo and Hotel foxtrot on Brown.'

Phew. I rubbed my temples and stretched back. I exchanged glances again with Jim, who was rubbing his hands at the prospect of finishing this job tonight. Now we should be able to sit back for an hour and a half, simply monitoring the situation. Better check the surveillance team.

'All stations, Zero. Check. Yankee?'

'OK, all quiet.' I didn't envy him, hovering thousands of feet up, eye glued to the little rubber hood of the powerful sight, thumb constantly adjusting the joystick.

'Quebec?'

'OK.'

'Golf?'

'OK. Static at the lay-by at Red One Four.'

Now the various team members would be mooching around independently, melting into the background in the small town, ready to react if any new situation arose but keeping themselves well away from the target area. The streets were busy with Saturday night revellers; even within the target the faint pulsing beat from the nearest bar's sound system could be felt. It struck me as incongruous, because in every other respect the shops and houses were trapped in a timewarp – in the nationalist border areas the Troubles seemed to have frozen everything as it had been in August 1969. The carpets, the clothes, the window displays, the architecture, it all looked rather shabby and neglected. Still, at least the young people obviously enjoyed themselves. As we sat listening to the sparse radio traffic, I continually updated my mapboard with the positions of the different callsigns.

Peter, one of the Special Branch officers, had been born and brought up in the area that we were working in tonight. In 1970 his family – Protestants – had moved to Belfast for their own safety, and he was studying the map with a wistful look. 'What a shame, eh?' he said quietly. He traced his finger down a broad valley near the border. 'I loved that valley. My brother and I used to fish for minnows in that wee burn there. Everyone about was so friendly. And what now? What have they achieved for theirselves? Goodness knows, if you dial 999 the police won't come, not until the soldiers have secured the area first, and the soldiers won't come until their engineers have cleared the route for bombs. So all they can do is ask the IRA godfathers to sort out the problem – and then some wee hoodlum gets a bullet in each knee, guilty or no.'

'Do you think the locals really support the aims of the IRA?' I asked.

'For a united Ireland? Yes, I'd think so. But not their methods, not in their hearts. Believe it or not, these are good folk, James, all bar the hardcore. They suffered a lot in the past from the dominance of the Protestants, little abuses and humiliations over housing and jobs and so on, until it boiled over into this. And now they suffer a different sort of humiliation because of the terrorists. Constant security force checkpoints and searches, still no jobs, no sympathy even – it's tragic really.'

I nodded at him then pressed the transmit button. 'Yankee, Zero. How much fuel have you left up there?' He should have had plenty to keep the heli up for the duration of the op, but it depended on the wind.

'Yankee. Graham reckons two hours' flying time at least.'

'Roger that.' I turned back to the policeman. 'Do you think in another fifteen years people like you and me'll still be sitting in an ops room here, running operations against the boyos?'

'God, I hope not. I've kids myself, I wouldn't wish this on them. It's too degrading. We're supposed to be civilised. Personally I reckon in the long run it'll come down to a question of economics.

When everyone in the province is wealthy enough to buy a smart car, a new kitchen and a foreign holiday, no one'll have the belly for this nonsense any more, they'll be too busy with themselves. I remember how my wife and I were when we bought our first house. We could hardly sleep, we'd be padding around the different rooms just touching things. No, I'm sure we'll get there in the end. Maybe we'll never defeat the terrorists once and for all, but they sure as hell can't defeat us either. And in the meantime life will ever so slowly get better and better, until one day someone like the guy we're after tonight will get a call from his commander for the next murder, and he'll say, "I'm sorry, I can't make that job, I've booked the family into Centreparcs next week, and I don't want to disappoint the kids."'

'Yeah, well,' I said weakly, 'I just hope you're right.' In a way, in front of him I felt embarrassed about the whole situation, like an outsider hearing about a family problem. It was as if we were doctors having to say, 'I'm sorry, but you've got a cancerous growth. We'll come and treat it all right, but the side-effects may kill you. There'll be no charge, of course – the state will pay.' And when we had had enough, we'd pass the case notes on to the next doctor and move on to something more congenial.

In the background Jim Bushmills was talking on his own radio net to his people at Lisburn, and to the team in the target, checking that they were adequately tweaking the tiny equipment that would be left behind.

Suddenly Tina's urgent whisper crackled over the net. 'Zero, Victor. Someone's just climbing over the rear wall from the alleyway!'

Jesus Christ, what's this then, I thought. It could be an ambush party coming in to get us. Let 'em come, I thought. As Tina had just demonstrated, we'd have the element of surprise on our side. They'd be mad to try to attack us from outside. No, if that was their intention, if they knew in advance we were coming, surely they'd have hidden inside the building and jumped us once we had started work, and if they'd only just spotted us they'd try to catch us on the way out.

'Victor. That's a second body over the wall. I think they're just kids, I can hear them talking.'

Kids? I looked at the two Special Branch officers, but they were shaking their heads. There were no kids we were aware of with any legitimate reason to come here, and certainly not over the back wall at this time of night. Bugger it, this was a serious situation. If one of the little bastards tried to break into the place, Tina would have no option but to stick her submachine gun up his nose and say, 'Back off, sonny. *We're* burgling this property tonight!' And then we'd be well and truly blown.

In the ops room we conferred briefly and came up with four options to scare them off, though I was aware they all had serious disadvantages: the entry team could turn some internal lights on to make it look occupied; the HMSU could scream past with their sirens going to try to scare them off; we could sit it out and see what happened next; or maybe we could somehow draw the neighbours' attention to them, perhaps by throwing something at their kitchen window and hoping that they'd investigate. I gave out these options over the net, and within seconds Ian came up on air, from where he was parked up on Orange.

'Zero, India. How about Rip and I having a look-see from the alley? Rip'll snarl and bark to order. Might chase 'em away.'

'Brilliant, give it a go.' That's an operator for you, I thought.

'Roger. India's foxtrot into the alley.'

'Victor, roger. They're still at the end of the yard, beside the oil tank. You'll be able to see them through the wooden gate.' That gate was thoroughly nailed shut, which was why we hadn't been able to use it ourselves, but I could see from the recent photos pinned in front of me that there were plenty of gaps in it.

Double-click from India. I was looking at the aerial blow-ups of the target. There was a shed in the corner of the yard; maybe that was what was of interest to them.

Now Ian was peering through a gap in the gate. He whispered, 'India. They're kids all right, about fifteen years, and pissed up by the look of them. I'll get rid of them.'

He put on his best Irish Borders accent and yelled at them through the gate: 'You boys get out of that yard now and take yourselves home before I tell your ma what you've been up to!'

Tina watched from a rear window as in a wild panic they dropped their cigarettes and fled back over the wall before scurrying up the alleyway, pursued into the distance by Rip's barks.

'Zero, India. They've fucked off. I'm going complete my wagon.'

'Roger, well done. All stations check. Yankee?'

'OK. Still no movement.'

'Kilo?' I ran through the rest of the callsigns, logging their positions once more. Now the streets of the town were becoming more boisterous as the Guinness began to take effect. The operators kept well clear of the bars and clubs.

Fifteen minutes later Jim pronounced himself satisfied with the job. I glanced at the clock. Eleven-fifteen – chucking out time. It couldn't have been much worse from our point of view!

'Zero, Delta. We're packing up now, ready for exit in five.'

'Zero, roger. Lima and walkers acknowledge.'

'Lima, at Yellow Three One towards Green.'

'Hotel's going foxtrot.'

'Tango's with Romeo.'

'India's foxtrot to Blue.'

Suddenly Will burst on to the net and my heart sank. 'Zero, Yankee. Standby, standby! I have Charlie 1, two up, lights on, manoeuvring at Alpha 2.'

'Zero.'

'Kilo.' Carl would confirm whether or not Bravo 1 was in the car, and he was very likely to be since it was now quite late. Shit, it was just typical. Why couldn't he have stayed there for another five minutes? It wasn't critical, so long as the extraction went smoothly, because he was a good fifteen minutes' drive from Alpha 1. Still, better play it safe now.

'Papa, Zero. Suggest you go mobile to Red One Six ready to set up a VCP.' Derek would ensure that if need be the HMSU would stop him long enough if everything fell apart.

'Roger. Papa's mobile.'

'Quebec's to Yellow One Seven.'

'Golf's towards Yellow Two Nine.' The surveillance team was fanning out now on the narrow roads, ready to take, no matter which way he went.

'Kilo. That's confirmed Bravo 1 and a female complete Charlie 1, at the junction and intending Yellow One Six.' Well, at least we knew now. The route to Alpha 1 was fairly straightforward from here – and fast at this time of night.

'Yankee has Charlie 1, Yellow One Six towards Yellow One Five.'

'Quebec's backing Yankee. Speed forty-five, fifty.'

Jake was beginning the exit preparations, and not before time. 'Delta's ready for exit.'

He and Tina had the technicians ready to go in the hallway,

having done a last sweep to make sure they hadn't left any items behind. Tina's camera, loaded with IR film and flash, had by now taken the necessary 'before and after' shots, so that we could be certain that there was no ostensible sign of our activities.

'Lima's on Green.'

'Romeo's at Blue Orange. There are four foxtrots at Yellow towards Purple, otherwise clear.' He and Suzy were now clutching beercans and weaving slowly up the street, his arm around her shoulder.

'Hotel. That's two foxtrots on Purple from Brown, but no problem.'

'Zero.'

'Yankee. Charlie 1 at Yellow One Four and straight.'

'India's static at Green Brown – all clear.'

'Romeo's approaching the target.'

'Lima's at Green Brown.' George would be standing now in the swaying darkness, grasping the inside handle of the van's side door.

'Hotel. That's two Charlies on Purple towards Brown.' Shit. If those two cars arrived at the junction just before Lima, their headlights would floodlight the target just as the team were piling out of the door. 'They're intending left! Abort, abort!' If they were turning left they would easily spot the exit drill.

'Lima's past the target, towards Brown Blue, going round again for pick-up.'

'Delta.'

'Yankee. That's Charlie 1 through Yellow One Three and straight.' Goddamn, he was returning even faster than we had anticipated.

'Zero, roger.' I studied the street plan in front of me. Bugger, it would take the van at least two minutes to do the circuit and get back to the target. If we had to abort again, we would be cutting it too fine for comfort; Jake might still be relocking the front door when Bravo 1 appeared.

'Papa's at Red One Six.' Well, Derek and the HMSU could always stop him to check his tyres or something, but it wouldn't look right, not in that area.

'Golf's to Red One Three.'

'Oscar's backing Yankee.'

'Quebec's off.'

'Zero.' And all the while, Pete and Suzy were snogging on the doorstep of the target. It was OK for a bit longer.

Lima was now skirting around to the north to come in on Brown. Again the walkers cleared the route in each direction.

'Lima's approaching Brown Green.'

'India. Clear from Green to the target.'

'Hotel. Clear to Purple Brown.'

'Romeo. OK south on Brown.'

'Lima. I've now got a Charlie backing me, out of Green.'

Shit. By sheer bad luck a car had pulled out immediately behind the van and was just feet from Andy's back bumper as he passed Yellow. It couldn't help but see the pick-up. I involuntarily held my breath. If Lima had to go around again we were going to be in trouble.

'I'm pulling over.' He pulled into the kerb briefly, forcing the car to overtake in the narrow street. Then, 'Mobile,' as he pulled out again, now behind the car. The van's headlights should dazzle anyone looking backwards from the car.

'All clear behind,' came now from India.

'Hotel's clear.'

'And Romeo.'

Silence descended. The faint *hish* of static came over the net. In the ops room we all sat or stood motionless, waiting for the next transmission. George should now be standing in the open doorway of the van, waiting to grab the MI5 lads, followed by Pete and Suzy.

Jake and Tina should now be on the doorstep . . .

'Pick-up complete. Lima's on Purple.'

I released a lungful of air and leaned forward to speak into the mike. 'Zero, roger. Yankee, where is he?'

'Approaching Red One Six.' This was our last chance to use the HMSU. If Jake encountered a problem relocking the Chubb, we could still be up shit creek. I had about three seconds left to make the decision.

'Papa, Zero. Stay complete – do not VCP.' We'd chance it. Jake was the most experienced lock-pick we had.

'Papa, roger.'

'Hotel's foxtrot on Brown to Blue. There's a group of yobbos approaching the target from Orange.'

'India. I'm foxtrot to back up Delta.' Ian was moving south so that if the yobs tried to interfere with Jake and Tina he could use Rip to protect them.

'Zero, roger. Hotel, go complete for an immediate pick-up of Delta Victor north on Brown.'

Tom double-clicked. His car was nearest the target, parked on Purple. If the yobs took an interest in Jake and Tina he could whip out and pick them up before things got out of control.

'Victor. It's OK, they've crossed to the other side intending Purple.' Tina sounded understandably relieved.

'Hotel.'

'Yankee. That's Charlie 1 approaching Blue.' He was less than a minute and a half away. Come on Jake, I willed.

'Delta. All done. We're foxtrot north on Brown.' From the lack of excitement in his voice he might have been saying 'pass the salt, please'. He was one cool cookie!

'Zero, roger. Everyone go complete, lift off, acknowledge.'

I felt completely drained, but it was nothing that a share of two barrels of beer wouldn't cure! As I cleared up the ops room, filing away the scattered paperwork, maps and photos, I ruminated that at least tomorrow was Sunday, and I could lie in for a bit, then maybe go for a run, followed by a leisurely brunch and a read of the papers.

Jim was packing up his radio equipment, and winked at me as I passed him. 'Piece of cake, wasn't it?'

'Yeah,' I replied. I thought for a moment, then added, grinning, 'Battenburg, I'd say! You know – little colourful bits stuck together with glue!'

Chapter Seven

A week later I was sitting in my basha cleaning my weapons when Carl dropped off a letter that had just arrived for me. Our mail was forwarded from another location and was always thoroughly sanitised, the address being replaced simply by the recipient's false Christian name. We routinely shredded mail once we had read it, because our domestic rubbish was disposed of within the province. However, I fervently hoped that I would be framing this letter, not shredding it. I ripped it open anxiously and scanned the few lines.

'Dear Mr Rennie . . . pleased to inform you . . . vacancy on the programme . . . if you wish to accept this offer . . .'

I found myself grinning with delight. This was the news I had been hoping for. Following two interviews, for which I had to fly back to the mainland, I was now being offered a place on the Graduate Trainee Programme of a major company. So now, for the first time in ages, it seemed, I needed to make an important decision solely about my own personal interests. I was at the junction of two diverging paths: should I stay in the army for the rest of my career, or leave while the going was firm and the sky clear? If I left now, I would still be young enough to start on the bottom rung of a new ladder – that much was obvious from the job offer. But then I thought, haven't I always been in a hurry to move on to the next thing? I'd hankered to join the army straight from school, then I'd pressed to go to University at the earliest opportunity, then I'd volunteered for 14 Company the moment the regular army bored me, and now here I was feeling that even a career in special forces, as far as that was possible for an officer, wasn't really what I was after. But if I left now, might I not want to change course yet again in a few years' time – and where would that leave me then? Maybe I was just a feckless malcontent. Why bury the foundations of a successful army career now, just when I had garnered experience that a lot of officers would give their eye teeth for? I'd always fancied myself as a general . . . and Jennifer always said she liked the look of me in uniform . . . .

I sat looking out of the window of my little sitting room, surrounded by the paraphernalia of my odd calling. I absentmindedly reassembled my pistol and slipped it back into my covert waistband holster. The comforting bulk of it reminded me that I had to get ready for a surveillance task shortly. I had put myself down as one of the team and Tim would be manning the ops desk.

As I stood in front of the full-length mirror in my dressing room, checking the concealment of the different items of equipment as I slotted each into its place around my clothing, I made my decision. I'd leave the army. This job was interesting enough, but it was lonely. Life in the regular army was full of good company, but the job was dull. So I'd leave now and start afresh with Jennifer. As soon as I got back from this task I'd tell Tim and then write formally to Colonel John, tendering my resignation.

I was fully occupied right up to the day of my departure. Two weeks before I was due to fly out of the province for the last time I had handed over the post of ops officer to Andy, an NCO of many tours' experience. This meant that I was available full-time as an operator again, and I enjoyed the constant activity out on the ground.

As part of our surveillance activities, we were continually inserting and servicing covert cameras, each created for its own very specific task. The ingenuity of our technicians knew no bounds, and they were expert at concealing complex camera rigs in everyday objects. We could command the cameras remotely, switching them on and off from the comfort of the ops room. Here we had a bank of monitors on which we could display the image from any selected camera, and some of them were set up to allow us to tilt, pan and zoom the image. It sometimes seemed bizarre to be sitting in the ops room during a surveillance task, following a terrorist around an operational area. This in no sense removed the need for a conventional surveillance team. Rather, it dramatically extended our capabilities in the hardest of areas.

There were two disadvantages to this use of high technology. Firstly, the insertion of each new camera was time-consuming because we had to go through a routine of tweaking the electronics until we received an acceptable image; and secondly there was always the risk that a piece of equipment would be pinged by the opposition, laying us open to the risk of a booby-trap or ambush when we next serviced it. So we sited cameras in pairs or more, covering each other. The general details of each individual location were passed in a sealed envelope to the local police or army base, to be opened in an emergency only on receipt of a codeword from us. It we saw, for example, that kids were playing around with an item, not realising what it was, one quick call would immediately despatch a local security force patrol to the spot to recover it.

The morning that I was due to leave Ulster for good I packed the last of my bags and prepared to go across to the stores to hand in my specialist kit and weapons. I was booked on to a late-afternoon flight and was due to fly out from the UK the next day with Jennifer on a short holiday. The Det had presented me with a silver cigarette box, thoughtfully inscribed, and I had just stowed it into my suitcase when the squawk from my intercom broke into my train of thought.

'James, it's Andy. We've got a problem with a piece of kit.' He named the site and instantly I could picture the spot, because I had only recently revised the emergency envelope, which contained photographs, a section of map and a sketch. 'It looks like it's kids. Can you come up to the ops room?'

'Rightoh.' I knew what was coming next. If kids had disturbed the kit, we needed to check whether they had damaged the intricate camouflage surrounding it. If not, we could leave it in place. But if they had disturbed it, we'd need to recover it pronto. The trouble was that an ordinary green army or police patrol would not be able to judge this adequately, and might inadvertently give the whole thing away. So it would need an operator's eye to decide the matter. I realised that if we sent a current operator – and if the kit was indeed now visible to passers-by – the operator would be identifying himself as belonging to the security forces if he strolled up in civvies and then carried the object away.

In the ops room Andy and the signallers had gathered around a monitor and were watching the picture transmitting from the tiny lens far away. The door and driveway of the target was still plainly visible, and when we panned around there were some kids playing with a football in the road.

'I reckon they may have hit it with the ball,' Andy said. 'The camera's on, but we can't see anything untoward. Pity we can't look directly backwards. For all we know they pinged it days ago and have just tipped up to bury a bomb under it!' A cheery thought!

'OK, I'll go and have a look at it,' I said. 'So long as you guarantee to get me on the flight home this afternoon!' I knew I was the only logical choice, because it wouldn't matter a jot if I was compromised now.

'Thanks. I've tasked a green army patrol to meet you in the local police station. They'll have a spare rifle for you.' There was no point drawing attention to myself, so I would dress in camouflage uniform and helmet and carry an ordinary self-loading rifle. 'The heli will drop you there as soon as you're ready.'

I grabbed a secure radio set, squirted the new code fill into it, and stuffed it into a camouflage backpack. Then I raced back to my basha, dug out my combat kit and patrol boots and changed like greased lightning.

It was a glorious summer's day as Graham piloted the heli up into the clear air and away. I drank in the emerald green scenery beneath the blue sky, realising that this was the last time I'd see this beautiful countryside from this angle. It was also the last time I'd ever be in uniform, or in the navigator's seat of a Gazelle for that matter. Half an hour later we spiralled rapidly down inside the tall grey walls of the RUC station on the outskirts of a republican village. It was quite common for local gunmen to take potshots at incoming helicopters here. Waiting on the hot grey tarmac was a sixteen-man patrol from the local infantry unit and two RUC constables.

A young second lieutenant, the patrol commander, greeted me warmly. It was obvious that he and his men were delighted to be involved in a special forces operation. I knew from my own experience that for these men it would be a welcome diversion from the tedium of routine patrolling.

I set up the radio inside the pack on my back and then briefed the whole patrol about what we should do. It was nothing very special because I would simply tag along in the middle of one of the bricks, acting like one of them. I indicated where the patrol should stop for a few minutes, giving me time to assess the kit in situ, and either recover it in my pack or leave it in place. They didn't need to know precisely what I was up to, although they could probably guess. Once I was done we would patrol in a wide loop back to the base.

We sprinted out of the main gates in ones and twos, and then settled down to bob and weave our way carefully into the town. I couldn't help smiling to myself. It seemed I'd gone full circle in my short military career. I'd started out doing basic military training at Sandhurst, then learnt how to be an officer. I'd commanded my platoon on patrols around West Belfast just like this one, and then operated individually on the ground on covert operations in 14 Company. Then I'd helped plan and run the ops, and now – on my last day in the army – I was back at square one, a humble grunt carrying an SLR, playing tail-end Charlie in a uniformed patrol!

We moved slowly along a back street. On one side was a tatty park, on the other a sparse row of drab houses. Heat and the smell of tarmac bounced up at us off the road, but still the soldiers were well spread out and very alert, scanning their arcs, rifle butts on their shoulders, occasionally rotating full circle as they walked. Soon we were nearing the target.

My brick commander, a fresh-faced lance corporal who looked about twenty, nodded his head in the direction of the target house and said to me quietly across the street, 'He's a bad devil that lives there!'

'Yeah I know. You guys make sure you keep an eye on him,' I replied.

Now I was alongside the camera position, and the four men in my brick spread out thirty metres either side of me as I surreptitiously examined the area. The kids had disappeared. As I approached the spot where the kit was concealed I was talking to Andy over the net. If it had been booby-trapped I might be able to pass some useful detail over before the bang!

Ah . . . there it was. The side of the camera's housing was distinctly visible now, where the camouflage had been shoved aside. There was no question about it. I quickly heaved the equipment out of its hiding place and into my bag. So that was that. I signalled to the brick commander that we had finished and the patrol set off again. I had a good look at the target as we scurried past, but there was no one at home. He was probably out drawing his dole money.

As we got to the end of the street a vehicle turned into the road, and I recognised it as the target's car. The lance corporal flagged it down and began to question the driver – the standard routine with suspected terrorists.

I couldn't resist it. I strolled up and took a really close look at him as he sat there, monosyllabically answering the soldier's questions. He caught my gaze for an instant and I held it, fascinated, staring at him. I'd been this close to him several times before, but I'd never been able to afford the luxury of looking really hard at him. He glanced away, uncomfortable now.

The brick commander was beginning to make a meal out of the process, probably for my benefit, so I nodded to him and indicated that we should move on. He handed the driving licence back to the driver through the open window.

As he reached for the handbrake I leaned in and gave him a big smile. 'Mind how you go now, sir,' I said. 'And just remember – you can run but you can't hide!'